THE BURIED SOUL

THE BURIED SOUL

SOUL

How Humans Invented Death

TIMOTHY TAYLOR

BEACON
150

BEACON PRESS

BOSTON

Beacon Press
25 Beacon Street
Boston, Massachusetts 02108-2892
www.beacon.org

Beacon Press books
are published under the auspices of
the Unitarian Universalist Association

08 07 06 05 04   8 7 6 5 4 3 2 1

This book is printed on acid-free paper that meets the uncoated paper
ANSI/NISO specifications for permanence as revised in 1992.

Typeset by Rowland Phototypesetting Ltd,
Bury St Edmunds, Suffolk

Library of Congress
Cataloging-in-Publication Data
Taylor, Timothy, 1960 July 10–
The buried soul: how humans invented death / Timothy Taylor.
p.   cm.
Originally published: London : Fourth Estate, 2002.
Includes bibliographical references and index.
ISBN 0-8070-4672-8 (cloth : alk. paper)
1. Funeral rites and ceremonies—History. 2. Funeral
rites and ceremonies, Ancient. 3. Burial. 4. Human remains
(Archaeology) 5. Human sacrifice—Comparitive studies.
6. Excavations (Archaeology) 7. Death—Social Aspects.
I. Title.

GT3150.T26 2004
393—dc22
2004043786

In memory of Ben Steed, 1976–2000

CONTENTS

Acknowledgements

'Acts of personal revelation would contribute greatly to our understanding of works of historical scholarship,' wrote Professor Stuart Piggott at the beginning of his classic archaeological survey, *Ancient Europe*, published in 1965. For giving me the courage to risk a few here, I must thank Leo Hollis and Christopher Potter at 4th Estate, Katinka Matson and John Brockman at Brockman Inc. and, most especially, my wife, Sarah Wright. I also thank my friends, Neville and Jean Steed, and their daughter Kirsty, for their deeper courage in allowing me to write about the death of Ben, to whom this book is dedicated in fond memory.

I owe special debts of gratitude to James Montgomery, for his help, advice and encouragement in relation to the chapters dealing with the translation and interpretation of a medieval Arabic text, Daphne Nash-Briggs, for diligent and constructive criticism during the preparation of the entire final draft, and to Paul Bloom, James Cox, and Chrissie Freeth, who each provided immensely valuable comments on successive drafts.

Others who have helped me whom I should like to thank by name are Miranda Aldhouse-Green, Tim Altmann, Peter Atkins, Charles Aukerman, Paul Bahn, John Baines, Kate Balmforth, Peter Bate, Anders Bergquist, Julie Bond, David Braund, Robin Briggs, Jean Brown, Chris Chippindale, Dave Cowland, Margaret Cox, Falko Daim, Andrew Docker, John Etté, Alix Firth, Herwig Friesinger, Alex Gibson, Sarah Hargreaves, Anne Hauzeur, Charlie Hawes, Carl Heron, Ian Hodder, Sarah Hough, Beth Humphries, Rob Janaway, Anton Kern, Daniela Kern, Chris Knüsel, Dan Korn, Mehdi Moussavi Kouhpar, John

Kruze, Bob Layton, Irina Levinskaya, Jamie Lewis, Graham Lord, Jane Lord, Chris Lukas, Dave Lucy, Elizabeth McCann, Linda McLean, Stuart Marshall, Roger Matthews, Peter Miller, Keith Moe, James Montgomery, Mike Morwood, Vyacheslav Murzin, Shannon Novak, Alvaro Mora Ottomano, Don Ortner, Osman at Catalhöyük, Irene O'Sullivan, Funda Odemis, Tegwen Owen, Mike Parker Pearson, Sue Pell, Ernst Pernicka, Paul Pettitt, Jim Phillips, Alistair Pike, Stuart Reevell, Howard Reid, Mike Richards, Gillian Riley, Jill Ross, Eric Sameit, Holger Schutkowski, Andrew Sherratt, Andre Singer, Michael Smith, Richard Solomons, Peter Stadtler, Chris Stringer, Jiří Svoboda, George Taylor, Nick Thorpe, Phillip Tobias, Peter Topping, Christina Toren, Elvira Toth, Gerhard Trnka, Anastasia Tsaliki, Gwyneth Vernon, Gillian Varndell, Michael Vickers, Suzanne Waugh, Abigail Wheatley, Ben Wheatley, Helen Wheatley, Victoria Wheatley, Tim White, Louise Woodstone, Josephine Taylor Wright, Rebecca Taylor Wright and Oleg Zhuravlyov.

I was granted study leave from the Department of Archaeological Sciences, University of Bradford, at an early stage; I would like to thank all those of my colleagues and students not specifically mentioned above for their support and enthusiasm throughout.

The title, *The Buried Soul*, is taken from the poet William Blake (*The Everlasting Gospel*, c. 1810, γ: line 100).

INTRODUCTION

Sentiments and Chronologies

... surely our Sentiments, – how we dream'd of, and were mistaken in, each other, – count for at least as much as our poor cold Chronologies.

THOMAS PYNCHON, *Mason & Dixon*[1]

———

I was six when my grandfather died and I was blamed for his death. I had come with my mother to stay with my grandparents for the Easter holidays. During the carving of the Sunday roast, my grandfather lost his temper with me, chased me round the chairs and wrestled me upstairs. I howled and fought every step of the way and was locked in a bedroom. Several months later, towards the end of summer, my mother told me that my grandfather had had a heart attack. We drove five hours to visit him in the John Radcliffe Hospital in Oxford. I remember that he jokingly offered me some of his medicated orange drink through a long clear plastic tube as he lay propped up in bed, apparently recovering. I never saw him again.

I knew that my grandfather's death was the worst thing that had ever happened in my world but I did not directly connect it to myself until a few days later. My father had gone home to Norfolk and my increasingly hysterical grandmother had retired

1

to bed, leaving me alone with my mother. I asked why Grandpa was dead and she told me I had killed him. Seething with grief and anger, she screamed that it was typical of my lack of thought for others that I did not know that 'Daddy' had been terribly out of breath after disciplining me, and that the effort had put a fatal strain on his heart. Confused and stunned, I wanted to believe that this was my 'daddy' she was talking about, but it was clear that she meant her daddy, not mine, and the horrible reality of what she had said at first sank in.

My mother's mantra, 'If you had not had that tantrum, none of this would ever have happened and he would still be alive today', was repeated at intervals even into my adult life. But no repetition was required to engrave it on my mind. I was at that magical, fragile age when children still half believe in the tooth fairy and Father Christmas. I took the implications of my bad-ness on board immediately. I understood that I had killed my mummy's daddy and that I was therefore a murderer. Too small to go to prison, my punishment was to be internal.

Ever since we became human we have used communal rituals to channel and focus the otherwise inexpressible emotions of the bereaved. To exclude the young from these rituals is to deny, to those least able to rationalize things through words, access to the longest-evolved means of coming to terms with grief. But in 1960s Britain, children were shielded from the physical reality of death: I was not taken to my grandfather's funeral and I do not know whether he was cremated or buried. Under the circumstances, that may have been a good thing, as I do not know how I would have coped had I attended his funeral as his nemesis.

Through my exclusion from the mourning process, 'closure' – the emotional coming to terms with death that has to occur before a person can move on – was put on hold. It remained so for sixteen years, until my relationship with the dead had become institutionalized. I became an archaeologist, turning skulls over in my hands, photographing grave goods and digging holes in the ground to retrieve and display what has been long forgotten. And so I began, unconsciously at first, to search for a balance between sentiments (my sense of the emotional), and chronologies (the discipline of dating the artefacts and events of prehistory).

This book is about the human response to death, in our earliest prehistory, in the present day, and at various points in between. From the mystery of the first ceremonial burials to the systematic desecration of vast cemeteries in antiquity, from human sacrifice and vampire beliefs to reverential funerary cannibalism, archaeology provides clues to what death – as we imagine it – was, what it is and what it could be.

Archaeology uncovers our responses to the human condition as it has developed since our divergence from the apes some 6 million years ago. At some moment in our biological and cultural evolution we became intelligent enough to formulate the idea of the soul, of something that was 'us' that continued after death, signalled only by its patent absence from each corpse. I am certain that the idea of the soul that modern humans have elaborated everywhere in the world first emerged in deep prehistory, some time after the advent of speech but long before the development of writing. In the absence of written history, only archaeology can provide evidence for how the idea was first acquired; but inferring ideas from objects rather than words is challenging and controversial, and involves making key assumptions in advance of the evidence. For example, that awareness of the inevitability of death could not have emerged before our hominid ancestors had acquired the power of speech.

There are widely differing estimates of when the power of speech evolved, or how to define it. Some place it at 2 million years ago, along with the origin of genus *Homo*. Others are uncomfortable with the idea that language could have emerged much before 40,000 years ago. Support can be found for both positions, and for a number of intermediate ones. But, whenever it happened, it is clear that once people could talk they could bring many more things into the world than at first appeared to be there, whether through objective observation or mystical conjecture. Belief in a disembodied identity or soul was the most significant of these. 'Why hast thou disquieted me, to bring me up?' – these words are ascribed to the dead Samuel in the Old Testament, after he has been conjured up by the witch of Endor.[2] Ancient necromancers typically used spells such as 'I summon you, dead'; and, even if 'the dead' did not always oblige, the words alone created an impression that the deceased somehow, somewhere, existed.

Like necromancy, archaeology attempts to conjure up the dead in order to learn something new, but it attempts to do so using scientific and rational procedures rather than esoteric chanting. The ambition of archaeology is to survey the entire cultural emergence of our species with a dispassionate scepticism, focusing on what people actually did rather than what they might choose to say about it were they still alive.

Nearly two centuries of painstaking excavation and analysis have revealed some extraordinary facts. For example, that while the first chipped stone tool was made 2.6 million years ago, the first ceremonial burial did not occur until 120,000 years ago. Or that, for 99.5 per cent of our existence as genus *Homo*, we lived as hunters and gatherers, and then, all in the space of the last 10,000 years, the first farming societies arose independently of one another, dotting the globe from China to western Asia to central America. Each solved the complex and intertwined problems of rising population levels and the loss of rich coastal hunting lands to rising, post-Ice Age, sea levels, by starting to cultivate their own food. These first farming societies were followed by complex civilizations that, again, arose independently, each with its own writing and counting systems, organized religion and refined, large-scale architecture. Amazingly, every early civilization had high priests, created religious monuments aligned in careful relationship to sun, moon and stars, and buried its dead using elaborate ceremonies. Human sacrifice was practised extensively in the ancient world – in Shang China, in the earliest phase of Egyptian civilization, in the Indus valley, among the Sumerians and by the Maya and the Aztecs.

It is hard to imagine how these similarities could exist without envisaging some secret unifying force. Bizarre myths and theories have arisen that claim to identify it. Some invoke the lost civilization of Atlantis, while others insist that humans received occult assistance from aliens. This 'para-archaeology', which selectively incorporates archaeological data to prove a prior supposition, has attempted to popularize the idea that the Great Pyramids of Egypt and similar monuments elsewhere, such as the pyramidical temples of the Aztecs in Mexico, and the ruins of Angkor Wat in Thailand, were designed by shadowy, inter-continental astronomer-priests. There are even those who believe that the Egyptian pyramids betray the fingerprints of Freemasons, who had previously built the Neolithic stone tombs of the Orkney islands off the north coast of Scotland.[3]

Nothing whatsoever historically links the monuments of the ancient Egyptians and the Aztecs. In time, they are further apart than Stonehenge is from Alfred the Great. The truth is that people on the banks of the Nile in 2500 BC and in the valley of Mexico in AD 1000 had independently developed some very basic ideas. Both civilizations realized, unsurprisingly, that large architectural structures were not only naturally more imposing than small ones, but culturally impressive too, because it took a lot of people, energy and organization to create them. Big monuments might therefore serve as places for communal ceremonies and for burying important leaders. Both civilizations also realized that large architectural structures that were narrower at the bottom than at the top were likely to fall over, whereas a broad base and progressively narrower upper levels might remain stable for a very long time. Having understood these sparse basics we can appreciate the differences between the originally polished, sharp, unclimbable Great Pyramids of Egypt and the far smaller Aztec temples with their flat tops reached by staircases. There is no secret unity to seek and no inherent mystery in our achievements. Similarities in religious architecture arise out of the typical responses of human beings when organized in particular ways (hierarchically, for instance) and faced with particular kinds of thing (death, for instance).

It is only human that we should want to turn what we see around us into something we can grasp with a minimum of effort. But this does not in itself explain the appeal of the wildest theories. Para-archaeology addresses a deeper fear: the fear of death. Running roughshod over the hard-won detail of established archaeological chronologies, analyses and inferences, these grand conspiracy theories nevertheless grapple with the big questions of being and time. Many of them dwell on the possibility that our ancestors knew the secret of immortality. And, if they have a kind of plausibility, it is because this is precisely what our ancestors were attempting to claim in many of their monuments.

Myths of astronomer-priests guarding the elixir of life are only one manifestation of a modern interest in immortality. The $100,000 Quarles Prize for the discovery of a genetic 'cure' for ageing was put up by the octogenarian Texan oil magnate, Miller Quarles, co-founder of the Geron Corporation, which aims to extend the average human lifespan to 150 years.[4] Quarles is not alone in his obsessive desire to go on living; others share his view of old age as a disease process and death as potentially avoidable. The adherents of fundamentalist religions, on the other hand, do not want to avoid it, and many of them actively promote martyrdom as the best guarantee of immortality.

Archaeology presents a microcosm of the broader ideological conflicts that currently rage over what we think we know about death. In dealing with mortality, both the scientific and humanistic sides of the discipline come up against faith and metaphysical questions. They uncover fault lines running off in unexpected directions. On one side are different kinds of claim to truth; on the other side are different kinds of doubt. Pitted alike against the secular certainties of laboratory science and religious assertions of a single transcendent truth is the post-modern claim that there is no such thing as truth at all, that everything is relative and open to a multitude of interpretations (including, logically and somewhat disconcertingly, absolutist interpretations themselves).

Because archaeology gets its hands dirty in the unequivocal

mess that people leave behind them, it is a powerful means of establishing real things that happened in the ancient past. Truth may sometimes be the most difficult thing in the world to discover but it nevertheless exists. The archaeological approach can attempt to determine it in the very recent past as well as in the very remote past. This is because, by viewing human behaviour over massive time periods, archaeology has created an unparalleled repository of knowledge about the huge range of human actions and responses.

The River Thames rises and falls with its estuary tides. At low water it reveals all manner of detritus to the eyes of Londoners. In the summer of 2001, an off-duty police worker was walking by the side of the river close to the Globe Theatre when she spotted what turned out to be the torso of a six-year-old boy of African origin.[5] His head, arms and legs had been severed in a practised five-point dismemberment that left short sections of protruding bone, terminating in neatly sawn and snapped ends. At around the same time, Dutch police recovered the torso of a girl of about eight, of European or mixed ethnic origin, in a Rotterdam waterway. Her head turned up some 100 kilometres distant but her limbs were never recovered. An international investigation began, concentrating on the possibility that a serial killer psychopath was on the loose, someone who might work in merchant shipping and be familiar with both port cities.

Archaeologists have a special angle not just on the accumulating fragments of potentially fugitive evidence, but also on the human actions and intentions that created them, and my view was sought in this case in order to provide a dimension beyond the purely forensic.[6] My immediate impression of the London torso murder was that a lone psychopath was an unlikely perpetrator. From my research, I knew that the ritual killing of children was not at all rare in the ancient world. There are examples on almost every continent, with particularly well attested cases among the Incas, the Aztecs and the Carthaginians. It is also more common today than many suppose, with several hundred documented cases from the 1990s from northern India, South Africa, and elsewhere.

The Thames torso had been dumped and parts of the body remained missing, indicating that the killing had taken place elsewhere, presumably somewhere the perpetrator(s) felt secure. If they were able to keep the amputated parts safe from discovery, why not the torso too? Why alert the police by dumping it near water in a major urban centre, where it would inevitably be discovered? The torso had been dressed, post-mortem, in orange shorts, making it more visible on the Thames mud. Whoever did this *wanted* this part of the child to be found, and this part only. Such behaviour could be manifested by a lone psychopath but then one would have to explain the coincidence involved in the fact that it exactly fits a known current cultural pattern of human sacrifice.

In 1994, in Boystown squatter camp, Cape Town, various remains from a five-year-old child were recovered by a forensic team. He had been killed by a ritual specialist or witchdoctor, known as an *isangoma* (in this case his uncle, although most isangomas are women) in order to produce ritual medicine, or *muti*.[7] Some muti comes from plants and some from animals. The most sought-after kind of human muti is made from children's body parts and its production follows strict rules. The perpetrating group should contain someone close to the child, such as a blood relative. After the parts have been cut away from the body, the elements (fingers, ears, genitalia, subcutaneous fat, parts of the scalp and so on) must be wrapped in different coloured cloths. For the muti to be powerful and effective, in the terms of those that believe in it, the victim must be kept alive through most of the dismemberment. In some variants the child should cry out in pain; in others, they are gagged, as the screaming is thought to dissipate the power of the muti. The victim is then strangled and further, post-mortem, dismemberment may take place. Finally, the torso is left by water. In the Boystown case, the torso was left in a metal trunk near a pool of water by the side of a freeway. A white bucket containing a short section of cervical spinal column, wrapped in red underpants, and other body parts wrapped in appropriate black, blue and green fabrics, were found in the isangoma's shack.

Although some muti murders have resulted in criminal prosecutions, attempts to criticize, or even investigate, human muti production are regarded by some as a failure to understand the moral values of a different culture, a culture whose conduct is as valid as our own. Scholtz, Phillips and Knobel, South African forensic pathologists with first-hand experience of the physical residues, say that muti 'is not regarded as a politically correct topic'.[8] The sacrifice of children to produce muti is defended as traditional among the Zulu and related tribes by some insiders. One indigenous cultural anthropologist, H. Ngubane, argues on the basis of thirty recent cases in Swaziland that muti killings should not be classed as murder *per se* and that white, imperialist laws put traditional isangomas and their associates in an invidious position. She feels that it should be acceptable for a member of a community to be sacrificed for the greater good, and she equates muti ritual killing with abortion or euthanasia.[9]

Perhaps, instead of imposing our values on others we should seek to understand the internal validity of the things they may do, however much we dislike them. Can we even presume to judge what the sacrificed child suffered? There is certainly a culturally learned dimension to human emotions. Adults in one culture may scream and tear their hair out during a funeral while those in another laugh and celebrate. Nevertheless, emotional expression arises out of what is innate. As Charles Darwin pointed out, we can usually read the most basic emotions – fear, pain, affection, guilt, grief, happiness, mistrust – in people of different cultures, whatever local nuances overlie them. They are unfiltered in young children, just as they are in those animals with whom we share our recent evolutionary history. (Darwin realized that we recognize pets' feelings by their facial expressions and that they show reciprocal knowledge of human feelings.)[10]

Whatever one's approach to the complex ethical issues of either abortion or euthanasia, both differ fundamentally from muti killing. Their proponents acknowledge the possibility of distress and seek to minimize it. Muti killing, by contrast, requires that distress be maximized. This is clear in the minds of those who practise it. The horrific agony of the child is seen both as an innate expression of animal terror and as a desired cultural outcome.

Human muti is sold for money, its different coloured wrappings signalling a variety of putative benefits. Six hundred rand can buy enough subcutaneous fat, cut in a strip from a child's thorax, to smear on the wheels of a taxi, providing supernatural insurance. Girls' genitalia are considered good for business, as they are symbolic of future fertility. Penises ensure sexual prowess. A child's ring finger may be used to ensure a good marriage. Heads may be buried in the foundations of a building to guard against collapse or fire, and brain muti can be prepared and eaten from the skull to confer special powers of acumen. In the mind of the believer, it is not the body part that is being purchased, but part of the child's soul.

The Rotterdam case turned out not to match these criteria closely: parts of the body turned up in two locations; neither had any colour coding; the torso and the head were both partially concealed; proximity to water counted for less because so many wastelands and derelict areas in Holland are adjacent to waterways. Two people have since been charged with the Dutch murder, which, despite some ritual aspects, was not a human sacrifice. In the London case, however, the orange colour of the boy's shorts served not simply to attract attention to his dismembered torso, but put out a specific signal to those for whose benefit the ritual was being conducted. In retrospect, it is easy to see that releasing details of the shorts to the media aided the transmission of this signal. The perpetrators wanted the torso to be found quickly and described publicly so that they could complete the process of ritual validation, demonstrating that this was not any torso, but one that had been shorn of body parts in traditional fashion. If people pay money to ensure their business ventures or criminal empires using human muti, they want to know that what they are getting did not come from a dead animal, a dodgy undertaker or a hospital morgue with lax security. The boy's genitals were intact, indicating that providing muti to enhance sexual prowess was not a priority, indeed, that whoever did it had no need to maximize the 'harvest' of muti materials. The Thames torso murder has the hallmarks of a deliberately commissioned ritual for the benefit of a single individual. Liaison between the Metropolitan Police and South African investigators has now strengthened the supposition that the murder was for muti.

Why such people should want to torture a child to death is an interesting question. There are many kinds of answer, but none more chillingly clear and logical than that a child, being innocent, has a good soul. The body of the child can be thought of as generously imbued with unfolding spirit. All its luck and aspiration lie in the future, whereas the perpetrators of muti murder are adults who feel as if their luck has run out and their spirits have been sapped. Believers in muti are convinced that there is a finite amount of luck or good fate in the world. By taking it from the child, in whom it is still overflowing, they believe that their own store of luck can be increased and their spirit revitalized.[11]

Archaeology provides a unique perspective on our human identity, but there is a danger of distortion. Signs of brutality are easier to recognize on a skeleton than signs of love, creating a danger that we will pay most attention to the grim. But, surprisingly, the distortion is the other way round. We diligently airbrush out the less palatable details of prehistory to construct a proud record of achievement for national museums to present to impressionable school parties. The Neolithic (the first farming period) is often portrayed as a time of peace and honest toil or, more popularly, as a utopian period of mother-goddess worship. But the discovery of a number of unmarked mass graves across Europe, the largest containing well over a hundred systematically butchered men, women and children,[12] evokes Rwanda more than Arcadia.

I have not shied away from making absolute moral judgements about the behaviour of our prehistoric ancestors, whatever religious beliefs and ritual justifications they may have had. The line between unacceptable excuses and culturally validated reasons forms a major focus of my investigation in this book. Examining why, precisely, some cultural communities may develop an apparent need for behaviour like child sacrifice, or descend into a cycle of tit-for-tat massacres – why, in short, they require victims – may help to prevent such things happening in future.

In using the word 'victims', I have turned against something I first learned as a student in social anthropology classes, namely that different cultures are never wrong in their difference, but simply 'other'. In its hand-wringing retreat from the imperialism and racism of much Victorian ethnography, social (or cultural) anthropology had, by the late 1970s, reached a high-water mark of what has since been dubbed political correctness. Almost any culturally validated behaviour could be viewed relativistically or, failing that, conveniently ignored.

One of the great standard works of the Victorian period, *The Origin of Civilization and the Primitive Condition of Man: Mental and Social Condition of Savages* by Sir John Lubbock (later Lord Avebury), has index entries for both cannibalism and sacrifice, the latter subdivided into 'Human sacrifices', 'Human sacrifices, abolition of', 'Sacrifices, human, confusion of the victim with the deity', and 'Sacrifices, human, in ancient times'. Yet my students search in vain for any mention of these themes in recent general works, except – rarely – in the special context of questioning their existence. Ferraro, Trevathon and Levy's *Anthropology: an Applied Perspective* (1994) is typical of the current crop of textbooks in failing to index not only cannibalism or human sacrifice, but even 'sacrifice' as a phenomenon at all. The ritual killing of animals, common to many religions worldwide, is thus overlooked. There is something patronizing about such avoidance. Modern Western academics signal that our civilization is happy to accept, or even glorify, indigenous peoples so long as we only acknowledge those differences that we ourselves can cope with – a packaged exoticism.

Archaeology, like anthropology, seeks to understand the motives of people from alien cultures, and archaeologists find it even easier to suspend judgement because the cultures they study are long gone. But if we refuse to say where we stand on child sacrifice among the ancient Inca of Peru, then we cannot complain about similar atrocities in our own era, and this means that we cannot learn from history.

In the tenth century AD a great Viking chieftain was buried on the banks of the Volga. Our detailed knowledge of this funeral rite comes from a graphic eyewitness account by the Arab writer, Ibn Faḍlān, and is independently supported by archaeology. In the middle section of this book, instead of concentrating on the chieftain, as many scholars have previously done, I examine the reasons for the horrific gang rape of a slave-girl by six warriors and her eventual killing by a mistress of ceremonies known as 'The Angel of Death'. This is a key part of the sequence of events that led up to the chieftain's final send-off to Valhalla, and is viewed by religious historians as reflecting normal Viking religious practice. One goes so far as to conclude that, at the brutal culmination of the rite, 'the happy girl is sent to Odin to be with her master', despite the fact that our informant witnesses the Viking men drumming on their shields with the express purpose of drowning out the continuous, terrified screaming. I argue that, by understanding the particular way in which the slave-girl was killed and by making no cultural apologies for it, we can provide ourselves with a key with which to unlock other mysteries. As with muti, the focus of the ritual was less on the physical body of the slave-girl than on the fate of the things understood as souls, both hers and the dead chieftain's.

The other mysteries that I consider in this book include the 34,000-year-old Combe Capelle skeleton, which preserves traces of a sequence of extraordinary events: an Ice Age hunter hacked to death with flint daggers, butchered for meat, and then accorded a ceremonial burial. Despite recent wholesale denial by an influential school of anthropology that humans, as a norm, ever indulged in cannibalism, a wealth of new and unequivocal evidence demonstrates that the phenomenon, also prevalent among chimpanzees (and many other animals), was widespread during the period of our biological evolution.

Butchered bones, from early australopithecines and *Homo erectus* as well as the later Neanderthals and early modern humans, display two distinct types of cut-marking 'signature'. One indicates aggressive, warfare-driven cannibalism and the other indicates reverential, funerary cannibalism. An example of the second type, among the near-modern species known as *Homo heidelbergensis*, from the site of Sima de los Huesos in Spain, constitutes the earliest known ritual behaviour anywhere in the world, dating to between 300,000 and 200,000 years ago. What began as an inherited primate behaviour that made straightforward nutritional and practical sense (why leave dead flesh around to attract predatory animals or benefit rival groups?) had become a palliative for supernatural fears. Eating one's own as well as eating one's enemies came, at some point in our history, to be seen as a means to control the threat and the power of the disembodied soul. Through ritual funerary cannibalism, spirit power could be reabsorbed and channelled.

Funerary cannibalism continued until very recent times, alongside a wide variety of alternative rituals for the disposal of the dead, such as exposure ('sky burial'), burial and cremation. But it is in those societies where the body is neither eaten nor buried nor burned, but actively stabilized through embalming and mummification, that we find the largest and most elaborate mausoleums.

One way of looking at the Great Pyramid of Khufu (or Cheops) is to see it as a 148 metre (486 foot) high exercise in grandiosity, stamping the power and prestige of the dead dynast and his living dynasty on the public mind. But look at it inside out and we see architectural containment on a vast scale – an isolation unit for a soul of immense disruptive potential. Once childlike and good, Khufu's adult spirit became backward-looking and malevolent. Then death freed it. In the language of refined belief, the soul of the Pharaoh is supposed to complete a sacred voyage to the other world, but this is not the only language people understand. At a more atavistic level, a force of overwhelming personality remains attached to the malevolent soul. It must be screened out of normal life at all costs, even if that means physically sealing it within millions of tons of masonry. Neither the specific complexities of ancient Egyptian theology (which had at least four different concepts of soul),[13] nor Khufu's personal complicity in building his own Great Pyramid, can dislodge the possibility of such a simple and powerful idea having been present, if not in the Egyptians' minds, then at least in their hearts.

The malevolence of the mature soul was an abiding concern in the later prehistoric periods and in the many pagan religions of historical times. From the Iron Age come the 'bog bodies', peat-preserved corpses of people killed with excessive violence in a number of quite distinct and simultaneous ways: poisoning, stabbing, strangling and drowning. Then there is the much more recent mystery of Lenin's embalming: an astonishingly complex and sustained ritual that established Stalin's credentials as the leader of a superpower. In the present day, there is the still-unfolding drama of 'Kennewick Man', a single skeleton washed by chance out of a Washington State river bank in 1996. Since then he has been fought over by the American army, archaeologists, American Indian tribes and Californian pagans, for the fundamental reason that no one knows who he is. Why did the bog bodies require a multiple cause of death? Why was the Soviet Union, despite the avowedly atheistic philosophy of communism, symbolically centred on the mysticism of ancestor worship, embodied by the Lenin mausoleum in Red Square? Why has Kennewick Man's identity disturbed people to the point where the US Corps of Engineers felt compelled to destroy and re-landscape the place where he was found?

The invention of death set loose not only souls but deities. To control and appease them, rituals were required that, in turn, encouraged the development of increasingly complex social structures. Running through this book is the conviction (not new) that our sense of propriety and our awareness of our own mortality are intimately connected. Having sight of our own deaths, we wonder how posterity will judge us. The French philosopher Jacques Derrida believes knowledge of mortality is the ultimate thing that limits us, showing how other limits – ethical constraints – can be set up in other places.[14] Just as death is final, so are our completed actions. Realizing their moral indelibility distinguishes the person who takes responsibility for their own freedom from the psychopath.

One of the most recent responses to personal, unavoidable mortalness[15] is archaeology itself. When we study it, the present becomes almost transparently thin as we reflect back through deep time. I earlier characterized archaeology in terms of 'dispassionate scepticism', but maybe I was wrong to use the word dispassionate. Emotional intelligence is as crucial as scientific objectivity in the struggle to understand the past.[16] We need sentiments *and* chronologies.

CHAPTER 1

Ascending Underground

... two pieces of tree fungus were also found with the Hauslabjoch corpse. The 'Iceman' had cut them from a piece of bracket fungus, perforated them, and threaded them onto a knotted leather or fur lace so that he could attach them to his belt ... tree fungus was, until quite recently, used in kindling fires as well as in wound dressings, due to its putative blood-clotting and anti-inflammatory effects.

MARKUS EGG AND KONRAD SPINDLER, *Die Gletschermumie*[1]

It was a long shot, and the arrow found its mark just as the man was turning to flee into the mountains. It missed his spine, but ripped through his shoulder blade, paralysing his left arm and rendering his own bow useless. More arrows whistled past as he wove and ducked, gaining height and cover, until he reached the snowline. He had layered, weatherproof clothing, insulated mountain boots and a bentwood frame-rucksack. He was still well armed. Having evaded pursuit, he paused to deal with the arrow. One critical tug left him staring at the fletched shaft in his bloody hand. His heart sank as he saw what he most feared – the tip was missing. His little first-aid kit was no use for this. At 3000 metres, the heavy bleeding had not stopped and, with a blizzard thickening, he collapsed.

This chilling snapshot of life in the Neolithic period – well organized, competitive, skill dependent, and often brutal – is confirmed by data from across Europe. The 2-centimetre flint arrowhead, recently revealed by tomography under the left scapula of Ötzi, the famous 'Iceman' discovered by climbers in 1991 on the mountain border of Italy and Austria, is hardly unique[2] – he was carrying a quiver full of stone-tipped arrows himself. Leaf-shaped and barbed flint arrowheads have been found deeply embedded in the pelvises and spines of Neolithic ('New Stone Age') skeletons from Spain, Saxony and Belgium.[3] Knapped with skill, the edge of a flint blade is sharper than steel. Cruelly virtuosic in design, impossible to remove without shearing through yet more vital tissue, these little points were the supreme anti-personnel weapon of their day.

The sources of natural flint were highly valued. In the pine forests of the Norfolk Breckland is a clearing cratered like the surface of the moon. The 400 or so dish-like depressions are riddled with rabbit warrens and full of rubble and nettles. This place is called Grime's Graves, from Grim – originally an Anglo-Saxon nickname for the pagan god, Woden (Odin to the Vikings). To the medieval mind, Grim was synonymous with the Devil, and Grime's Graves were his delvings. Less superstitious local people thought that the Vikings must once have camped in the clearing, digging winter quarters. Today we know that the depressions were made by people forgotten by early chroniclers, whose existence was not hinted at in any monastic text.[4] Each crater marks where a wide shaft once cut vertically through the rock. These were, in fact, prehistoric mine shafts, as the intrepid antiquarian Canon Greenwell proved in 1868 when he unblocked the pit that is named after him and made the first scientific observations.

In August 2001, as part of a team of specialists, I descended Greenwell's Pit. From the outside it looks like a small missile silo. On top of the flat circle of concrete that caps the shaft is a heavily padlocked steel trapdoor. Beneath it, a steel ladder drops 40 feet through a surprisingly wide space. Standing on the compressed chalk at the bottom is like being in an underground church. Rough-hewn arches on all sides lead into low winding galleries cut into the floorstone – the layer of top-quality flint that the miners were after. Flint was widely traded in the Neolithic period. It came from more than a dozen British mines, as well as from sources in the Holy Cross mountains of Poland, the Low Countries and central France. The first farming revolution was in full swing and, apart from arrowheads and knife blades, flint was knapped into axes for the forest clearance needed to create fields and pastures. The timber was mostly burned, firing kilns to make pottery, the new storage and cooking material. Investment in land and herds created a new kind of wealth, and new kinds of competition and jealousy.

In Greenwell's Pit, carefully reserved pillars of the natural rock support the snaking galleries. Violence may have been a central part of life in the Neolithic, but the miners at Grime's Graves, whether slaves or free agents, dug with an eye to personal safety.[5] In none of the seven shafts so far investigated has a skeleton been found crushed under a collapsed roof (although a skeleton of a woman with a broken neck in a Neolithic mine shaft at Cissbury, on the south coast of Britain, indicates that such mining was never risk free). Crawling to the far end of one of the galleries and looking left, it is possible to discern, sharply outlined against the strikingly fresh-looking sandy material of an ancient roof-fall, a red-deer antler pick, firmly jammed into the floor. Whoever it once belonged to seems to have worked as much flint as they could before leaving. They could see diminishing returns and increasing danger ahead. Perhaps they left in a hurry but, in any case, the decision was made to abandon this particular pit, and begin again afresh nearby. It is not known how many pits would have been open at any one time but it seems likely that, throughout the 1,000 years of extraction at the site, one or two pits must always have been reaching exhaustion as others were just being opened.

Ötzi, the Iceman, already possessed a copper axe alongside his flint dagger. In 3300 BC metalwork was new technology in central

Greenwell's Pit: discarded Neolithic antler picks and fragments of flint.
(Photo: author)

Europe, and it was a full thousand years later that metal, now as the harder alloy, bronze, began to appear in Britain. The Stone Age was finally ending and, around 2000 BC, the last pit at Grime's Graves was abandoned and the entire workings fell into disuse. During the final phase, somebody buried the cranium of an extremely aged mare in a small pit under the debris around the lip of a mine shaft. The lower jaw was missing, but the few remaining teeth show clearly that she was over 35 years old when she died (which is very old for a horse). Archaeologists found that the cranium had been placed on top of chalk blocks, three of which carried deeply engraved lines that may have had some symbolic meaning.[6]

Archaeology brings to light many different kinds of objects, each requiring an interpretation. They can be unequivocally practical or purely symbolic. On many occasions they are both, but sometimes – perhaps too often – their original purpose eludes us. We have to pick through the ruins of the past and define significance. The roof-fall and the pick seem to make sense against the background of mine workings that were planned rationally, with both safety and efficiency in mind. But much archaeological evidence is like this aged mare's head, ambiguous and difficult.

The mare is the earliest domesticated horse yet discovered in England, matched in antiquity only by fragments of horse bone from the impressive Neolithic tomb complex of Newgrange in Ireland. Horses had been domesticated on the steppes, far to the east, and began to appear in Atlantic Europe during the 'Beaker' period, when metals too made their first appearance alongside distinctive pottery drinking mugs or beakers. Metal daggers and horses may have been part of the same phenomenon, possibly status symbols of an invading elite.[7] Although archaeologists have revealed the basic facts about the technology and chronology of ancient flint extraction, the horse cranium leaves us stumped. Only one part of this ancient beast – the bit that housed its brain – was buried. This suggests an animal not just treasured into old age, but kept for long as a trophy after death, as first the lower jaw and then most of the teeth fell away before eventual burial at the pit edge. We do not know, and may never know, why it was put there.

The horse cranium at Grime's Graves hints at something that all archaeologists know but many of us prefer to forget much of the time: that what survives to be excavated is often a tiny and highly unrepresentative fraction of what once was. The cranium is not likely to have belonged to the only horse in England in 2000 BC, but it is the only one whose cranium has been discovered. Many things crucial to our ancestors do not survive at all, or go unrecognized. Tens of thousands of flint artefacts are catalogued in museums, but we know that Grime's Graves alone produced nearly 18,000 tons of flint, representing an output of finished tools equivalent to between 5 and 10 million axes.[8] The vast majority of utilitarian artefacts were reused, their function perhaps altering in the process. A long chain of resharpening, fragmentation, reduction and incorporation in the soil means that, over a period of thousands of years, nearly all prehistoric tools end up not in a glass display cabinet but as anonymous debris. Archaeology is an underground ascent to knowledge – knowledge won back from the excavated shards of the past. Their degree of fragmentation can only be guessed at, but the unpredictable and challenging reality of what excavation reveals cannot be doubted.

Humans have become fragmented and lost too. For every period that produces dramatic and interesting burials to display in museums, there is another period from which we have virtually nothing at all. The round barrows of the Bronze Age, which began to be built at the time that Grime's Graves was going out of use, preserve the bodies of a select few. In the subsequent Iron Age period, the absence is even more marked. Despite impressive hillforts and the widespread evidence of manufacturing industry that indicate high population levels, entire regions of Britain lack a single identifiable burial.[9]

Human prehistory is an almost unimaginably vast period, and it is easy for the dead to go missing. The millions and millions of axes from Grime's Graves and other mines were all needed and used. But only a tiny fraction of the people who wielded them are represented by the bones in museums and archaeological laboratories. In the last 10,000 years alone, it is estimated that 100 billion human beings have died[10] and far fewer than 0.01 per cent are accounted for.

As Darwin overturned the idea that humans were created fully formed and replaced it with his revolutionary theory of a long, slow evolution from an ape ancestor, archaeology overturned the 6,000-year chronology suggested by the Old Testament. This, just about graspable, sweep of Judaeo-Christian history was replaced with a prehistory of culture measured backwards over several million years.

Surveying time from present to past, according to the best current archaeological evidence, we can plot a reverse evolution where we lose writing some 5,000 years ago, lose permanent settlements and the idea of farming some 10,000 years ago, lose durable art some 35,000 years ago, lose our need of, or capacity for, ceremonial burial some time between 35,000 and 130,000

22

years ago. We lose our anatomical 'modernity' around 150,000 years ago but, as 'early archaic *Homo sapiens*', we can still make wooden hunting spears 400,000 years ago. Some 900,000 years ago, as *Homo erectus*, we can still traverse the open ocean by raft or boat. But before 1.5 million years ago a whole third of our brain capacity has gone. Our ability to make stone tools has been lost by around 2.5 million years ago, along with the right to be dubbed genus *Homo*: we are relegated to the *Australopithecines*. Our ability to walk upright, and with it the freedom to move while throwing, holding or pointing, leaves us in the period from 4.5 to 6 million years ago.[11] Somewhere along the line we must have lost our clothes, our hairless skin, our powers of song, speech, laughter and weeping, our ability to believe in God and any clear understanding of the inevitability of personal death.

Archaeologists can deduce certain things about attitudes to death at the time that the first pit was sunk at Grime's Graves, around 3000 BC. At Haddenham, in the nearby Cambridgeshire Fen, the first farmers had been burying their dead all jumbled together in a mounded-up communal tomb or long barrow. Excavations by the archaeologist Ian Hodder and his team reveal that the Haddenham barrow was periodically re-entered by its builders and the bones inside rearranged. A careful audit of the types of bones present in the barrow showed that only the bigger ones were present – predominantly long bones and crania (skulls minus lower jaws). This indicated that the barrow had been a repository for bones that had been wholly separated from corpses and which were most probably already dry and white when they arrived.

Wild nature helped clean the bones. Halfway across Britain, at Stoney Middleton in the Peak District, archaeologists have excavated a natural stone platform covered with small and fragmentary human remains that date from the same period as the Haddenham barrow. It seems that birds of prey were encouraged to pick the dead clean before the larger bones (those which had not been removed by the scavengers or fallen down cracks) were taken to be stored in three charnel houses discovered nearby. A similar two-stage ritual may have occurred at Haddenham although, in the absence of a convenient natural rock locals may have used an artificial exposure platform, perhaps a wooden scaffold like those constructed for the same purpose by some Plains Indian tribes.[12]

By the time that Grime's Graves and other flint mines were going out of use and the first metal was making its appearance, there had been a transformation in belief. No longer were bones picked bare, collected up, and communally housed. The wealthy (often men of mature years) preferred to carry their individual identities into death with them. These warriors were buried with their bodies intact, accompanied only by personal items – new-style bronze daggers, wrist-guards for archery, cloak pins and decorated clay drinking beakers. Their bodies are found hunched in the foetal position in small pits under round barrows. It is hard to escape the thought that they believed they would be reborn from their swollen earth mounds into some other world, like babies emerging from the womb.

It would be easy to see these changes as reflecting an upheaval in which peaceful and communal agrarian societies were disrupted by exploitative, male-dominated, elite invaders (and just such a scenario has been persuasively sketched by the archaeologist Marija Gimbutas).[13] But the dramatic switch from communal long barrows to individual round barrows is perhaps not as straightforward as it at first seems. If the new type of burial was a form of propaganda, a fashion statement that said it was OK to keep hold of one's own body and one's own property in death, then the old type of burial may have been propaganda of a different sort. People who are truly community-minded do not need big monuments to advertise the fact. The shared long-mounds are every bit as dominant in the landscape as the private round barrows that followed them. Although their scattered, mix-and-match skeletons *appear* communal, they probably never housed more than a subset of the community.

One of my students has recently tried to determine how many

people could be fitted into the famous prehistoric grave chambers of the Orkney Isles, in use at around the same time as Grime's Graves was being mined. The research shows that the impressive megalithic structures such as Maes Howe, Isbister and Quanterness could, theoretically, have held the entire island dead of the Neolithic, if the bones were neatly packed, charnel-house wise. But the detailed archaeological evidence suggests otherwise. Maes Howe was probably more temple or cathedral than grave, with its ceremonial niches displaying the skulls of a select few.[14] At Quanterness, the remains of more than 150 people were found, but there was room for many, many more. Although 'collective', such a tomb catered in practice for a subsection of the population. The fresh corpses of the chosen ones may initially have been dug into sand dunes rather than exposed (unlike at Stoney Middleton, the bones lack gnaw- or claw-marks).[15]

It is not unknown for people who live by rivers or on small islands to let water do the work of burial for ordinary people. The final resting place of the majority of the Neolithic Orkney Islanders may have been similar to that observed by nineteenth-century anthropologists in Melanesia. In the Solomon Islands

Maes Howe, Orkney: Neolithic burial mound. (Photo: author)

The vaulted Maes Howe chamber showing a niche for human bones.
(Photo: author)

and New Hebrides (modern Vanuatu), it was customary 'to cast the bodies of common people into the sea, while . . . the bodies of important persons are placed on wooden platforms surrounded by palisades and are so kept until only the bones remain'.[16] At Haddenham and Stoney Middleton less important people may have been put in rivers when they died (although there are a number of other possibilities).

If the Neolithic 'collective' tombs projected the idea of sharing and belonging in order to distract attention from the fact that wealth and power were actually becoming more concentrated, then the openly individualistic Beaker burials might reflect the growing confidence of the rich. As in Melanesia, it may have been thought that only the elite had souls that could join the ancestors with their personality intact. The individual identity of the majority was dissolved in death.

Every year, the literary agent and science commentator, John Brockman, poses a trick (or, at least, tricky) question to his contributors on *The Edge* website (www.edge.org//questioncenter). His 2001 question was 'What questions have gone away?' I responded:

A question that has gone away (almost): 'How can I stop the soul of the deceased reanimating the body?', explaining:

At a particular point (yet to be clearly defined) in human cultural evolution, a specific idea took hold that there were two, partially separable, elements present in a living creature: the material body and the force that animated it. On the death of the body the animating force would, naturally, desire the continuation of this-worldly action and struggle to reassert itself (just as one might strive to retrieve a flint axe one had accidentally dropped). If the soul (or spirit) succeeded, it would also seek to repossess its property, including its spouse, and reassert its material appetites.

The desire of the disembodied soul was viewed as dangerous by the living, who had by all means to enchant, cajole, fight off, sedate, or otherwise distract and disable it. This requirement to keep the soul from the body after death did not last for ever, only so long as the flesh lay on the bones. For the progress of the body's decomposition was seen as analogous to the slow progress the soul made toward the threshold of the Otherworld. When the bones were white (or were sent up in smoke or whatever the rite in that community was), then it was deemed that the person had finally left this life and was no longer a danger to the living. Thus it was that for most of recent human history (roughly the last 35,000 years) funerary rites were twofold: the primary rites zoned off the freshly dead and instantiated the delicate ritual powers designed to keep the unquiet soul at bay; the secondary rites, occurring after weeks or months (or, sometimes – in the case of people who had wielded tremendous worldly power – years), firmly and finally incorporated the deceased into the realm of the ancestors.

Since the rise of science and scepticism, the idea of the

danger of the disembodied soul has, for an increasing number of communities, simply evaporated. But there is a law of conservation of questions. 'How can I stop the soul of the deceased reanimating the body?' is now being replaced with 'How can I live so long that my life becomes indefinite?', a question previously only asked by the most arrogant pharaohs and emperors.

We have forgotten what it is like to be really and truly afraid of malevelovent, disembodied human spirits, to feel haunted by ghosts. The Neolithic rites at Haddenham look strangely complex to us now. Indeed, a previous generation of archaeologists failed to realize that the bones were finally placed in the barrows as the culmination of highly elaborate rituals. Even the apparently straightforward Beaker rite only represents the last phase of what was a longer process: the identification of a prehistoric owl pellet inside the skull of a burial excavated at Bredon Hill demonstrates beyond doubt that, although the skeleton was kept intact, the flesh must have been long gone from it by the time it was interred under the barrow.[17]

It is now clear that all the traditional funeral rites studied by anthropologists the world over, whether they involve burial or not, have a shared logic – a common funeral choreography of hidden depth designed to protect the living against the dead. Elements of these rites still persist in the developed Western world even though their original purpose has long been forgotten. Attending the corpse and constantly reciting prayers in its presence, from the time of death to the time of burial, is still a requirement of Jewish law. The origin of the practice lies far back, when its specific purpose may have been to keep the soul from wandering away from the body and thus haunting others. Because the soul might follow a person if they left the house, the immediate family had to 'sit shmira' (or 'shiva') for seven days, not going out, and doing nothing but receiving visits of condolence. Today, the idea that an interruption in prayers or in sitting shmira would expose the bereaved to supernatural dangers is not, as far as I know, widely held; it is possible to visit the synagogue in this period to pray. The continued observance of such rites serves instead to signal respect and religious seriousness, to structure grief into mourning, to display commitment to traditional form, and to keep the dead company in a loving and humane way. Sitting shmira is no longer driven by heartfelt existential terror.[18]

In order to understand the Neolithic exposure platforms and long barrows we have to accept the reality of such terror in ancient peoples' minds. That, in turn, poses a question: at what point did we, as a species, start to believe in something like an immortal soul? Chimpanzees do not have such a belief, nor the capacity for it. Did we, as humans, 'invent death' when we first began to speak? Perhaps it was when we first began to bury the corpses of our dead. The last suggestion is seductive. To investigate it, it is necessary to track back to an early period of hominid prehistory, after our divergence from the other apes but before we became fully human, to a point some 2.6 million years ago. It was the time of the first chipped stone tools and a time when burial, if it occurred, was geological not ritual.

'I knew at a glance that what lay in my hands was no ordinary anthropoidal brain. Here in lime-consolidated sand was the replica of a brain three times as large as that of a baboon and considerably bigger than that of any adult chimpanzee. The startling image of the convolutions and furrows of the brain and the blood vessels of the skull was clearly visible,'[19] wrote the anatomist Raymond Dart of his discovery in 1924 of a 'missing link' in Buxton Limeworks, near Taung in South Africa. It was the fossilized cast of the inside of a young hominid cranium, still attached to most of the facial skeleton. A full set of milk teeth, with the molars just beginning to erupt, indicated an age at death of around three or four.

Dart rightly concluded that the 'Taung child' represented a new species, which he named *Australopithecus africanus* ('Southern ape of Africa'). But he was probably wrong to assume, because the fossil was found among a mass of broken animal bones, that the Taung australopithecines had specialized in game hunting. Recent reanalysis of the bone jumble suggests that it was created by a large bird of prey, probably a crowned eagle. The little australopithecines, for all their upright walking and intelligence, were a long way from the top of the food chain. Scavenging, foraging and the hunting of creatures smaller than themselves – monkeys, perhaps – were more their style.

Just discernible on Dart's fossil are marks where talons punched through the thin cranium into the extraordinarily precocious brain. Biomechanical tests on the lifting capacity of crowned eagles suggest that the child was eviscerated before being carried off.[20] There is no reason to suspect that such evisceration and the transportation of remains was not a common event. What was more unusual was that this particular young hominid's head fell among the remains of previous meals below the eyrie and was covered up before the eagle had really picked it over properly. Then, 2.6 million years later, an even less likely event occurred: it was found by a quarryman and recognized by Dart when he opened a consignment of fossils which he had asked to have sent to him.

When they died, there was little to stop ape-men, ape-women and ape-children from being torn to pieces. The dead were edible. Vultures, hyenas, crocodiles, rodents, insects, fish and bacteria each took the meat, blood and fat they wanted. What remained was scattered and trampled, then shattered and powdered by wind and rain. From time to time, small pieces of apparently inconsequential bone would become coated in mud or volcanic ash, and, by degrees, harden into stony fossils. The only near-complete skeletons of early hominids (two australopithecines, from Sterkfontein in South Africa and Hadar in Ethiopia – the 'Lucy' bones – and one *Homo ergaster* specimen, from Narioko-tome in Kenya)[21] were probably preserved by sudden events, such as flash floods, which can sweep an individual to their death and deposit them downstream, more or less in one piece, under layers of protective sediment.

The Taung child was killed and unceremoniously dumped.

But there is nothing to suggest that, had she or he died in the bosom of the community, there would have been anything like a funeral. What happened was probably similar to what happens among wild chimpanzees nowadays where the bodies of those who are not carried off by predators and who may have died weakened by disease are left. The chimpanzees may prod the body of the deceased to see if it moves and keep a vigil for a while, but eventually they will abandon the remains to scavengers.

Fast-forwarding through time from 2.6 million years ago to 26,000 years ago, we see a dramatic contrast. Humans just as intelligent as we are now had evolved and established themselves right across the Old World. It was no longer conceivable that a dead person would ordinarily be left lying around to be dragged off by hyenas or foxes. Approaching the height of the last Ice Age in Europe (the mid-Upper Palaeolithic period), we find wonderful cave paintings mixing naturalism with depictions of strange beast-men or masked shamans, implying the existence of a system of supernatural beliefs. By this time there is abundant evidence of ceremonial burial. Perhaps the most famous of around 150 discovered so far is the 'triple burial' from the open-air hunting site of Dolní Věstonice in the Czech Republic – a carefully posed interment of three young people, their faces covered in masks of red ochre, decorated with pierced fox teeth.

The community at Dolní Věstonice was made up of relative newcomers to Europe – anatomically modern *Homo sapiens* (AMHS) of Cro-Magnon type, who had, by degrees, been squeezing out the old, well-established population of Neander-thals. The Neanderthals, a robust, cold-adapted human form that evolved in parallel with AMHS before becoming extinct, had had most of Europe to themselves for the previous 100,000 years or more. The status of Neanderthals as a species remains the subject of one of the most long-running and hard-fought contro-versies in archaeology. It has been popular to consider them rather dim-witted. Their stone tools are made in a style, the 'Mousterian', that is considered unaesthetic and monotonous, and they appear not to have made durable art (at least, none of the cave paintings so far discovered has been attributed to their hand).

If one accepted the clear inferiority of Neanderthals, then the most obvious implication of the sudden appearance of ceremonial burials in Europe was that spiritual belief came into being – uniquely – in the brains of the incoming AMHS people. In John Pfeiffer's influential phrase, one could imagine that there had perhaps been a 'Creative Explosion', a critical moment when art and myth were born.[22] If this was so, then revering the dead by burying them with grave goods might suddenly have seemed the proper thing to do. Yet it is ironic, if not paradoxical, that, for many scholars, the ultimate proof of our arrival as rational beings should be the emergence of religious behaviour – something that must be considered irrational by many of the atheistic scholars who make this connection. As with so many neat ideas, the main problem with the 'Creative Explosion' is that it fits the data very poorly. Hints that this is so have been accumulating over a considerable period.

When, in the early 1960s, Ralph and Rose Solecki excavated what they believed was a deliberate burial, containing the pollen remains of multicoloured bouquets of wild hollyhocks and juniper along with other flowers and medicinal herbs, they caused a sensation. Not just because the bones in Shanidar cave in the remote Baradost mountains of Iraq were at least 60,000 years old – more than twice as old as the Upper Palaeolithic burials of Europe – but because they belonged to an adult male Neanderthal. Before this no one had really considered that Neanderthals might have been capable of spirituality.

The 'grave of flowers' was one of a number of remarkable finds at Shanidar. Among nine skeletons recovered was one of an adult who had sustained crippling injuries and who could not have survived without the constant attention of a close-knit community. In *Shanidar: The First Flower People*, published in 1971, Ralph Solecki argued not only that his Neanderthals had a kind of spirituality, but that they had belonged to a peaceful, loving society, where even the disabled were valued. Solecki provocatively implied that Neanderthals were morally superior to us – or at least to those modern humans who were at that time leading the United States in its bloody losing battle over Vietnam.

Solecki's data have been repeatedly challenged. The patches of flower pollen that were identified in samples taken from the area above the skeleton and which Solecki interpreted as the remains of funerary wreaths could have perhaps arrived in the cave by other means – windblown, or dropped from the pelts of sheltering animals.[23] The cave was large enough to house a small village of refugee Kurds during the 1970s but was dangerous. There is evidence, presented by Solecki himself, that some, at least, of the Neanderthals who lived there long before were killed in roof-falls.[24] This means that the evidence for 'natural' versus 'cultural' burial is not clear-cut. Scholars who rate the Neanderthals as intellectually inferior have rejected the ritual interpretation of a series of claimed cave burials from France to Uzbekistan and from the Crimea to the Levant. The absence of obvious grave goods at these sites opens the possibility that the excavated skeletons, many of which were incomplete, were no more than the result of random preservation following accidental death.

Scepticism about Shanidar suited the influential school of thought that held that Neanderthals were dumb, in both the literal and colloquial senses. Despite the fact that Neanderthals' brains were the same size as ours are now, it has been argued that they lacked the ability to speak a proper language.[25] The Neanderthal speech issue seems finally to have been settled by the identification of a Neanderthal hyoid bone, part of the larynx and instrumental in creating the kind of vocal range we have today.[26] Recent ground-breaking analysis of ancient mitochondrial DNA (mtDNA) from a Neanderthal baby found in Mezmaiskaya cave, Russia, suggests (along with two previous results) a degree of genetic difference between modern humans and Neanderthals which might indicate that they were a separate species,[27] but there is also evidence that Neanderthals and AMHS interbred. Early anatomically modern *Homo sapiens* and Neanderthals coexisted in the Near East, western Asia and Europe for tens of thousands of years: perhaps closely – a skeleton from Abrigo do Lagar Velho, Portugal, of a little boy who died 24,500 years ago displays Neanderthal and modern human features in roughly equal part.[28]

It is not just our knowledge of Neanderthals but the entire parameters of the burial debate that have shifted since Solecki's book came out. At 60,000 years old, although more than twice as old as Dolní Věstonice, Shanidar is only half as old as the most recent estimate for the age of the earliest burials. A number of skeletons of early anatomically modern humans buried in Skhūl cave in Israel were excavated in the 1930s by the pioneer Palaeolithic archaeologist, Dorothy Garrod, but it has only been through the recent application of a battery of advanced dating techniques – thermoluminescence, electron spin resonance, and uranium-series – that it has been possible to date them. Chris Stringer of the Natural History Museum in London, and his colleague, Rainer Grün of the Australian National University, estimate the date of interment of the Skhūl 9 skeleton, found with a pig's jaw and a fire-burnt flint tool, to have been around 120,000 years ago.[29] This fits well with a series of date estimates from other Levantine burial sites – Qafzeh near Nazareth, and Tabun on Mount Carmel.[30]

The fact that the skeletons at Skhūl and at Qafzeh are of the AMHS type – considered directly ancestral to the Cro-Magnons whose later ceremonial burials at sites like Dolní Věstonice are so striking – leads Grün and Stringer to the conclusion that symbolic burial is a 'modern human behaviour'. Yet the third early site mentioned, Tabun, has produced bones with strongly Neanderthal features as well as bones of more modern appearance in different layers of deposit. The Neanderthal remains at Tabun may be even earlier than the early AMHS humans at Skhūl and Qafzeh, but the way that they were preserved and excavated means that doubts must remain as to their status as deliberate burials.[31]

The continuing controversy over whether it was early AMHS or Neanderthals who first developed the capacity for burial misses a crucial point. Identifying the first reverential burial is important, because burial is likely to be connected to the existence of religious belief, and the existence of religious belief has implications for intellectual development. But the attractively simple idea that the things archaeologists label 'burials' actually provide good evidence for the emergence of religious sensibility among our remote ancestors is logically and fatally flawed. Absence of burial does not prove absence of religion.

By making the parallel between his caring, spiritual Neanderthals and the ethics of the Vietnam War, Solecki brought us to the heart of the matter. We have an emotional engagement with burials that makes it hard for us to see beyond them, to imagine what else they might be other than the remains of either accidents or funerals. It would be surprising if the first burials meant the same to the prehistoric people who may have dug them as our burials mean to us, over 100,000 years later.

Even in the recent past, ceremonial burial need not imply a funeral, nor that someone has already died. When an important building was constructed in eighteenth-century Fiji, living people – prisoners of war – were made to stand in the bottom of the deep foundation pits, each clasping one of the great corner posts upright, and were buried alive in that position.[32] At Nitriánsky Hradok, a fortified Bronze Age citadel in western Slovakia, archaeologists found a 4-metre-deep pit, like an underground room. At the bottom were the skeletons of ten adults, kneeling in a circle. They had raised their hands before their faces, not in chaotic struggle but neatly and uniformly as if calmly praying, while the earth was shovelled in on top of them. With the pit nearly full, a dog was sacrificed with a battleaxe, and both axe and dog also covered over, capping the extraordinary scene below.[33]

People do not need to bury their dead in order to show reverence to them or to their gods, and are not necessarily manifesting religious belief if they do bury them. So, while the religiously devout may be cremated and have their ashes scattered, at 'humanist' funerals people who did not hold any religious beliefs at all are buried by relatives and friends who may also hold no religious beliefs.[34]

Some burials lack any humane respect and serve purely to conceal. In 2001, Robert Mugabe's Zimbabwean army, fighting over cobalt and diamonds in the Democratic Republic of Congo, were ordered to dispose of battlefield fatalities as efficiently as they could without ceremony, preserving the illusion among the families back home that they were still alive and that the war was going well. One day, perhaps, these men will have funerals, but probably without their corpses being present. Even a body in a grave can be a cover-up for war atrocity – a thing made to look funeral-like in order to deflect an unwelcome investigation (many burials of this kind have been revealed in the aftermath of the recent conflict and genocide in Kosovo).[35]

Similar disposal patterns are evident in the prehistoric period, as in the Neolithic mass graves already mentioned in the Introduction. But the unmarked mass burial of massacre victims in the prehistoric period was probably thought of as having a twofold purpose. Beyond the cheap and practical disposal of corpses was the positive denial of a place in the afterlife. Death was an opportunity for rebirth, but only if the correct rituals were gone through.

The idea of death as a form of birth, and funerary ceremony as a kind of supernatural midwifery, brings us back to sacrifice. It is not just important people who are thought to be reborn, but deities too: 'Death is a portal through which gods and men alike must pass to escape the decrepitude of age and attain the vigour of eternal youth,' wrote Sir James Frazer in his provocative late Victorian masterpiece, *The Scapegoat* (Part 6 of *The Golden Bough*). In many cultures studied by social anthropologists, sacrificial animals or humans are deified before death. The animal or person identified with the god is able, through its death, to remove sin from the living community. Jesus Christ – Frazer argued – was one in a long line.

Reconsidering the burial of the horse's head at Grime's Graves

36

in this light, the ideas of 'horse' and 'burial' can both be questioned. I do not mean that what was found is not – in our terms – a buried horse cranium. But it could have been a horse that was believed to be possessed of the spirit of a goddess (a horse-deity like the – much later – Celtic *Epona*). Or, like the biblical scapegoat in the Book of Leviticus, the mare could have had the entire community's sins loaded on to her head to nullify them when she died. In that sense, the ceremony at the pit edge may not have been a reverential disposal of an old horse, but an act of social renewal. Then again, the mare may have been a tribal totem: while she lived, she may have been thought of as not merely a horse, but a creature possessed by a human ghost. In this case, the strange burial may have been the final phase of a long-drawn-out *human* funeral rite.

Philosophers of science recognize the 'interpretive dilemma' in all attempts at archaeological explanation: in order to interpret something, I must have decided that there is something to interpret. Inevitably, by focusing on that something, I will have already formed some idea of what it is. I say I want to investigate the meaning of this or that burial, but I have already decided the most significant thing about it when I called it a 'burial'. The possibility of understanding anything new and surprising is dramatically lessened.

To comprehend the profounder things about prehistory, it is important to understand how different the thoughts and feelings that Ötzi had in his last few minutes may have been to those that we would be likely to have if we found ourselves in a similar situation. It is easy to imagine a familiar gamut of emotions: anger at having lost in combat, fear in relation to the pain, shock when the tip-less shaft comes out, determination to survive, and, finally, resignation in the face of death. But, although Ötzi must have felt pain in the same physiological way that modern people do, his attitude to it is likely to have been bound up with belief in opposing supernatural forces. Modern anger in such a situation would tend to be secular, directed towards earthly causes and failures – the aggressor and/or ourselves. Ötzi's anger was probably sacred, directed at a tutelary spirit – an ancestral guardian to whom he had diligently sacrificed and who had at last failed him; as consciousness faded, he may have been impatient to meet this guardian in the afterlife to find out what had gone so badly wrong.

CHAPTER 2

A Skeleton Illuminated by Lightning

For of the soul the body form doth take;
For soul is form, and doth the body make.

Edmund Spenser, *An Hymn in Honour of Beauty*[1]

———

Purple storm clouds roll in over steep, pine-forested crags. In a small clearing, a skeleton is illuminated by a flash of lightning. Torrential rain starts to fill an opened grave. Alone, I wrestle with a billowing sheet of white plastic in the wild undergrowth and methodically secure it in place with heavy rocks, covering the skeleton from view.

The summer of 1982 was my fourth season working in Austria. I had just graduated with an Archaeology and Anthropology degree from Cambridge and was being employed as part of a University of Vienna team investigating the great medieval settlement known as Gars/Thunau. The site is defended by a massive rampart to the west and to the east by precipices that fall to the River Kamp far below. What was once a thriving town of Christianized Slavs is now upland meadow – the Holzwiese. Previous excavations on the Holzwiese had revealed large numbers of potsherds and the remains of wattle-and-daub houses. The skeletons of a child and a broken-necked woman had also been found, dumped on top of what had been a domestic rubbish pit,[2] and another adult female skeleton appeared to have been trapped in the remains of a burnt-down building.

Invading Magyar horsemen from the Hungarian plain had destroyed the entire settlement, along with its Carolingian church, in the first half of the tenth century. Over time, the ramparts became overgrown and the dreadful events were slowly forgotten. Local farmers still held that the Holzwiese was haunted but whether because of some faint folk memory or because they occasionally turned up bones is hard to say.

We were digging in the lower part of the Holzwiese, not far

Excavations on the Holzwiese at Gars/Thunau, Austria.
(Photo: author)

from the steep drop to the Kamp, in what turned out to be the precinct of the lost church. Centuries of intermittent ploughing on the meadow had reduced the original ground level so much that we had not dug more than a spade's depth when we came across the grave. The first sign was the characteristic darker oblong of earth and then we began to uncover the skeleton. It was on its back, in a relaxed and tidy position, without grave goods, suggesting a Christian rite.

As we worked through the afternoon, using trowels, paint-brushes and spatulas to expose the skull and ribs and clean the earth away from the vertebrae, the atmosphere grew humid, the unmistakable lead-up to a violent central European summer storm. *In situ* drawing and photography had to wait as the priority was to protect the grave. We covered the excavation over with plastic sheeting, weighting the edges with large stones, and set off up the steep forest path, carrying our equipment. As we reached the farm track leading to the camp, a VW Golf thundered to a halt and three local lads jumped out. The previous night, drinking with members of the football club in the nearby village of Tautendorf, I had agreed to show some of them the skeleton. The public education aspect of archaeology was taken seriously by the dig director, Professor Herwig Friesinger, and site tours were encouraged.

The four of us drove back as far as the car could manage, and made the rest of the descent on foot. Volleys of rain spattered the leaves and the temperature fell. As the sky darkened, the white plastic protecting the skeleton became visible through the tree trunks, rippling uneasily. The three visitors formed a little group, standing further from the edge of the excavation than was strictly necessary. As I removed the stones, the storm broke, the wind whipped the sheeting out of my hands, and a massive flash of lightning lit up the excavation. The skeleton flickered horribly in its grave and the footballers turned tail, and ran back up into the trees. I shouted after them for help but in vain. I was left alone to pull the flapping plastic out of the undergrowth and secure it back in place single-handed. Drenched, I returned to the camp, where some puzzlement was expressed over the way that the VW Golf had hurtled back up the track at such a crazy pace, without its occupants even stopping for a beer. Like a medieval *memento mori* – anonymous bones displayed in church with a Latin motto expressing a sentiment of the type 'Remember that you have to die' – the excavated skeleton was a reminder for a more secular age of the horrid finality of death.

Whoever it was that we exhumed that day, they had believed the world to be flat, overarched by the literal heavens. Today, we can gaze at the near boundless extent of deep space and heaven remains invisible. Maybe the universe is pure mechanism with no need of a divine creator, and we are mere sub-mechanisms within it. The chemist Peter Atkins thinks so: 'The universe can emerge out of nothing, without intervention. By chance.'[3] But even chance has to come from somewhere,[4] and there appear to be other qualities in the universe, such as love, beauty and truth, that are not the rarefied products of matter, energy, space and time, however defined and divided. Pages of obscure equations do not account for our powerful sense that we exist.

What we may once have seen as the core of our identity, the soul, is, nevertheless, increasingly hard to believe in. As the wellsprings of personality and action are purportedly laid bare by science, there seems as little space for the soul in the body as for God in the universe. Paradoxically, the very things that persuaded the ancients that we had souls – the dream flights and visions produced by the use of drugs or sacred herbs, which presaged the grander spirit flight of death itself – are the same phenomena used by cognitive scientists as evidence that the concept of 'dualism', of mind and body as a dichotomy, is artificial. Mainstream science sees consciousness as a wholly material and chemical creation. As a result, we feel that the only things that can extend or enhance our experience of being are material and chemical too. Happiness is pursued through the manipulation of brain chemistry, while the promotion of everything from vitamin supplements to advanced gene therapy and cryogenic chambers encourages us to dream, if not of immortality, then of the imminent possibility of indefinitely postponed mortality.

The urge to continue existing for ever is not uniquely modern. It is embodied in the pyramids of Egypt, the underground palace complex of the dead First Emperor of China at Mount Li, and in the sacrifice of more than 360 horses to provide mounts and mare's milk in perpetuity for the Iron Age Scythian chieftain buried at Ulski Aul, north of the Black Sea. Nevertheless the nature of the aspiration for immortality today is different. Science asserts that death, when it comes, is truly the end. By picking apart its causes – a lethal gene here, a hormone imbalance there – the secular medical establishment presents death to us, not as a mystery that mirrors the mystery of life, but as a set of definable physical degradation processes. Each of these marks a challenge to be overcome.

Hospitals are where the modern world dreams of death. Our experiences of drugs and anaesthetics shape our view of mortality as profoundly as trance dances shaped those of our ancestors. Illuminated by X-rays rather than lightning, we see our own skeletons buried in our living flesh. We are the first people to have such personalized mementi mori, such secularized altered states.[5] But far from demystifying mortal life, photo-revelation only makes it more inscrutable. Just as our telescopes cannot discern God in heaven, X-rays reveal nothing of the human spirit. If we expect the soul to be buried somewhere in the body we are disappointed, unless we identify it with the dense contents of the skull itself.

On 2 April 2000, the John Radcliffe Hospital in Oxford admitted that, back in 1984, it had removed the brain of Marc Clynes (a baby who died of SIDS – Sudden Infant Death Syndrome), and thrown it out in medical waste, without his parents' consent or knowledge. Marc's mother, Barbie, is reported as saying 'We are not religious but I believe your soul is your brain. How can you bury someone if they haven't got their soul?'[6]

The idea that the theft of a baby's brain is, practically speaking, the theft of its soul is a complex one. In his book *Consciousness*

Explained, artificial intelligence (AI) guru Daniel Dennett argues that our feeling of selfhood is an illusion. For Dennett, the feeling I have of being 'me' stems from the fact that I have a 'centre of narrative gravity' – a place I call myself – a virtual 'X' in the midst of my brain's computational activities that is a convention only, as indistinguishable from what surrounds it as the snow at the precise North Pole is from the rest of the Arctic waste. On this reckoning, the core of my identity, a thing that I could, if I liked, choose to think of as my soul, is not something that really exists. For Dennett, the meaning of 'soul' can in reality be no more than an expression for consciousness itself, and consciousness is, in turn, seen to be an effect of neural metabolism. When organic death switches the metabolism off, consciousness ceases and that is that. In these terms, Marc's brain was his soul, if that is what we decide to call it.

The particle physicist and religious thinker John Polkinghorne has memorably objected to Dennett's view, saying: 'I do not regard our notion of selfhood as being just a convenient manner of speaking (by whom? one might ask).'[7] Polkinghorne does not think the soul is the brain or any apparent focus within it: 'My soul is the real me, but that is neither a spiritual entity temporarily housed in the physical husk of my body, nor is it just the matter that makes up my body'; the soul and the body are not separate. Viewed like this, Marc's brain never was his soul, but it was once an integral part of it. Although couched in academic language, this is a mainstream view.

'Everyone in Tinseltown is getting pinched, lifted and pulled. The trade-off is that something of your soul in your face goes away. You end up, in the last analysis, looking body-snatched'[8] – the actor and film maker Robert Redford's indictment of plastic surgery echoes the thought expressed by the philosopher Ludwig Wittgenstein: 'The human body is the best picture of the human soul.'[9] This, in turn, harks back to the poet Edmund Spenser ('For of the soul the body form doth take;/For soul is form, and doth the body make'), developing a medieval idea approved of by the theologian Thomas Aquinas.[10] Cosmetic surgery, like AI research, looks at human essentials in terms of mechanism and repairability. Both may run risks in the trade-off between a little bit of living history, old yet vital, and its substitution with a little bit of technology that is of its time, new for a moment yet unalive.

It is so hard to imagine life without a body that the Catholic Church recently provided guidance on how to do it, restating the idea as 'the continuation and subsistence, after death, of the spiritual element, endowed with consciousness and will, in such a way that, although lacking the complement of its own body for a time, the "human I" itself subsists.'[11] The possibility of such a state has been imagined for millennia. The sixth-century BC Greek mathematician Pythagoras supported the idea of metempsychosis, in which our immortal souls strive, through a series of reincarnations, to free themselves from the 'wheel of becoming'. The Buddha, Gautama Siddartha, was a contemporary of Pythagoras who believed much the same thing, and both may have been building on a body of magico-religious thinking that was shared by Iron Age communities in Eurasia.[12] Recent popular thinking in the West on the possibility of being able to leave our bodies has been dominated by the medical context again, and reports of near-death experiences.

Not long after my grandfather's death, I remember undergoing an operation in the Jenny Lind children's hospital in Norwich. Drowsy after a pre-op, I was placed on a metal gurney and wheeled away down long, echoing, Victorian corridors, punctuated by swing-doors. A nurse bent over me outside the final pair of doors and, warning me of 'a little scratch', plunged a needle into the back of my left hand. There was no time to scream – not even a recollection of the needle coming back out.

In retrospect, the moment of becoming unconscious had a quite distinct quality: an almost audible, almost visual sensation that gave way to a muffled aftershock as my ears reopened in a great airy ward and my eyes tipped me into the upturned hull of the soaring roof. Pale daylight filtered through dim, iron-rimmed panes. The bed pushed my own weight up against my back, and

I mentally righted myself in space, feeling a detached satisfaction in being alive. Seeing now that I had been cut open and sewn up, I wondered how it could be that my body had been physical for the surgeons but more absent from me than ever in the deepest sleep. I asked myself if the absence I had felt while under anaesthetic was what death was, minus the waking up bit.

My general anaesthetic revealed a new kind of limit to conscious life to me. But it did not reveal the nature of death. It was just an experience of a particular mental edge, after which I felt as if I had been restarted. Like a jump-cut in a car-chase movie, it was as if a section of journey was missing: two roads that did not normally join up had been connected. Other people have spoken of altered states in hospital in terms of crossing a boundary into another kind of space entirely. There is no jump-cut: the film keeps running, but the point of vision changes, rising above the body to look at it from outside and then, turning from the body, moving towards a shining light. Perhaps the most notorious such claim of modern times was made in 1988 by A.J. 'Freddie' Ayer.

The doyen of Oxford philosophy, A.J. Ayer, had an almost legendary hostility to anything that could remotely be considered mystical. His 1936 book *Language, Truth and Logic* was the classic statement of 'logical positivism' which held that meaningful statements about the world had either to be testable by observation or to be analytically true – wholly logical when set out as a linguistic argument. When he found himself in hospital for a short spell with the food less than adequate, an ex-lover smuggled some smoked salmon in to him; he choked on it, nearly died and had what is known as a 'near-death experience' (NDE).

The event appears to have provoked Ayer's spectacular conversion from an anti-mystical, baldly modernist philosophy to belief in life after death. In an article for the *Sunday Telegraph* entitled 'What I saw when I was dead', Ayer talked about the feeling of moving out of his own body towards a bright light and later seeing the River Styx that in classical mythology forms the boundary between this world and Hades, the Land of the

Dead.[13] This is all typical of the near-death experience, although those who lack Freddie Ayer's classical education do not see the Styx but are more likely to be welcomed into an English rose garden before regretfully turning their backs and abruptly regaining their bodies in hospital. For the Chinese, a mist resolves into the moment of passing a bureaucratic exam with flying colours and their return to the everyday involves a recall by the presiding mandarin, who informs them of a clerical error.[14]

Because NDEs meet cultural expectations (entering rose gardens and achieving bureaucratic promotion are just some among many stereotypical versions), it has been suggested that they can only be an extreme form of reverie, part of the mind's final shut-down phase before the total oblivion of death. It has also been claimed that people who know something in advance about the usual form that NDEs take are less likely to experience them if they find themselves in near-death situations. This can be interpreted to mean that those who are forewarned of the mind's illusory power *in extremis* are somehow inoculated against it. But an omnipotent God could design a point of death that consistently met expectations and secret desires, whether that involved a spectacular display or a mundane drift into unconsciousness.

No one who reports a near death experience is actually near enough death to die, so the experience could be one of our survival mechanisms, calming the mind so that it can overcome a moment of extreme physical crisis. All we can really say is that near death experiences are a special case of 'out of body' experience. These are widely reported by victims of profound violent or sexual abuse during childhood, as well as by shamans, who regard them as trance flights in the spirit world. The ancient Egyptians believed that something like an NDE happened every night, when the soul of the sleeper rose up out of the body, attached only by a silver cord: dreams were revealed to the soul while in this special out-of-body state.

Visions can happen without the sensation of disembodiment, and these, too, can be interpreted as evidence for a world beyond the everyday. The recently bereaved often have the experience of a visit by their dead loved one. The fact that the Victorians 'saw' fairies and were enthusiastic about, and fearful of, spectres, while few of either are reported today, might suggest cultural rather than supernatural principles at work.[15] It is very hard to separate out the physical metabolism, the psyche that arises from and acts on it, and the cultural etiquette that frames and controls external inputs and internal outlook. All we know is that the human brain has a hallucinatory power, but precisely what stimulates it in each case, and what people consequently feel about particular apparitions – what they believe they were and what they meant – is private, sensitive in every way, and ultimately impossible for science to analyse.

The Victorians were notoriously interested in death, and not just in their own culture. The way that indigenous ('savage' and 'barbarous') peoples dealt with death was reported in great detail by social anthropologists such as A.R. Brown, Sir James Frazer and W.H.R. Rivers. They observed that the Koryak of Siberia and the Pennefather River Aborigines of Queensland, along with other tribal peoples in other parts of the world, believed in more than one soul per person – for instance, a benevolent one that goes quietly to the afterlife and a malevolent one that hangs over the dead body.[16] They also noted that the kind of soul(s) that people are considered to possess – indeed the possibility of having a soul at all – varies with age, gender and rank. When a woman dies among the Windessi of New Guinea 'both her spirits go down to the nether world, but one of the two souls of a man may pass into another man, who thus acquires unusual and mysterious gifts'.[17] Ideas of similar complexity exist in Ancient Egyptian theology, the philosophy of Plato, and in St Paul's distinction of spirit from soul.

When the Koryak, Pennefather River Aborigine, and Windessi peoples spoke about the things that anthropologists called 'soul', 'ghost' and 'spirit', their conversation was undoubtedly subtly shaded.[18] Ethnographic descriptions are translations from a language not just of foreign words but foreign acts. Even so, there is no doubt that beliefs about animating principles that reside in our bodies and may at certain times, in certain ways, to certain degrees, become separable are widespread.

In every culture it is possible to behave disrespectfully towards the dead, despite the fact that there is no testable empirical proof that 'the dead' exist beyond their physical remains. Showing disrespect to a deity is similar, and involves a similar dual uncertainty. 'Having shown that men are incapable of proving the existence of God, we know that they cannot disprove him either,' wrote the German philosopher Immanuel Kant.[19] The same goes for souls. Although science has been famously able to disprove many things previously promoted as true by religion, such as the idea that our earth is situated at the centre of the universe, it is unable to either prove or disprove the existence of the soul. Science may speculate but cannot rule on whether there is 'life after death'. The words and the concepts that they appear to label are too slippery.

Modern speculation about death is not aided by the fact that Western cultures have grown unfamiliar with death 'in the flesh'. Despite wall-to-wall news media and feature film depictions, it is quite possible to live a full and long life in a major centre of population without ever seeing an actual dead human, either accidentally or electively, and some people do. By contrast, no medieval town was complete without its gallows, where death was publicly displayed both as a process and as a state.

Medieval law reflected the fact that killing was such a habitual phenomenon that penalties needed to be fine-tuned down to the level of the youngest potential perpetrator: 'Now an infant kills a man by accident. If an infant kills by accident he shall be fined nine marks, and nothing to king or hundred [the district administration]. If he is seven years or less and kills with intent, he shall be fined four marks and a half; if he kills by accident, he shall be fined three marks to the aggrieved party alone. If there is injury, but not homicide, then no compensation shall be paid for injuries.' These lines from the fourteenth-century law code of King Magnus Eriksson of Sweden, which goes on to discuss the position if the infant denies the killing,[20] fit the picture painted by a range of skeletal data from archaeological excavations indicating that children were not uncommonly in the thick of mortal combat in historic and prehistoric periods. Magnus himself had been a monarch since the age of three, and must have been swinging swords and axes from the time that he began to walk.

Compare this awareness to the modern period and the case of a young man who stabbed his mother to death with a kitchen knife in the garden of their rural Berkshire home.[21] In his statement to the police he explained how, even before he was convinced she was dead, he had opened her chest cavity and cut out her heart to eat it. Finding that he did not like the taste he went into the house to fry it, but it still tasted unpleasant and he gave up. Curiously, the post-mortem examination established that the woman's heart remained intact. However, exhibit SPG/15, retrieved from the crime scene with vegetation adhering to it, and already partially decomposed, turned out to be a 9 × 7 centimetre piece of lung. The case betrays both an incompetence in killing (the son was unsure at what point his mother died) and ignorance of basic anatomy.

Perhaps our animal spirits, if they are left with few constructive outlets, have a tendency to spill over uncontrollably, in psychopathy. People took a much more habitual responsibility for death, including their own, in the medieval period. As the French historian Philippe Ariès argued, an individual was obliged to detect their own impending death and make proper arrangements for it, receiving visitors, giving blessings, asking forgiveness, making final bequests, and receiving the sacraments, before dying with composure. Books such as the seventeenth-century *The Art to Dye Well* encouraged men and women to make themselves masters of their own deaths.[22] Today we farm out death to experts, part of whose role may be to obscure its imminence from the dying patient. Death is seen as a tragic failure rather than as the necessary culmination of a good life.

The difference between the medieval and the modern is not just about control or self-control of the body. It reflects a shift in attitudes concerning the idea of the soul and its imagined ultimate destination. Modern Western culture frees us to live existences in which decisive physical action and heartfelt belief are sidelined to a point where it is consumer luxuries rather than honour that are 'to die for'.

For materialists, when someone dies, there is, abruptly, in place of a person, a bag of bone and gas and meat and fluid which, according to the cause of death, the nature of the last meal, the ambient temperature and humidity and so on, begins to swell, fart, burp and stink.[23] Death is an embarrassment, levelling City bankers and convicted felons: the corpse mocks our pretence to have been anything at all. But there is an alternative point of view, expressed most sharply in religious fundamentalism, where the conditions under which one becomes a corpse – the way one dies – are the basic affidavits of continuing to exist as an honourable person.

In November 1997, a group of tourists was visiting the Temple of Hatshepsut in the Valley of the Queens. Without warning, a small group of young men appeared, chanting the name of Allah and firing machine-guns. They forced young children to kneel before their parents and then shot them. They mocked a man before decapitating him in front of his daughter. They laughed as they raped and then cut the throats of several young women. Finally they were themselves shot dead by armed Egyptian police. We know these details because some of the tourists, by playing dead, survived the massacre, adding eyewitness testimony to the forensic and police evidence. The al-Jamaya al-Islamiyya, who carried out the atrocity, are (or were) Islamic fundamentalists, part of a network of organizations funded by Osama Bin Laden. The activities in the Valley of the Queens were a sign of their growing confidence.

Fundamentalists are convinced that their belief is absolutely right and others are absolutely wrong; in this all fundamentalist movements are remarkably similar. The term first began to be applied to Christian communities in parts of the USA in the 1920s, and it has recently been extended to cover certain brands

51

of Islam, Hinduism, Buddhism and Judaism. Group members are often prepared to countenance, and sometimes prepared to carry out, the killing of non-believers; they are also sometimes willing to die.

There are obviously complex psychological reasons behind any individual's attraction to martyrdom. Dominating their thought world is the idea of salvation. But this does not account for why one true believer is predisposed towards it while for another it remains low on the list of ambitions. Nor does it explain why Christian fundamentalists seem less prone to martyr themselves nowadays than Islamic fundamentalists. Other things must therefore be involved. Martyrdom may perhaps present a reputable solution to the problem of suicide in a society in which suicide *per se* is considered the most dishonourable form of death. The idea may also, strangely enough, hold out a promise of pleasure. Sorely frustrated by the sensory austerity of religious authoritarianism, one reason that the testosterone-driven al-Jamaya al-Islamiyya males may have done what they did is that – unlike Christian fundamentalist conceptions of a cerebral and celibate, harp-playing posterity in heaven – Islamic scriptures can be interpreted as promising the supremely sensual delights of a luxurious Paradise for those who die prosecuting *jihad*.

The words *can be interpreted* are important: prophetic discourse is always open to interpretation. On the basis of her reading of the powerful and beautiful passages concerning the Day of Judgment, Rabi'a al-Adawiyya (AD 717–801), the freed slave who founded the Sufist tradition in Islam, concluded that the true lover of God (Allah) can have no space for despising the world and that a sincere, authentic life is incompatible with acting either out of hope of reward or, equally, out of fear of punishment.[24] It is likely that the Valley of the Queens killers, on the other hand, were principally motivated by belief in the immediate personal translation of their souls to Paradise on martyrdom. They believed that their actions (which Rabi'a al-Adawiyya would certainly have deemed both mad and evil) were right and just, part of a cosmic struggle against the secular

Western world. The Qur'ān, taken literally, promises that men will be welcomed into Paradise by 'maidens, chaste, restraining their glances, whom no man or *jinn* before them has touched'.[25] For the al-Jamaya al-Islamiyya, rape, torture and murder may have become, in their imaginings, a means to arrive at a beautiful place of crystal fountains where they would be served sherbet for eternity by naked women, under the benevolent and direct gaze of God himself.

All fundamentalist movements are closely linked by their attitude to death, their adherents immovably convinced that death is not just not the end, but the only true beginning.[26] The critical nature of entry into the life beyond is determined by the sort of spiritual stock that has been built up in this life, with the greatest credit being awarded for rigid conformity and the execution of uncomfortable, dangerous or intolerant actions. These actions may also attempt to purge the world of perceived evil, making it a simulacrum of the world beyond. Part of the logic of fundamentalist struggles is the idea that there will not be room for everyone in the beyond, whether it is Paradise or Heaven, and that the souls of non-believers are of less value than those of the group members, who, through submission to Allah or God, consider themselves alone to be truly human.

The religious metaphysics that privileges the salvation of the invisible above all things can be seen as the pathological counterpart of shallow consumerism, which values possessions and appearances. The Western governmental and media response to the atrocity in the Valley of the Queens was as secular as could be imagined. It did not focus on the composure and bravery that some of the victims showed in facing their inevitable deaths – the less pleasant details were too uncomfortable to dwell on – but on whether Egypt should have been deemed a safe destination for tourists.

Where consumerism meets fundamentalism we see, on the one hand, a denial of the sovereignty of death and, on the other hand, a denial of the importance of life. These are polar opposites, each unbalanced on its own. Ancient writers wrote about the necessity of balancing life with death, pleasure with pain, darkness with light. Unsurprisingly, Sigmund Freud, in ransacking classical mythology to create a science of clinical health, seized on the idea of balance and attempted to rebrand it. What he came up with was the almost wilfully obscure concept of the 'death drive' (*Thanatos*),[27] the primordial equal and opposite to the 'sex drive' (*Eros*).

In Freud's time, it was Eros that caused the stir: discussion of sex was suppressed while death was writ large across European society. But today, in part as a result of Freud, the tables have turned. Sex is in the ascendancy and it is death which is the embarrassment. Only Eros has survived in the system of Freudian psychoanalysis that developed, predominantly in the United States, after Freud's death. As Bruno Bettelheim has remarked:

> To imagine, as many Americans do, that psychoanalysis makes it possible to build a satisfying life on a belief in the sexual, or life, drive alone is to misunderstand Freud completely. Just as an exclusive preoccupation with the death drive would make us morbidly depressed and ineffective, an exclusive preoccupation with the sexual, or life, drive can only lead to a shallow, narcissistic existence, because it evades reality and robs life of what makes every moment of it uniquely significant – the fact that it might be our last one.[28]

The historical shift in the West from sacred to secular, from a belief in the perfected soul freed at death towards an emphasis on the perfected body, ruined by it, has left us peculiarly confused. The confusion is currently being played out in the heart of my own discipline in the 'reburial' issue – the conflicting and competing claims of archaeologists and those who identify themselves as the distant descendants of the people whose bones archaeologists excavate. The early Christian skeleton on the Holzwiese was not exhumed for spiritual reasons but excavated as part of a scientific agenda, to satisfy our backwards-looking curiosity. Unconsciously, however, such uncovery may serve to generate a vicarious familiarity with death. The ability to interpret and, in a sense, control the prehistoric dead may be a modern kind of consolation in the face of uncertainty and disempowerment concerning our own mortality.

Despite their differences, the archaeology of human bones and the religious logic of the *memento mori* share something crucial – the idea that bones are things *left behind* by people. As the plastic sheeting was torn out of my hand and the lightning flashed, a thing that had become separated off – the skeleton – was revealed. The footballers' response was genuine. In staying to replace the plastic sheeting, I was ignoring the vibrancy of the uncovered ritual. The static presence spoke volumes for the existence of a corresponding and active absence. The human skeleton almost forces us to shape an image of equal and opposite power in our mind's eye, an image of what has most critically gone – not, in essence, flesh or blood, but vitality and movement or, in a word, the soul.

Medieval charnel houses, Tarot cards, archaeological investigations – the image of the skeleton has become such a familiar personification of death that we no longer think it odd, although it can be shocking. Yet if we did not happen to already believe that the soul is a separable entity, then we might not choose burial or cremation for a corpse. Rejecting any suggestion that death forces a division, we might view the dead body not so much as dead, but rather as a person in a special state of spirit-imbued latency, like a sleeper dreaming. The absence of regular burial from most of world prehistory may not be a symptom of spiritual or mental incapacity, or of the vagaries of archaeological preservation. It may be a signal that, for most of the time that genus *Homo* has been on the planet, there was a more obvious way to deal with death.

CHAPTER 3

The Edible Dead

Often, in the back country of Montana a hole will be dug and the body, in a plain pine coffin or perhaps just wrapped in a tie-dyed cloth, will be lowered into the ground. Instead of a tombstone, a fruit tree is planted over the body. The roots are nourished by the return of that body into the earth from which it was sustained. And in the years to follow, eating the fruit from that tree will be like partaking in that loved one. It touches on the ritual of the Eucharist.

STEPHEN LEVINE, *Who Dies?*[1]

In Hereford Cathedral hangs the Mappa Mundi, the finest surviving medieval map of the world. Veined by dark rivers and seas, and held within a thin rind of encircling ocean studded with squashed amorphous islands, the yellow-brown earth on the undulating vellum is reminiscent of a giant cow pat. The map is the work of one Richard of Haldingham who, in his own words, 'made it and set it out, that he may be granted bliss in heaven'.

Haldingham enhanced the outlandish character of distant cities, mountains and countries with images of unfamiliar beasts and men, and carefully labelled them in spidery Latin. Just above Scythia, on the banks of the River Jaxartes, and with their victim's head gazing blankly up at them, the cannibals appear: a dis-

56

turbing miniature image of two people enthusiastically tucking into a meal of freshly butchered human legs and arms from which the blood runs free and red. Near them is a bear, roaming in mountains labelled as the Carpathians – one of the last places in Europe where bears still roam free today – and beyond that the city of Prague is marked. But Haldingham also inked fictions: a griffin, a manticore and a minotaur.

Despite denial and dissent, there is now overwhelming biological, anthropological and archaeological evidence that cannibalism was once all around us. New imaging techniques have allowed us to see more clearly than ever before that some hominid bones are striated with deliberate cut marks – marks made with stone tools when the bone was still fresh and 'green'. The fact that such marks have been observed on different continents and date to a range of different periods has prompted Chris Stringer, of the Natural History Museum, London, to remark in a recent interview that 'the fossil record is only a tiny sample of the people who lived in the past. If we are picking up butchery in this very sparse sample of humans and human behaviour in the past, then it cannot have been a very rare event.'[2] Cannibalism may even explain why so few of the bones of our ancestors were preserved recognizably in burials or anywhere else. Bones make poor eating, but smashing and splitting them for brains and marrow increases fragmentation while cooking hastens the destruction of bone collagen.

Archaeologists have to infer behaviour from mute remains. We cannot obtain photographs of people eating each other in prehistory, so any claim that cannibalism took place has to be based on plausible explanations of what we call signatures – patterns of marking, breaking and preservation believed to correlate with a given activity. Cut marks on long bones or evidence for skulls having been cooked or altered to remove brains are both potential cannibalism signatures. Plausibility, in turn, is connected to what we think we know about behaviour from what we now see around us. Because cannibalism is not easily observable in today's world, being represented only at the psychopathic fringes, we may remain doubtful that it was ever a custom among our ancestors.

Maps like the Mappa Mundi were well known to Christopher Columbus. He disbelieved their flat-earth geometry, but took careful note of their social geography, because he thought it might provide him with valuable clues as to his relative position on what was in reality a spinning globe. The little man-eating vignette, captioned 'Essedenes', was one of the more important because it referred to a tribe first mentioned by the fifth-century BC writer Herodotus, who lived in the Black Sea lands of Scythia. Beyond these lay China and the lands of the Great Khan. Columbus and his Spanish backers were rivals of the Portuguese, who had recently broken the Mongol control of the lucrative Spice Island trade by sailing south round both Africa and India to reach the East Indies directly. Columbus' apparently contrary plan was to sail west in order to reach Asia. On reaching what we now know as the Caribbean, he was told of an infamous tribe referred to variously as *Caribes*, *Canibes*, or *Canibales*, said to eat human flesh. This vastly excited him as he thought that man-eaters could be located nowhere else but Asia, being the *Khan*-ibales, the most savage subjects of the Great Khan himself.[3]

By painful degrees it dawned on his contemporaries that Columbus was wrong about what he claimed to have found. Nevertheless rumours of people-eating abounded in the Americas, suggesting that more than one nation indulged in the practice. Henceforth always known as *cannibalism*, it quickly became a – perhaps *the* – shorthand for branding people as savage and uncivilized, fair game for European 'betterment' and exploitation wherever they lived.

The classic cartoon of white missionaries bubbling in the South Sea island cauldron is an extraordinarily durable icon of cannibalism. Responding to it and to the tales of Victorian travellers who inspired it, the social anthropologist William Arens in his book *The Man-Eating Myth* declared, 'I am dubious about the actual existence of this act as an accepted practice for any time or place.' Published in 1979, *The Man-Eating Myth* noted the racism of nineteenth-century ethnographers and called into doubt every-thing they described. From this time onward, as I have shown in the discussion of muti killing, some social anthropologists, sensitive to their discipline's colonialist past, began to deny, ignore the existence of, or generously reinterpret a range of human activities. These were too extreme to be condoned under the banner of amiable cultural diversity, and included clitoridec-tomy (amelioratively renamed 'female circumcision'), human sac-rifice and cannibalism. Arens' thesis was that the label 'cannibal' was actually an accusation – a deliberately derogatory, and often imperialist, exercise in name-calling that had no basis in fact. Stories of cannibal kings were libels on happy forest-dwelling tribespeople.

Long before Arens, anthropologists had recognized cases where the label 'cannibal' was denigratory and untrue. But Arens' criteria for rejection were blanket and, at times, bizarre. For example, he cast doubt on Hans Staden's famous seven-teenth-century account of cannibalism among the Tupi of coastal Brazil for the explicitly stated reason that in it most of the pur-ported butchery and consumption were done by women rather than men, and that this was inherently unbelievable. His short book was extraordinarily influential, not because it was soundly argued, but because it was what a new generation wanted to hear, despite the fact that many senior social anthropologists thought it an academic sleight of hand. Among a sheaf of poor professional reviews, one (from P.G. Rivière in the journal *Man*) called it 'a dangerous book. With little work and less scholarship, it may well be the origin of a myth.'[4] And so it turned out. Arens' ideas were accepted in vague form by many who lacked the expertise to assess his claims and judgements including, unfortunately, many archaeologists.

As late as 1977 the human-origins scholar Richard Leakey was quite at ease with evidence suggesting that *Homo erectus*, known from the fossil bones of 'Peking Man' preserved in Zhoukoudian (or Choukoutien) Cave dating to between a quarter and a half million years ago, were cannibalized: 'many of the limb bones were shattered. So too were some of the skulls. But in a number of them the opening through which the spinal cord runs had clearly been enlarged – a difficult task, calling for particular care ... Peking Man probably did eat the brains of his fellows.' Leakey argued that this was a ritual behaviour, but was open minded about 'whether the aim of the feat was to gain power over enemies by devouring the brains of the vanquished, or to maintain a bond of continuity with a deceased relative'.[5] Post-Arens, no one felt able to interpret the evidence in this way any more.[6] *The Oxford Companion to Archaeology* of 1996 is typical in sidestepping the issue entirely: its entry on Zhoukoudian fails even to mention the existence of the remarkable enlargement of the hole, the *foramen magnum*, at the base of the skulls.

To throw new light on this controversy, we have to turn our backs for a while on both the archaeological evidence and the disputed accounts of anthropologists, and instead assess the evolutionary and behavioural background to human nutrition and inter-species aggression. Remarkable insights are afforded by our closest evolutionary relatives, the chimpanzees, and one sub-species of them in particular, *Pan troglodytes schweinfurthii*, communities of which were first discovered for European science by the German scholar Georg August Schweinfurth in 1869–70 in the territory of the Niam Niam (now the border region of Sudan and Central African Republic).[7]

I remember the spectacle of the chimpanzees' tea party at London Zoo, where the creatures were (as in some zoos and circuses they still are) dressed up in human clothes and trained in a genteel repertoire of cucumber sandwiches – and less genteel bananas – for the entertainment and edification of the paying public. It now seems sad and sick, but the attraction of the tea party was always its ambivalence, demonstrating the chimps' curious similarity to us at the same time as underlining the yawning behavioural and intellectual divide that evolution had opened up. The chimps' behaviour threw into relief standards of politeness and honour among humans, negatively as well as positively. It used to be an accepted fact that chimpanzees did not kill each

60

other or engage in homosexual acts, and some moralists saw in this a warning about the unnatural wickedness and decadence of human society.

But, outside captivity, chimpanzees behave quite differently. We know this now because, in 1960, Jane Goodall began to study wild chimpanzees as part of a programme aimed at understanding the behavioural background to human evolution. The study was so successful and revealing that it has now been running for over forty years in Gombe National Park on the eastern border of Tanzania, towards the southern end of the natural range of the sub-species that Schweinfurth identified. As studied by Goodall and her co-workers, the chimpanzees of Gombe are perhaps the best known non-human wild animals in the world. Individuals have been given names and their ancestry over two or three generations is carefully documented. The picture that has emerged is of complex behaviours and community relations, of a creature capable of bravery and kindness, which can experience bereavement and happiness, and which can and does kill members of its own species, sometimes eating them.

The society of the Gombe chimps, like human societies, has changed over time, most notably in 1970 when it split into two communities, the Kasakela and the Kahama. Within the Kasakela community, the mother and daughter outfit of Passion and Pom are the best known and most habitual cannibals. These two females have been directly observed killing and eating three infants belonging to other mothers in their own community, and were circumstantially linked with the disappearance of seven other infants, which they are presumed to have eaten, partially or completely. The killing and partial eating of three further infants by various Kasakela males has also been recorded, as has cannibalism in communities unconnected to the Gombe study area. Goodall writes that 'cannibalism has been observed in Uganda and at Mahale, where infants were killed not only by males of different unit-groups, but also by males of the same unit-group'.[8]

Chimpanzees are competitive as well as cooperative apes who

regularly inflict physical injuries on one another at the same time as being capable of gentleness and what human observers might well interpret as compassion. They have a taste for fresh meat – a taste that is known to lead to organized hunting expeditions, especially to corner, catch and eat other, weaker primates (young baboons are a food of preference for chimpanzees). In genetic terms, killing other mothers' infants confers a competitive advantage – it makes space for more of one's own offspring. In nutritional terms, the energy expended in killing them can be replaced by eating them. It makes sense, but there is a catch.

Goodall and other researchers have poignantly shown how the death of a parent or infant, even a step-parent or adopted infant (not an infrequent relationship at Gombe) caused grief. Goodall speaks of chimpanzees suffering depression and lethargy, and it is not unknown for juvenile chimpanzees, who could care for themselves if they wished, to pine and starve themselves to death following the death of their adult carer. Although some emotions are recognizable across species' divides, as Darwin suspected (a view that has been powerfully supported by Paul Ekman in his annotated edition of Darwin's *The Expression of the Emotions in Man and Animals*),[9] whether such behaviour should be considered as 'mourning a loved one' is hard to say.

Chimpanzees are social animals, so it is understandable that the abrupt severance of attachment that an unexpected death causes produces psychological trauma. The behaviour of Pom and Passion has caused grief and anger among other chimpanzees and has therefore probably been limited by what the community as a whole can tolerate. Concerted action could have driven Pom and Passion out of the community, but the chimpanzees do not have the potential for group decision-making or solidarity that a human community might have in a similar situation.

Jane Goodall's own discomfort registers in her scientifically accurate descriptions of the worst behaviours of the chimpanzees that she loves. She has championed their cause and spoken out at a global level against their suffering in captivity for both human entertainment and laboratory research. But although she would like to be able to see Pom and Passion as aberrant, the chimp equivalents of psychopaths, she is too honest to reject the conclusion that chimpanzee cannibalism has a brutal evolutionary logic for victors and their kin. This conclusion is echoed by Chris Boehm of the University of Arizona, who argues that cannibalism among chimpanzees must be considered as standard rather than aberrant behaviour. The risks involved, such as disease and social censure, are massively outweighed by the bloodline benefits – the ability to promote one's own genes at the expense of those of others. Such benefits even outweigh the risk of accidentally cannibalizing one's own kin from time to time.

If this logic is correct, then it should hold true for other species too. From seagulls to lions, spiders to marsh harriers, beetles to mice, cannibalism has now been observed in over 1,300 species of animal in the wild, including 75 species of mammal, and the numbers are growing as zoologists learn what to look out for.[10] Cannibalism is an integral part of many biological systems, so widespread in the natural world that it must be considered a basic mode of animal behaviour.

Cannibalism can be triggered by simple nutritional and survival needs, or can even be entirely casual, as when spawning fish eat large numbers of their almost infinitely plentiful fry. Such creatures produce myriad offspring and care almost nothing for them individually. The marine biologist Grant Gilmore has shown that sand tiger shark foetuses feed on each other *in utero*. Mammals, on the other hand, are a little more complex. If a mouse litter is threatened by a cat, the female mouse may eat her litter – cashing in on the energy value of her babies herself in order to escape and start another family in a safer location. And, as Robert Elwood of Queen's University, Belfast, has shown, female gerbils will indiscriminately eat gerbil young until they give birth, at which point inhibitor hormones kick in and operate until the mother is able to identify her own litter.[11]

In creatures like chimpanzees who produce even fewer offspring and invest more heavily in their survival and who display a higher level of social cooperation and more directed competition ('constructive aggression'),[12] cannibalism takes more varied forms. Because there are several reasons for cannibalism in higher animals there is unlikely to be a specific cannibalism gene. Any inhibition on cannibalism is, similarly, likely to arise out of an assessment of advantage and disadvantage under particular conditions.

The things we once thought we knew about the chimps at the tea party turn out to be untrue. Primates are complex and their behaviour flexible. For example, their sexual behaviour in the wild is now known to include masturbation (males and females in several species), lesbian liaisons (especially Japanese macaques), male homosexual acts (several species), male on female rape (orang-utans) and further variations.[13] The reasons for these behaviours – pleasure, reproductive success, dominance, social bonding, routine learning – are varied and depend on circumstances. The same is true of cannibalism which, like 'sex', is a single word that covers a range of behaviours and intentions. In humans it has been claimed to relate to nutritional necessity (survival cannibalism), psychological imbalance (psychotic cannibalism), aggression (hunting enemies and eating them), spirituality (eating the dead as a funeral practice; partaking of human sacrifices), sensual pleasure (gustatory or culinary cannibalism), health concerns (medicinal cannibalism), and combinations of these.

Cannibalism would not occur in any form unless knowledge of self-edibility was implicit and instinctual among mammals. Beyond suckling or the licking of wounds, our edibility is confirmed by placenta-eating. This is a standard mammalian behaviour for replacing protein, minerals and hormones after birth and was a widespread – probably once universal – pre-modern practice among human populations. Therapeutic benefits, especially for averting post-natal depression, are reasonably claimed for it, and it is beginning to resurface in the West as something people are prepared to talk about: a childbirth celebration meal featuring a fried placenta recipe was recently screened on British television.[14]

This understanding of ourselves as potentially nutritious under-pins the most basic form of cannibalism – survival cannibalism. The best-known recent case of this was in October 1972, when a rugby team and their supporters from a wealthy Uruguayan Catholic school crash-landed in a remote region of the Andes: six-teen of the original forty-five passengers managed to survive almost three months, long after the search for them had been aban-doned, by eating their dead. Basic knowledge of edibility also comes into play in criminal or psychopathic cannibalism, already met with in the Berkshire murder case, and, in *The Man-Eating Myth*, Arens accepted that both these sorts of cannibalism did indeed occur (although he downplayed their incidence and significance).

Arens' central claim was not that cannibalism did not exist but that it was never an 'accepted practice' in any of the ways that previous generations of anthropologists had claimed it to be. He admitted that – rarely – acts of forced or aberrant canni-balism took place, but he insisted that all eye-witness accounts of societies in which it was an accepted custom ('custom canni-balism') were suspect. This included that of Georg Schweinfurth, after whom Jane Goodall's chimps are named. Although Schweinfurth did not know what we now know about these primates, he did write that the Niam Niam tribe, in whose terri-tory he first recognized them, were cannibals.

There is no sense in denying that Schweinfurth, along with his contemporary, Paul Du Chaillu (who also discovered a sub-species of chimpanzee), thought in racial terms and was interested in natural varieties within animal species, including those that might exist among humans. Supported by the Humboldt Foun-dation in Berlin, Schweinfurth was on a mission to collect human skulls and produce a scientific typology that would detail the location and extent of racial differences. The tribes that Schwein-furth and Du Chaillu described, such as the Bongo-Bongo and the Fang, really existed. The detailed accounts they wrote of life among these tribes have a genuine feel. The picture that emerges is of societies in which only some people are cannibals, while others will share no drinking vessel with cannibals in their own community.

Du Chaillu, a religious and philanthropic American trader, says that he was at first disinclined to believe in reports of cannibalism among the Fang (or Fan), who lived in what is today Gabon and Equatorial Guinea, but in his 1861 account he describes entering a village where he 'perceived some bloody remains which looked to me human . . . I passed on, still incredulous. Presently we passed a woman who solved all doubt. She bore with her a piece of the thigh of a human body, just as we should go to market and carry thence a roast or steak.'[15] Du Chaillu reports that a man who had obviously died of disease was eaten, the villagers confirming 'without embarrassment' that it was normal to eat disease victims. He says that, as known gustatory cannibals, the Fang were often offered dead slaves by neighbouring non-cannibal communities, and they paid for these with ivory. He goes on to describe how the dead were exchanged between Fang villages, so that people did not eat their own. Although Du Chaillu does not seem to have known it, his observation echoes a pattern of exchange well known in China, where the phrase 'to exchange children' – with the tacit understanding 'to eat' – is the standard expression designating a time of famine and hardship.[16]

It would be wrong to think that the Europeans' disinclination to believe in cannibalism went unnoticed in the communities they visited. Munza, the king of Monbuttu (or Mangbettu; on the modern borders of Zaire, Central African Republic and Sudan) for example, is reported by Schweinfurth to have taken whites' distaste in witnessing cannibalism seriously enough to keep it out of the public eye during their visits. Schweinfurth says that he only found out what was going on because of his deep frustration over the fact that he had to reject so many of the native skulls he had paid to have brought to him because they had been widened underneath in the area of the foramen magnum (in the same manner as at Zhoukoudian), to extract the brains. Seemingly oblivious to the fact that people may have been killed to order to supply him, he is unlikely to have feigned his complaint that many skulls were still moist and smelt of cooking.

Cannibal accounts were not limited to the Americas and Africa. In 1772, with two ships – the *Resolution* and the *Adventure* – James Cook set sail on the second of his three great expeditions of maritime exploration. His first had already revealed the existence of New Zealand and Australia to Europeans and he was returning to verify the entire geography of the Southern Ocean. At sea for three whole years he lost only one crew member out of 118 and covered a distance equal to a triple equatorial circumference of the earth. In the Pacific he plotted the precise latitude and longitude of Easter Island, visited the Marquesas, Tonga, Tahiti, and 'discovered' New Caledonia, the Isle of Pines and Norfolk Island.

Cook was a sympathetic and humane man who was usually well liked by the inhabitants of the islands he contacted. Ironically, it was his eventual deification by the Hawaiians that led to his death in 1779: having allowed himself to be seen as the personification of their winter god Lono, and having received ceremonial offerings in that role, a broken mast forced his return in spring, when the opposing god, Ku, was believed to be in the ascendant. Cook's untimely reappearance, like Santa Claus at Easter, led to tension as a result of which some of his officers were drawn into a scuffle. It escalated and Cook was beaten to death in a chaotic skirmish on the beach at Kealakekua.[17]

Cook's death was all the more poignant because his exploratory success was based, to a considerable degree, on listening carefully to what people had to say. He did not find unmapped islands by chance but because he questioned the natives of previously visited islands. He needed to be an acute judge of veracity and of the potential deviousness of human nature. Therefore, like Paul Du Chaillu in Africa nearly a century later, Cook was highly sceptical when he first heard cannibal accusations levelled at the Fijians and Maoris.

Unlike Du Chaillu, Cook was not a race theorist. As a child

of the Enlightenment, he believed in the 'Equality of Man', and dreamed of finding 'noble savages'. Yet, according to the sources we have, human flesh was twice cooked on board the *Resolution* and eaten on the quarterdeck in the shocked presence of the crew, as part of a demonstration by the Maoris that this was, indeed, what they did and that they were proud of it. Cook wrote an apologia for them in his log, stressing their honesty, their 'state of civilization', and the fact that it was only their enemies that they roasted: 'I firmly believe they eat the flesh of no others.'[18] The astronomer William Wales, who was also with the expedition, was blunter in his assessment:

> They do not, as I supposed to be the Case, eat them only on the spot whilst under the Impulse of that wild frenzy which they have shewn us they can & do work themselves into in their Engagements; but in cool Blood ... It cannot be through want of Animal food; because they everyday caught as much fish as served both themselves and us: they have moreover plenty of fine Dogs which they were at the time selling us for mere trifles ... [T]heir practice of this horrid Action is from Choice.[19]

Whatever 'Arensite' anthropologists may find it comfortable or fashionable to believe, it is simply not true that the ethnographic record of cannibalism was solely created by Europeans reporting on native peoples that they considered barbarous and may have wanted to brand as inferior. Nevertheless, if all apparent first-hand accounts of cannibalism were solely commentaries by Europeans on non-European indigenous peoples then we might suspect systematic prejudice. Again, they are not.

Cook's third expedition began not in the South Seas but as a search for the Northwest Passage, revealing and naming King George Sound and Prince William Sound. His pioneering work in the Arctic was extended from the 1820s onwards by Sir John Franklin. Then, in 1845, Franklin and his two ships, the *Erebus* and the *Terror*, disappeared. In 1854, one Dr Rae, on a sledging expedition near Repulse Bay, met a group of Inuk (Inuit) Eskimos who said that white men had been seen dragging a boat southward along the frozen coast of King William Island; they gave him a small selection of belongings which were later identified as having belonged to Franklin's crew. They also reported that the starving sailors had been falling down as they walked and subsequently eating each other. One Inuk hunter named In-nook-poo-zhe-jook spoke of finding long boots 'that came up high as the knees and that in some was cooked human flesh'; another Inuk, Eveeshuk, described bodies of which 'a great many had their flesh cut off as if some one or other had cut it off to eat', and a third, Ogzeuckjeuwock, 'saw bones from legs and arms that appeared to have been sawn off'.[20]

Although the Eskimo information concerning the fate of the Franklin party was accepted as an important clue that the expedition had failed, their reports of cannibalism were dismissed as a slander on the character of British sailors. In 1859 it was established that Franklin had been close to breaking through the Northwest Passage when his ships had become icebound. He himself had died on 11 June 1847 and the remainder of his crew had abandoned the frozen ships on 22 April 1848 to take their chances on the ice. None survived.

The belief that it was innately impossible for British sailors to eat each other and that the Eskimos were liars persisted until 1981 when an archaeological survey of parts of King William Island led by Owen Beattie of the University of Alberta recovered a human thigh bone with clear cut-marks.[21] But, with the impact of Arens' welcome book fresh in people's minds, frostbite surgery or an Inuk attack were the only explanations that the academic world was at first prepared to entertain. Beattie persisted, uncovering evidence that went against the grain, demonstrating, across a number of definitively identified frozen camp sites of the Franklin expedition sailors, a pattern of butchery that is wholly consistent with the Inuk account. The archaeology starkly reveals that bits of limb were carried as packed food as the doomed survivors struggled on in appalling weather, only to suffer further casualties. These new corpses were eaten as well.

Beattie's work shows how archaeology can produce physical data that can settle competing claims to truth. The 'signature' from the sites he has been studying is that of survival cannibalism. The idea that there might be a specific archaeological signature for the aggressive, man-hunting cannibalism Cook knew about was suggested in 1951 by E.W. Gifford of the University of California at Berkeley. By looking at the relative amounts of animal and human bone in domestic refuse or midden sites on Fiji, Gifford concluded that 'except for fish, man was the most popular of the vertebrate animals used for food'. This conclusion – the same as William Wales' for the Maori, but arrived at by independent means – has been confirmed by David DeGusta, who has demonstrated a tight match between the archaeology of kitchen middens and the style and method of human butchery and meat preparation as recorded in Fijian folklore and ethnography. DeGusta's bone analyses at the site of Navatu show that, between 50 BC and AD 1900, there are two clear patterns of contemporaneously deposited human remains – the remains of meals, made from the 'enemies' whom Cook spoke of, and those which belong to reverential burials.[22]

The same archaeological signature, suggesting killed and eaten enemies, has also been identified by archaeologists working in the American south-west. Human bones from Anasazi and Fremont Indian sites dating to just 1,000 years ago are considered by scholars such as Tim White, Christy and Jacqueline Turner, and Shannon Novak to display a pattern of systematic butchery and cooking. This has angered modern Hopi and Pueblo tribespeople who say that their oral history recalls their Anasazi ancestors as peaceful farmers. Yet at the Cowboy Wash site a distinctive protein, human myoglobin, only found in quantity in human heart muscle, has been identified in a coprolite (a piece of fossil excrement) from a pit containing cooked human bone. Although Arensite sceptics have argued that the coprolite was either not of human origin or was produced by someone suffering some dire disease that somehow caused their own myoglobin to be

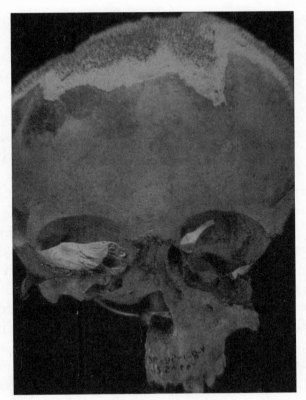

Cannibalized skull of a child from the Fremont culture, Utah.
(Photo: Shannon Novak)

present in their excreta, the adjacent evidence of skulls systematically used to 'self-cook' the brains inside is hard to interpret as
anything but cannibalism.[23]

Recent reports of aggressive Bornean cannibalism echo historical ones from the American south-west in noting how people
who are hunted and eaten are considered by their attackers to
be no more than animals.[24] In a sense, having demoted the victims
from membership of humanity, the practice of killing and eating
them is no longer quite cannibalism as we might think of it. Such
cannibals, happy to hunt enemies, definitively balk at killing
and eating certain kinds of forest animals that are considered to
embody ancestral human spirits.

At Cowboy Wash and at Navatu the human bones ended up in refuse deposits along with animal bones because they were the enemy. But there is another, equally well documented pattern of cannibalism, where cannibalized bones are not just dumped. This is where the dead who are eaten are not enemies but deceased loved ones. The best-known modern example of reverential funerary cannibalism, as it is called, was documented by D. Carleton Gajdusek among the Fore people of the eastern highlands of New Guinea. It was based not just on anthropological accounts and observations but on epidemiology.

The Fore were in the middle of a mystery epidemic, suffering uncontrollable shakes that led to paralysis and a painful death. In a paper in the journal *Science*, Gajdusek argued that the degenerative nervous disease called kuru that afflicted them was connected to the eating of the spinal and brain tissue of the dead. Kuru is similar to 'mad cow' or new-variant Creutzfeldt-Jakob Disease (CJD) in having a long incubation period and a long, harrowing, invariably fatal final phase.[25] It was most manifest among older women, but had broadened into the population of younger people of both sexes. This epidemiological pattern was consistent with women being in charge of the funerary rites.

Shirley Lindenbaum, who also studied the Fore, recognized that women's central role in food preparation and the care of children explained the incubation of kuru in the younger generation, including males who could not have been adult participants in funerary rites but who had nevertheless ingested human nerve tissue. Lindenbaum considers that the women were 'gourmet cannibals' who ate the dead because they were 'delicious', but they ate *everything*, including stomach contents, faeces and bones.[26] This was the edible dead's funeral after all – the women were the grave.

Among the Gimi-speaking people of New Guinea, studied by Gillian Gillison, it was also women who mainly ate human flesh, predominantly that of important males who had died. Male cannibals were referred to as 'nothing men', of low status and like women: 'eating human meat drained a man of his strength so that he was limply helpless before his enemies on the battle-field'.[27] Gillison describes how the funerary cannibalism of Gimi women took place in the men's house, usually strictly off limits, in the presence of the men's usually secret penis-shaped ritual flutes. Their funerary feast represented a dramatization of a battle between the sexes. Normally, men thought themselves in charge, but the tables were turned following the death of an important male. After the cannibal feast, the men would drive the women back out of their hut, collect up the bones of their dead brother and place them in a hole in a tree or a little cave – some natural place thought to be like a vagina where their souls would be reborn into the life of the forest.

In Gillison's careful study we begin to see that cannibalism can be central to the religious and social life of a community. She writes:

> cannibalism was the first stage in a process to regenerate the dead, part of the means to maintain the continuity of existence by transferring human vitality to other living things. This transmigration was carried out through metaphorical sexual intercourse, in which the man's whole body functioned as a penis: by 'going inside' women cannibals, his body was transformed into a dispersible set of spirit-laden bones; by 'going inside' symbolic female orifices in the forest, his bones bore issue, that is, the spirit within them caused rivers to flow and animals and plants to appear spontaneously in the world.[28]

Such accounts bring home how sophisticated cannibalism may be, playing a central role in religious belief and the rituals that order society. Seeing things symbolically is typically human, and a symbolic dimension can easily be injected into cannibalism even if it was not there originally. This happened in the case of the Andes air crash cannibals when, on their return to Montevideo, their novel means of survival met with growing disquiet. Seizing the opportunity, one of their number, a trainee lawyer called Pancho Delgado, silenced all criticism at a press conference, saying: 'when the moment came when we did not have any more food . . . we thought to ourselves that if Jesus at His last supper had shared His flesh and blood with His apostles, then it was a sign to us that we should do the same – take the flesh and blood as an intimate communion between us all.'[29]

In the standard interpretation of the Last Supper, the bread and wine are a pre-memorializing symbol of the intended sacrifice that Jesus will make to end all blood sacrifice. Sacrificial cannibalism is thus signalled as the ultimate taboo (hence its fascination for Satanists). But the symbolism of the Eucharist is, like all symbols, mutable. So, although Delgado's theology was not explicitly endorsed by the Vatican, its newspaper, the *Osservatore Romano*, for 27 December 1973, carried an article containing curial advice from Father Gino Concetti. His conclusion was that *anthropophagy in extremis* (cannibalism in extreme circumstances) need not necessarily be a sin, either of omission or commission. That is, those who had not eaten human meat and had perished, even though they had survived the initial impact, were not to be thought of as having committed suicide (a sin), but neither had the survivors sinned from a Catholic perspective. The body after death was a husk, and to eat it was a matter of free choice.

But in an interview thirty years later another survivor, Carlos Paez, said:

> I remember Pancho Delgado – when he came here, [he held] a big press conference and he [used the term] communion . . . For me it wasn't like this. We were hungry, we were cold and we needed to live – these were the most important factors in our decision . . . I don't even think that Delgado himself believed [what he said] – it was just a very gentle way of saying things, and it was very diplomatic. All the families were waiting for answers, and it was a good thing to say, but it wasn't true. Really it wasn't.[30]

Demonstrating the possibility of different and conflicting interpretations of cannibalism within a single community is a great strength of Pierre Clastres' 1972 book, *Chronique des indiens Guayaki*, about the Guayaki Indian tribe of the Atchei Gatu (Ache) cannibals of Paraguay. Clastres lived on and off with the Ache from 1963, describing in often unremitting detail a culture in which both child sacrifice and cannibalism had long been central features. We are forced to recall the atavistic behaviour of the chimpanzees of Gombe when Clastres describes how an 18-month-old Atchei boy was eaten against the wishes of his mother, Baipugi. Whether his death had been entirely natural was a moot point; he had been sick, but his death was sudden and attributed to his being smothered by a hostile ancestral ghost; it was his stepfather who insisted on cutting him up for an apotropaic (evil-averting) cannibalistic rite. Baipugi did not eat any of him, but she led Clastres to where the ritual had been held, away from the camp. He writes:

> Baipugi fell to her knees and wept over the death of her child. Then she pointed to where the fire had been; 'Those are the ashes, the ashes of the bones that were burned.' The skull and the little skeleton had been broken and thrown into the fire. But not everything had burned up. The woman gently sifted through the dead ashes with the tips of her fingers and pointed to a fragment; 'This is my child's shoulder blade. And here is a piece of his head and the bone from his leg.' The tears were pouring down her cheeks, little by little washing away the black mourning paint.[31]

As humans, we may justify our behaviour by siphoning it up into the realms of ritual, lending it symbolic value, when much of it originates in brutal genetic realities.

But epicurianism should not be overlooked either. Cannibals enjoy eating human flesh. Gillison notes this for the Gimi, Lindenbaum for the Fore, Christina Toren for the Fijians, and so on. It is very fatty, which is a quality particularly valued in nutrition/survival terms. The Atchei told Pierre Clastres that 'it is very sweet, even better than the meat of wild pig' – closest to the domestic pig of the whites and with more good fat (*kyra gatu*) than any animal of the forest.[32]

So how far back do the various types of cannibalism go? Chimpanzees kill and eat each other in a habitual and aggressive way that – in terms of unconscious biological imperatives – could be as much about wiping out genetic competition as providing nutrition. But these two things connect. In the story of human evolution there is the recurring problem of squaring the evolution of our powerful brains with our oddly inefficient metabolism. In order to stand up and then develop lungs that can be controlled to allow speech, we had to shorten our gut length considerably, making it more difficult for us to absorb energy. Yet the evolution of bigger brains, which required vast energy supplies, happened at the same time.

Our hominid ancestors must have required high-quality, low-risk food for thought. Smaller and less threatening versions of themselves, whether rival species or subordinate group members, would have been a logical choice. Baboons are not the preferred food of chimps for nothing – just as little fish are eaten by bigger fish, so baboon brains provide the protein for chimp brains. It should be an expectation of human evolution that cannibalism, inherited as part of the primate legacy from Miocene apes, a behaviour which has continued in several variants into the present day, played an important role.

The very earliest evidence for intentional death-related behaviour anywhere in the world dates to just over two million years ago and comes in the form of a fossil skull of an early hominid (closely similar to an east African *Homo habilis*) from Sterkfontein in South Africa. Specimen Stw 53 displays deliberate cut marks. These are not fatal weapon wounds, the product of a frenzied attack, nor accidental; they were done when the individual was freshly dead, and quite deliberately to cut the masseter muscle to remove the lower jaw.[33] The implication that they represent butchery for nutrition seems unavoidable. The issue of cannibalism is a little more difficult, as the Sterkfontein site preserves the fossils of australopithecines too, with whom early *Homo* was in competition, and we do not know enough about the tool-using capacities of australopithecines. Their brains were larger than chimpanzees' brains, and chimps use tools to get at food. So the Stw 53 cut marks could indicate inter-species competition.

However, australopithecines had become extinct by the time another individual was butchered: a fossilized cranial vault of early archaic *Homo sapiens*, from Bodo in Ethiopia, dates to around 600,000 years ago. Found among stone tools and butchered hippopotamus skeletons, the Bodo cranium is covered in cut marks. The seventeen identified stone tool cuts have to be interpreted as 'patterned intentional defleshing . . . by a hominid(s) with stone tool(s)'.[34] Just pre-dating the controversial and now lost crania of *Homo erectus* from Zhoukoudian in China, which have already been mentioned, are the extensively butchered remains of *Homo antecessor* from the rugged Gran Dolina (Sierra de Atapuerca) in Spain, dated by palaeomagnetism to some time before 780,000 years ago. Although hyenas were definitely present at this site, and seem to have been competing with the early humans, hyenas do not use stone tools. Both human and animal bones appear to have been treated in the same way, displaying light cut marks, peeling, chopping and percussive smashing.[35]

Nearby, in the same spectacular Gran Dolina site complex, is the cave shaft of Sima de los Huesos, where similar cut marks have been found on thousands of bones of the more modern *Homo heidelbergensis*, probably dating to between 300,000 and 200,000 years ago. Dozens of people seem to have been defleshed and deliberately deposited intact in the deep natural shaft. The absence of discarded stone tools, or similarly butchered animal bones, does not suggest a domestic setting (survival cannibalism, for example) while the total lack of other predated animal bones rules out the possibility that natural scavengers or predators could have accumulated them. Ritual cannibalism seems to have

The Bodo cranium. (Photo: Tim White)

been taking place, but whether funerary or related to some kind of ceremonial killing is unclear. But whichever of these it is, it is the earliest unequivocal evidence of a death ritual anywhere in the world. We shall never know the precise thinking behind the defleshing of Stw 53 and Bodo, but here at Sima de los Huesos the cave shaft was carefully chosen and used over many years for an exclusive and deliberate purpose.

It has been argued that the Sima de los Huesos shaft provides clues to an 'incipient funerary practice'[36] but the systematic nature of the butchery and the character of the bodies – mainly adults in their prime (although the excavation of the site and its analysis are incomplete as I write) – leaves open the possibility either that chosen members of the occupying group were at times ritually killed, eaten and offered to the shaft or that members of other groups were caught for this purpose. What we can say beyond doubt is that the first death-related ritual identified any-

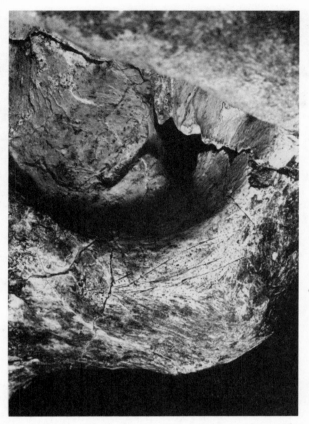

Cut marks on the Bodo cranium. (Photo: Tim White)

where in the world was not a simple formal burial but a complex practice involving cannibalism.

Much more recent bones, belonging to fully anatomically modern *Homo sapiens* from Gough's (New) Cave in the Cheddar Gorge, dating to between 14,000 and 12,500 years ago, show how human and animal food preparation followed the same procedures. Cut marks on the inner surface of the lower jaws of deer, left when the nutritious tongue was removed, are matched by cut marks in the same place on the inside of human mandibles that are mixed in with them. Cut marks on human crania, designed to free the meaty masseter or cheek muscle, shed further light on the butchery pattern.[37] It is hard to say whether this was

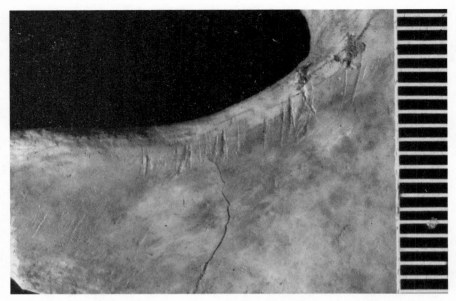

Cut marks on the inside surface of a modern human lower jaw bone from Gough's (New) Cave, Cheddar. (Photo: Chris Stringer)

survival cannibalism or actual people-hunting. Similar evidence comes from the transitional Mesolithic-Neolithic site at Fontbrégoua Cave in south-eastern France, excavated by Paola Villa, where humans, wild deer and domesticated sheep were all butchered in closely analogous ways. The remains of between eight and twelve processed humans were found together in a particular layer of the site, unlike the butchered animals, which were found throughout a number of layers. This could indicate that here, at least, the cannibalism was more a response to ultimate hardship, similar to the Franklin expedition and Andes air crash examples.[38]

All this takes us back to the Mappa Mundi and the medieval iconography of cannibalism. What are the two little cannibals doing in Hereford Cathedral? Were they desperately hungry, or practising their own religion? Or are they fictions like the manticore, minotaur and griffin? Herodotus, writing in the fifth century BC, says that, among the Issedones – the Iron Age nomads depicted on the Mappa Mundi whom he describes as living towards the eastern end of the Kazakh steppe – 'When a man's father dies, the relatives all bring sheep and goats, and, having killed these, they chop up the flesh and cut up too the flesh of their host's father and, mixing all together, serve up a feast.'[39]

Herodotus names two other peoples whom we might label cannibals. The Massagetae, who lived north and east of the Caspian Sea, were like the Issedones in that 'when a man grows very old, all his relatives come together and kill him, and sheep and goats along with him, and stew all the meat together and have a banquet of it'. The Androphagoi, on the other hand, were the literal 'man-eaters'; of them Herodotus says, slightly cryptically, that 'they are the only one of [the people in this region] who eat human flesh'. Such an apparent muddle might lead one to doubt that he knew what he was talking about, but all becomes clear from a careful consideration of the original Greek. Herodotus was distinguishing people who practise reverential funerary cannibalism (Issedones, Massagetae) from people who eat human flesh as a dietary choice (Androphagoi). Given the prevalence of slaving in Scythia,[40] the Androphagoi may have stood in relation to their neighbours much as the west African Fang did to theirs, eating up the dead whom no one wanted.

There is controversy over the potential archaeological match-up with Herodotus' description, and processed human bones from a number of Scythian Iron Age sites are currently under review.[41] Pure archaeological evidence of reverential funerary cannibalism is more ambiguous than evidence of either non-ritual nutritive cannibalism or aggressive warfare-driven cannibalism because of the potential confusion caused by the curious practice of ritual funerary defleshing which does not, apparently, end in eating. 'When a young man dies in Frazer Island (Great Sandy Island, Queensland) the survivors first skin him, then cut off his flesh, and finally extract the marrow from his bones. The skin, flesh, and marrow are distributed among his relatives and are carried about to ward off evil. But when the old and "stale" die, their bodies are placed in the boughs of trees.'[42] Unfortunately, our source does not tell us the eventual end of the meat and fat, whether it rots, or is fed to animals, or buried somewhere. It seems that the ritual must represent a carry-over from a time when the flesh was eaten, before the final consumption of the meat went out of fashion or became no longer nutritionally necessary.

Ritual funerary defleshing without tasting is the standard Arensite interpretation of cut marks on human bones. Cut marks have been recognized in a burial of the Uyuk culture at Amyrlyg in southern Siberia, dating to the third century BC – potential successors to Herodotus' Issedones. The bones have been analysed by Jim Mallory and E.M. Murphy of Queen's University, Belfast, who – perhaps suffering the aftermath of the Arens effect – suggest that the cut marks indicate non-cannibalistic funerary defleshing, noting that none of the long bones were split for marrow extraction, and none of the skulls was cooked as they were on American sites like Cowboy Wash.[43]

Yet Herodotus is quite explicit in saying that it was meat alone – κρέα/krea – that was cut off for cooking, an action that would leave traces wholly consistent with the archaeologically analysed cut marks. The Massagetan practice he describes, of hastening the end of an old relative, has many resonances in the anthropology of death worldwide.[44] What Herodotus' careful description and the archaeology that is congruent with it reveal is the fine-grained complexity of human death-related behaviour.

In another part of his majestic *History*, Herodotus uses the motif of funerary cannibalism to make a sophisticated and compelling point about human culture in general, saying:

Darius [the Great of Persia], during his own rule, called together some of the Greeks who were in attendance on him and asked what they would take to eat their dead fathers. They said that no price in the world would make them do so. After that Darius summoned those of the Indians who are called Callatians, who *do* eat their parents, and, in the presence of the Greeks (who understood the conversation through an interpreter), asked them what price would make them burn their dead fathers with fire. They shouted aloud, 'Don't mention such horrors!' These are matters of settled custom, and I think Pindar [the poet] was right when he says, 'Custom is king of all.'[45]

Herodotus captures the sense of outrage among the Greeks and Indians who are faced with the challenge of doing death differently. Nothing is static. Burial practices, like everything else, change over time. But we are loath to be the ones to change them, and certainly not at the behest of an outsider. For the Yanomamo of the Amazon basin, the idea of burying dead children in damp rainforest earth and abandoning them to rot, cold and lonely, is as horrifying a thought as it is for us to imagine doing what they do, cooking and eating their dead children and drinking down their calcined bones in plantain soup, keeping them warm and comforted inside them. Darius, the ruler of the Achaemenid empire, must have taken a special interest in the extent to which his tributary peoples would assimilate to a universal Persian standard of behaviour: he wanted to know how much they honoured their identity – a concern that has as much political relevance today as it did then.

Funerary rites are a powerful way of stressing the ethnic identity of the living – an opportunity for showing outsiders that they are just that, outsiders; the Greeks, the living symbols of pyre burial, were made to be present and to understand when the Callatians were asked to name a price for giving up their reverential funerary cannibalism. To change custom would mean that the Callatian dead would be buried like Greeks – they would become Greek-like in death and the Callatians would, by degrees, lose their ancestors. With them they would then lose their history and their identity. The offer of money to change such customs was, as Darius surely knew, particularly offensive as it suggests that honour can be bought and bereavement commodified. The reason Herodotus mentions this story at all is to demonstrate Darius' realism in contrast to the old king, Cambyses – a 'violently distracted' ruler who unwisely 'set about the mockery of what other men hold sacred and customary'.

But societies do change. Were that not the case, William Arens' assertion of the non-existence of custom cannibalism would have had no supporters. The abandonment of cannibalism in the case of the Gimi of the New Guinea eastern highlands is especially fascinating. Centrally, it was connected with a shift in belief during the 1960s when Australia came to be considered the place of the true afterlife, from which dead Gimi men must eventually return to be with their kin. Gillian Gillison writes that:

> Women's reasons for renouncing cannibalism under the edict of the Australian Administration were similar to their reasons for having practiced it. As one woman explained: You see, when a man dies that is not the end (of him). He exists. If we do not eat him, he will return (to us as a white man) ... In the past we did not understand (this) and so we ate the dead. The White man came and explained these things to us ... (that) our dead go to stay in Australia and come back (here) later as White men. (Knowing this), we do not cut up the dead any more.[46]

Missionary disapproval probably spurred the abandonment of reverential funerary cannibalism in many places for similar reasons. Nineteenth-century ethnographies record that non-white indigenous peoples in many parts of the world believed in reincarnation as whites.

The inconsistency and variety of the archaeological record, especially during the last one million years, suggests that we are picking up faint signals from the birth of culture, which was connected in some way with our expanding brains and the increasing psychological trauma of death. Not all ancestral humans cannibalized their dead. Many fossil bones do not show the pattern. After 120,000 years ago, there is evidence of at least two distinct patterns in the bits of human bodies we find: there are deliberate burials, both of Neanderthals and of anatomically modern humans, and there is evidence of cannibalism in both groups as well. But that is the most interesting thing. The evolution of options – the ability to conceptualize alternative fates – is central to who we are. It is this that makes human culture distinct from the so-called culture of apes.

Cannibalism, from being an unreflective norm of survival and competition, as among chimpanzees today, came to be imbued with certain values and elaborated in certain ways. Elaboration, meaning a correct and complicated way of doing it, implied ever more wrong ways and the latent possibility of creating a total taboo. With the advent of the food-producing revolution we call farming, the taboo came into being and spread through an increasing number of societies – societies that had discovered a new and powerful use for corpses.

CHAPTER 4

The Foreign Witness

Like a racist, I believed that a strong man could regard
the faiths of others as an opportunity for harmless day-
dreaming and no more.

UMBERTO ECO, *Foucault's Pendulum*[1]

In 1923, at Mashhad in Iran, the diplomat and scholar, Ahmed
Zeki Validi Togan found a remarkable manuscript which
described events witnessed in northern Russia a thousand years
before, around the year AD 921. Its writer, Ibn Faḍlān, claimed
to have been invited to witness a Viking chieftain being cremated
on his boat on the banks of the River Volga. He describes in detail
a ceremony that culminated in the elaborately choreographed
multiple rape and ritualized killing of a slave-girl.[2] The account
has the recognizable ring of authenticity. It fits both with recent
archaeological discoveries and with something Ibn Faḍlān himself could not have known – the inner structure of the secret
cult of the Viking warrior god, Odin.

'I have never seen more perfect physiques than theirs – they
are like palm trees, fair and reddish,' wrote Ibn Faḍlān:

> the man wears a cloak with which he covers one half of his
> body, leaving one of his arms uncovered. Every one of them
> carries an axe, a sword and a dagger ... Each woman wears

a disc on her breast made of either iron, silver, copper or gold, in relation to her husband's financial wealth and social worth. Each disc has a ring to which a dagger is attached ... Around their necks they wear bands of gold and silver. Whenever a man's wealth reaches ten thousand *dirhams*, he has a band made for his wife ... Sometimes one woman may wear many bands around her neck.

The dead chieftain belonged to a Viking tribe or people whom the Arabs called the Rus (or Rūsiyyah), who probably originated in eastern Sweden. The Norse word *vikingr* means warrior and the Vikings were as much a movement as a distinct ethnic group. As ship-borne raiders they moved west from the eighth century AD, leaving Scandinavia to eventually settle in Britain, Ireland, Iceland, Greenland and beyond. The Rus were a group who chose to travel south and east, sailing their longships down the great rivers of the land that would eventually be named 'Russia' after them. Their numbers may have been swollen by young men from the Baltic coast, for their business was exciting and lucrative: raiding, slaving, trading and fighting as mercenaries.

Ibn Faḍlān tells of how they would moor their ships and erect large communal houses on the banks of the rivers. Each Rus trader as he arrived would set out food, milk and a potent drink called *nabidh* (the precise constituents of which will be discussed later) before a wooden idol, prostrate himself and list the number of slave-girls and sable pelts he had with him and how much he was hoping to get for them, 'I want you to send me a merchant who ... will buy from me as I wish, and will not haggle over the price I fix.' Over 80,000 Arab silver coins – *dirhams* – minted as far away as Baghdad, Samarkand and Tashkent, have been found in Scandinavia, reflecting this massive trade in which slaves were a key element.[3]

In youth, captured boys and girls may have been predominantly sex slaves: the Arabic word *jariyah*, translated here as slave-girl, also meant concubine, while *ghulam* – serving lad, slave-boy or equerry – is a term used in homoerotic Arabic poetry from the ninth century on. Ibn Faḍlān says that between ten and twenty of the Rus would live together in one of their newly built riverside houses: 'Each of them has a couch on which he sits, and beside him sits one of the slave-girls for trading. One man will have sex with his slave-girl while his companion looks on. Sometimes a group of them comes to do this, each in front of the other.'

The Vikings later glorified this time in their poetic epics: *Yngvar's Saga* tells of one Swedish adventurer who tried to find the source of the River Dvina, which runs east from the Baltic towards the headwaters of the Dniepr and Volga (see map, p.89). How far he got is unknown[4] but others successfully moved southwards, down the Volga and Dniepr, and founded the great city of Kiev, now the capital of Ukraine. Vikings attacked Byzantium with appalling savagery in AD 860, later becoming the principal suppliers of her slaves, and a contingent of them had reached Baghdad in AD 846 – over seventy-five years before Ibn Faḍlān set out on his journey to the north.

Ibn Faḍlān was part of an Arab embassy sent by the Caliph of Baghdad to the kingdom of the Volga Bulgars near modern-day Kazan. The Bulgars were an invading military aristocracy of Turkic origin, another group of whom later conferred their name on Bulgaria. The Arab visit was connected to a complex power struggle in which religion and economics intertwined: the Bulgars were considering adopting a more orthodox version of Islam in return for military support against their rivals and sometime overlords, the Khazars, whose official religion was Judaism. Ibn Faḍlān's aim, beyond any diplomacy involving the Bulgars, could have been to forge direct links with the Viking Rus slavers. One of his companions, Takīn al-Turkī, 'the Prince', had previously traded metallic ore in the area.[5]

Archaeological evidence indicates that slave raiding first appeared with the advent of farming in the Neolithic period. By the early medieval era slavery was big business across Europe, and much of the export was to the Near East. Arab scholars travelled widely in Europe in the period during which the Slavic

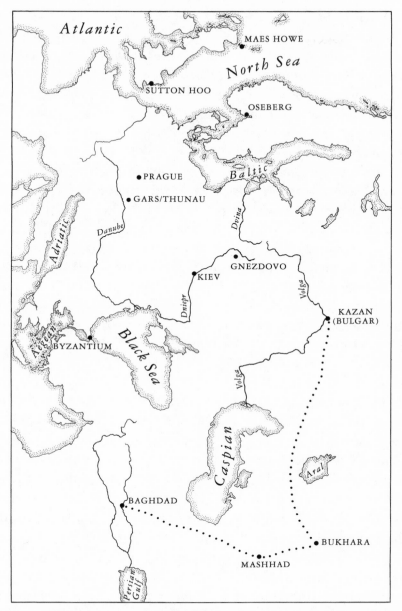

*Map showing the route of Ibn Faḍlān from Baghdad to meet the
Volga Bulgars and Viking Rus near Kazan.*

hillfort of Gars/Thunau in lower Austria (where I excavated the early Christian skeleton) was being overrun. The broken-necked and burnt victims discovered on the Holzwiese may well have been killed while vainly defending their children against being sold at the great slave market that, according to the geographer Ibrahim Ibn Yakub, had developed in Prague. It was the Slavs who were particularly targeted – their name became synonymous with slavery – and the slave-girl whose last hours Ibn Faḍlān recorded was probably from one of the Slavic-speaking tribes.

Ibn Faḍlān was an educated soldier of fortune,[6] and his account, written for his patrons back in Baghdad, probably had a practical purpose. The tone is factual, discursively detailed and blunt, as it needed to be if it was to be useful to other Arabs wanting to benefit from a potentially lucrative, dangerous and highly complex economic and geopolitical situation. The description of a Rus chieftain's funeral in Ibn Faḍlān's *Risala*, or epistle, is the only eyewitness account we have of the ceremonial of a pagan European ship burial, something otherwise only known about from excavations:

> I was told that when their chieftains die, the least they do is to cremate them. I was very keen to verify this, when I learned of the death of one of their great men. They placed him in his grave [*qabr*] and erected a canopy over it for ten days, until they had finished making and sewing his [funeral garments].
>
> In the case of a poor man they build a small boat, place him inside and burn it. In the case of a rich man, they gather together his possessions and divide them into three, one third for his family, one third to use for [his funeral] garments, and one third with which they purchase *nabidh* which they drink on the day when his slave-girl kills herself and is cremated together with her master. (They are addicted to *nabidh*, which they drink night and day. Sometimes one of them dies with the cup still in his hand.)
>
> When their chieftain dies, his family ask his slave-girls

and slave-boys, 'Who among you will die with him?' and some of them reply, 'I shall.' Having said this, it becomes incumbent upon the person and it is impossible ever to turn back. Should the person try to, he is not permitted to do so. It is usually slave-girls who make this offer.

When the man whom I mentioned earlier died, they said to his slave-girls, 'Who will die with him?' and one of them said, 'I shall.' So they placed two slave-girls in charge of her to take care of her and accompany her wherever she went, even to the point of occasionally washing her feet with their own hands. They set about attending to the dead man, preparing his clothes for him and setting right all he needed. Every day the slave-girl would drink *nabidh* and would sing merrily and cheerfully.

On the day when he and the slave-girl were to be burned I arrived at the river where his ship was. To my surprise I discovered that it had been beached and that four planks of birch [*khadank*] and other types of wood had been erected for it. Around them wood had been placed in such a way as to resemble scaffolding [*anābir*]. Then the ship was hauled and placed on top of this wood. They advanced, going to and fro [around the boat] uttering words which I did not understand, while he was still in his grave and had not been exhumed.

Then they produced a couch and placed it on the ship, covering it with quilts [made of] Byzantine silk brocade and cushions [made of] Byzantine silk brocade. Then a crone arrived whom they called the 'Angel of Death' [*Malak al Maut*] and she spread on the couch the coverings we have mentioned. She is responsible for having his [garments] sewn up and putting him in order and it is she who kills the slave-girls. I myself saw her: a gloomy, corpulent woman, neither young nor old.

When they came to his grave, they removed the soil from the wood and then removed the wood, exhuming him [still dressed] in the *izār* in which he had died. I could see that he had turned black because of the coldness of the ground. They also placed *nabidh*, fruit and a pandora [*ṭunbūr*] beside him in the grave, all of which they took out. Surprisingly, he had not begun to stink and only his colour had deteriorated. They clothed him in trousers, leggings [*rān*], boots, a *qurṭaq*, and a silk caftan with golden buttons, and placed a silk sable [trimmed] cap [*qalansuwwah*] on his head. They carried him inside the pavilion on the ship and laid him to rest on the quilt, propping him with cushions. Then they brought *nabidh*, fruit and sweet basil [*rayhān*] and placed them beside him. Next they brought bread, meat and onions, which they cast in front of him, a dog, which they cut in two and which they threw onto the ship, and all of his weaponry, which they placed beside him. They then brought two mounts, made them gallop until they began to sweat, cut them up into pieces and threw the flesh onto the ship. They next fetched two cows, which they also cut up into pieces and threw on board, and a cock and a hen, which they slaughtered and cast into it.

Meanwhile, the slave-girl who wished to be killed was coming and going, entering one pavilion after another. The owner of the pavilion would have intercourse with her and say to her, 'Tell your master that I have done this purely out of love for you.'

At the time of the evening prayer on Friday they brought the slave-girl to a thing that they had constructed, like a door-frame. She placed her feet on the hands of the men and was raised above that door-frame. She said something and they brought her down. Then they lifted her up a second time and she did what she had done the first time. They brought her down and then lifted her up a third time and she did what she had done on the first two occasions. They next handed her a hen. She cut off its head and threw it away. They took the hen and threw it on board the ship.

I quizzed the interpreter about her actions and he said, 'The first time they lifted her, she said, "Behold, I see my father and my mother." The second time she said, "Behold, I see all of my dead kindred, seated." The third time she said, "Behold, I see my master, seated in Paradise. Paradise is beautiful and verdant. He is accompanied by his men and his male-slaves. He summons me, so bring me to him."' So they brought her to the ship and she removed two bracelets that she was wearing, handing them to the woman called the 'Angel of Death', the one who was to kill her. She also removed two anklets that she was wearing, handing them to the two slave-girls who had waited upon her: they were the daughters of the crone known as 'Angel of Death'. Then they lifted her onto the ship but did not bring her into the pavilion. The men came with their shields and sticks and handed her a cup of *nabidh* over which she chanted and then drank. The interpreter said to me, 'Thereby she bids her female companions farewell.' She was handed another cup, which she took and chanted for a long time, while the crone urged her to drink it and to enter the pavilion in which her master lay. I saw that she was befuddled and wanted to enter the pavilion but she had [only] put her head into the pavilion [while her body remained outside it]. The crone grabbed hold of her head and dragged her into the pavilion, entering it at the same time. The men began to bang their shields with the sticks so that her screams could not be heard and so terrify the other slave-girls, who would not, then, seek to die with their masters.

Six men entered the pavilion and all had intercourse with the slave-girl. They laid her down beside her master and two of them took hold of her feet, two her hands. The crone called the 'Angel of Death' placed a rope around her neck in such a way that the ends crossed one another [*mukhāl-afan*] and handed it to two [of the men] to pull on it. She advanced with a broad-bladed dagger and began to thrust it in and out between her ribs, now here, now there, while the two men throttled her with the rope until she died.

Then the deceased's next of kin approached and took hold

of a piece of wood and set fire to it. He walked backwards, with the back of his neck to the ship, his face to the people, with the lighted piece of wood in one hand and the other on the gate of his anus, being completely naked. He ignited the wood that had been set up under the ship after they had placed the slave-girl whom they had killed beside her master. Then the people came forward with sticks and firewood. Each one carried a stick the end of which he had set fire to and which he threw in amongst the wood. The wood caught fire, and then the ship, the pavilion, the man, the slave-girl and all it contained. A dreadful wind arose and the flames leapt higher and blazed fiercely.

One of the Rūsiyyah stood beside me and I heard him speaking to my interpreter. I quizzed him about what he had said, and he replied, 'He said, "You Arabs are a foolish lot!"' So I said, 'Why is that?' and he replied, 'Because you purposely take those who are dearest to you and whom you hold in highest esteem and throw them under the earth, where they are eaten by the earth, by vermin and by worms, whereas we burn them in the fire there and then, so that they enter Paradise immediately.' Then he laughed loud and long. I quizzed him about that [i.e. the entry into Paradise] and he said, 'Because of the love which my Lord feels for him. He has sent the wind to take him away within an hour.' Actually, it took scarcely an hour for the ship, the firewood, the slave-girl and her master to be burnt to ashes, and then dust of ashes.

They built something like a round hillock over the ship, which they had pulled out of the water, and placed in the middle of it a large piece of birch [*khadank*] on which they wrote the name of the man and the name of the King of the Rūs. Then they left.

This demands to be believed as a true account of what occurred that day. Ibn Faḍlān may be cagey about his reasons for being among the Rus but it seems certain that he was among them and

94

was invited to this particular funeral: not only does his description tally with the findings of archaeology but it contains a mystery that he himself was unaware of, the solution to which reveals just how powerful the idea of the disembodied soul had become among the barbarian peoples of Europe.

Ibn Faḍlān, through his interpreter, was made privy to a degree of inside information as the ritual proceeded. When he says that the slave-girl went in to each of the pavilion-owners – the tent-lords – to have sex with them, he does not imply that he witnessed the sex in person, as he may have done in the communal trade houses. It also seems unlikely that the tent-lords were speaking loudly enough for him to hear the words from outside. The words that are spoken to the slave-girl about love by each tent-lord as he had sex with her must be considered traditional and well known to those Rus outside the tents who are explaining to Ibn Faḍlān what is going on. Faḍlān's interpreter may have been his companion Takīn al-Turkī. In the Turkic languages, Takīn is an honorific title meaning 'prince' and it may be that this character, with his interest in metals, had good contacts among the Rus, from which an invitation to the funeral might have come.

The Rus act as Ibn Faḍlān's guide at the ceremony, interpreting the events as they occur. It is never clear precisely how much of the slave-girl's ordeal Ibn Faḍlān can see at any given point in the ritual. It is unlikely that he was allowed on the ceremonial ship, let alone inside the death pavilion erected on it, so his graphic description of the killing is probably based on putting together what he glimpsed and heard, what he saw or was shown before and after, and what he gleaned from information volunteered during the rite, or given in answer to his questions.

The funeral rite that Ibn Faḍlān describes is Scandinavian. The Norse scholar, Morten Lund Warmind, believes that it was directed to the god Odin, and was designed to send the chieftain well equipped to Valhalla, Odin's great hall of feasting heroes.[7] The way to Valhalla was by ship or by fire, and sometimes both elements were combined in a single ritual. Ship or boat burial was a prestigious rite but not uncommon. There are 200 known cemeteries in Scandinavia dating to the ninth to eleventh centuries AD that have been found to contain one or more boat burials. Some were truly spectacular ships, like the one preserved by waterlogging at Oseberg, Norway (see map, p.89), which contained the bodies of two women, perhaps a high priestess and her elderly, sacrificed, maidservant.[8] Outside Scandinavia there is the 'royal' ship burial at Sutton Hoo in Suffolk, England, but the largest Viking-age burial complex known is in western Russia, at the great trade centre of Gnezdovo, strategically situated on the upper Dniepr river. Of about 4,500 burial mounds identified in the pine forest here, some 700 have been excavated and the one known as Burial Mound 13 held a boat cremation containing the remains of a Viking chieftain and a young woman, in a rite similar to the one that Ibn Faḍlān describes.[9]

Ibn Faḍlān's account of the Viking Rus is less than flattering. To him their habits and rituals seem rough and brutal ('the filthiest of all Allah's creatures: they do not clean themselves after excreting or urinating or wash themselves when in a state of ritual impurity [i.e. after sex]'). Defensively, perhaps, Morten Lund Warmind takes Ibn Faḍlān to task for what he perceives as a patronizing attitude, warning that the Arab writes so persuasively that it is difficult not to be seduced by his view of the proceedings. Warmind interprets Ibn Faḍlān's stance as that of 'the horrified civilized person among barbarians' and argues that Ibn Faḍlān failed to appreciate the finer cultural aspects of the slave-girl's death. It is worth looking in detail at what Warmind says about the ritual killing. Although perceptive in some ways, it contains elements of emotional denial that, as we have already seen in the cases of muti and cannibalism, characterize modern anthropological relativism.

Warmind refuses to respond with horror and this undermines his ability to understand the psychic, physical and emotional states of the characters involved, in particular the slave-girl. He claims that the 'more mundane observations such as that the old woman hurries the girl, and that she appears drugged, confused

96

A Viking picture stone from Alskog, Gotland, showing a longship (below) and Odin, surrounded by Valkyries, riding his eight-legged horse towards Valhalla (above). (Drawing: George Taylor)

and less willing to undergo the ordeal as it draws ever closer, are hardly part of the ritual itself'. These would, Warmind assures us, 'have been overlooked by insiders as unfortunate hitches, just as we would see it if a priest stuttered while saying the blessing or spilled the wine during the Eucharist. The actual death, the strangling and the stabbing have long been recognized as the Odinic way of sacrificing kings. The happy girl is sent to Odin to be with her master.'[10] The surprising reason for this claimed happiness, which Warmind infers from the ritual, is that 'the slave-girl – as a prerequisite for her sacrifice – is lifted up into the highest social layers. She is given nabidh to drink – a sign of kingly status – and she is given rings, which she later distributes.' It is not accidental that Warmind calls her a 'slave-girl' before this supposed elevation and 'girl' at the point of death: as he sees it, she has become the wife of the great chief himself.

Warmind's understanding of the rite involves taking a lenient and ostensibly non-judgmental view. He seems to be saying that, if only Ibn Faḍlān had understood and respected native values more, he would have seen that what transpired was perfectly legitimate within the context of the ritual. It is the ritualized nature of the act rather than the act itself which is important: 'On the superficial level, the girl is made drunk, raped, stabbed and strangled while the men beat on their shields to drown her screams. However, there are important details which show us that these barbarians are in fact only different, not uncivilized.'

In order to make this interpretation stick, Warmind has to play down the slave-girl's terror and the idea that this horror was masked by sound: 'The noise which accompanies the rite itself is seen by the civilized as a barbarian trick, so that the supply of voluntary slave-girls should never be exhausted', whereas it is – according to Warmind – 'a well-known feature in Germanic rituals, corresponding to modern applause . . . The sound must be understood as one of the ways of marking out the holy sphere.' Ibn Faḍlān probably knew that the drumming was 'ritual' even better than we do today, and did not think to spell it out. Unlike Warmind, he was aware of something else, namely that rituals may serve practical functions. There is no reason to believe that his explanation is anything other than a fair account of what the Rus told him: that the drumming drowned the sounds of screaming and disguised the terrifying aspects of the prodecure from the remaining slave-girls who might possibly be invited to take on the same role at a later date.

My distaste for Warmind's analysis is all the stronger because

I do not feel that Ibn Faḍlān's account *is* particularly sympathetic towards the slave-girl. The position of women in Baghdad in the tenth century was not enviable by modern standards. Arab society was strongly gender-demarcated, with men exercising ultimate authority in the majority of contexts; it was also a hierarchical society, with a super-rich elite serviced by slaves and tied retainers. Ibn Faḍlān does not express any disgust concerning the slave-girl's death and keeps his own counsel. He listens politely, as an observant special guest. His account is compelling precisely because it is rather clinical – detailed but aloof.

Sensing the atrocious in what Ibn Faḍlān describes, we naturally recoil. None of the textbooks which mention or reproduce his account actually face up to what was entailed. The archaeologist Zdeněk Váňa is typical in speaking of Ibn Faḍlān's 'colourful and dramatic description' in which 'the corpse was burnt on a ship together with numerous offerings and a sacrificed female slave' yet avoiding mentioning the rapes or the *Malak al Maut*. In fact, the Angel of Death lurks ineffectually in the background of a reconstruction drawing that accompanies Váňa's text. The picture shows a sword, not mentioned by Ibn Faḍlān, resting next to the slave-girl, lending the scene the ambience of Arthurian legend. She reclines serenely in flowing robes with a fine girdle about her waist and a circlet in her hair, dead but untroubled by noose or stab wound.[11]

Echoing the sentimentality of Pre-Raphaelite romance, it seems the slave-girl chooses her pagan death freely, for the highest motive: love. A similar sort of glossing over is found in other descriptions of ancient ritual killings. Of the twenty-three retainers found sacrificed in the grave pit of Queen Puabi near the ziggurat of Ur, the standard texts say that 'The victims may well have been not only content but even proud to follow their masters ... however surprising we may find such a practice, it was relatively widespread and characterizes an evolutionary stage of highly hierarchical societies.'[12] And, writing about the live burial of the ten kneeling, apparently praying, individuals in the Bronze Age pit at Nitriánsky Hradok (mentioned in

Chapter 1) my colleague Andrew Sherratt says that they 'must have been interred willingly' because there are 'no signs of struggle or disorder'.[13]

Regimented submission need not necessarily be 'willing'. The kneeling people who were buried alive at Nitriánsky Hradok and the retainers killed in the grave pit of Queen Puabi could have been driven by altruism or by fear. They could have been complying to protect their children from being forced to take their places. Or they may have felt that their sacrifice would protect loved ones from imagined supernatural dangers. Andrew Sherratt rightly points out that the people in the pit belonged to a culture (the Baden) in which both alcohol and narcotic and psychotropic drugs were widely used in ritual, and that ceremonial pottery vessels in the death pit may indicate the use of drugs or alcohol, or a mixture of both, during an early phase of the procedure. Coercion, hierarchy and mind-altering substances would have been interwoven with inner metaphysical convictions to the point at which the word 'willing' falls wholly short of the reality. The psychology of compliance *in extremis*, where a person acts in a way that may seem at odds with their own best chances of personal survival, is complex. But ritual exerts its own powerful coercion, as the mass human sacrifices of the Aztecs show.

In the years 1519 and 1520, Bernal Díaz, author of *The Conquest of Mexico*, was among a group of 600 or so Spaniards – *conquistadores* – who, under the leadership of Hernan Cortés, penetrated to the heart of the Aztecs' empire and imprisoned their king, Moctezoma. Diaz writes of the horror of the soldiers when they entered the temple precincts of the Aztecs' spectacular sacred city of Tenochtitlan, built on artificial islands connected by causeways in the middle of a lake. He describes 'a pyramidal mound or tumulus, having a complicated framework of timber on its broad summit. On this was strung an immense number of human skulls, which belonged to the victims, mostly prisoners of war, who had perished on the accursed stone of sacrifice. One of the soldiers had the patience to count the number of these ghastly trophies, and reported it to be one hundred and thirty-six thousand!'[14]

The Tenochtitlan skyline was dominated by the 60-metre-high twin towers of the pyramid temples of Tlaloc and Huitzlipochtli, the rain god and the great ancestral hero. Sacrifices to them could involve the killing of 20,000 people in a single ceremony. There is no reason to doubt the general accuracy of the skull count Diaz records. The Aztecs' own explanatory texts, such as the one now known as the *Florentine Codex*, support Bernal Díaz' account in recording that victims were typically pinned down on the killing stone and had their still-beating hearts excised. Sacrifices to Tlaloc were different: here children took pride of place within the ritual.

When Cortés first saw it, Tenochtitlan, now buried under Mexico City, had a population of around 300,000,[15] and was dominated by the Aztecs, or Mexica. This people, speaking a Mexican language, believed that they had originated from an

Aztec temple pyramid with human sacrifice as seen by the Spanish (Codex Magliabechiano). *(Source: Nuttall 1903)*

Aztec ritual cannibalism as seen by the Spanish (Codex Magliabechiano). *(Source: Nuttall 1903)*

island called Aztlan (hence the archaism 'Aztec'), although whether this ever really existed is not known. By the early sixteenth century the Mexica controlled a large tract of Mesoamerica. Tenochtitlan symbolized the mythical island of Aztlan and so rain to feed the surrounding lake, as well as for agriculture, was of paramount importance.

Wherever in the Mexica territories they came from, all the small children who had been born under a particular day-sign and who, at birth, had a double cow lick of hair, were sold into temple kindergartens by their mothers. Chosen to become 'bloodied flowers of maize', they were brought up by priests who eventually revealed to them exactly how they were to meet their death, not by excision of the heart, but by having their throats cut. The children had to recognize the horror of their own impending death because their tears and wailing were essential to the success of the ritual, a fitting homage to the god who would send his own precious raindrop tears to regenerate the earth.

The historian Inga Clendinnen, one of the foremost experts on Mexica ritual, writes, 'the onlookers wept as the children destined for Tlaloc the Rain God were carried weeping in their litters, and wept as the terrified wailing choked and stopped'.[16] Although it appears to be theatrical and insincere, the adults' collective grief was in some way genuine – in their minds the belief was fixed that if these children were not given up then the cosmic order would collapse and every living thing would be plunged into chaotic darkness. The ritual for Tlaloc was a true sacrifice in that something precious was being given up as part of a supernatural exchange.

Whatever its theological justification, the rites of Tlaloc involved what I would term atrocity in the *Oxford English Dictionary* definition of the word: 'savage enormity, horrible or heinous wickedness'. It is fashionable to say that, of course, the Mexica would not have accepted such a definition themselves, and that in their morality the rites of Tlaloc were right and necessary. The Mexica did not make any pretence that their child victims died 'happy'; they overtly recognized human emotional negatives, terror and extreme distress, as a central part of what they deemed necessary for their rituals.

Theological philosophers, such as Jan Patočka and Jacques Derrida, distinguish religions which consider human freedom as inseparable from the exercise of reflective moral responsibility for actions,[17] from orgiastic and unfree types of religion, cult and ritual, which are forms of what can be termed 'demonic sacralization'. It is an item of anti-imperialist faith to say that the dismantling of the Aztec empire by the Spanish was a tragic moment in the history of Mesoamerican indigenous peoples. But it is difficult to assert with a clear conscience that the Roman Catholicism that swept away the human sacrifices of Aztec religion was not, for all its hypocrisies, repressions and failings, better than what it replaced.

The Rus ceremony as recorded by Ibn Faḍlān was different from the Aztec ritual, not least because the girl had to face the horror alone. And it was also unlike the rituals at Ur and

Nitriánsky Hradok, where the sacrificial victims kept their composure, for whatever reason. Warmind's idea that the girl – a victim of enslavement – willingly volunteers to die in a ceremony that will de-victimize her and make her the Rus chieftain's social equal is a grotesque parody of what Ibn Faḍlān actually describes: drug- or alcohol-influenced consent, followed by confusion and terror. There is a match between what we can tell of the mental state that was induced in the slave-girl at death and what is known of the desired ultimate mental state of the muti victims, like the one whose torso was found on the banks of the Thames.

We do not know what choices faced the slave-girl when she became the one to volunteer. Drugged and disoriented, she was prompted through the 'lifting' ceremony to accept the physical reality of the otherworld. But how genuinely persuaded was she? Her responses, 'Behold, I see my father and my mother' and 'Behold, I see all of my dead kindred, seated' may be specific and true to the circumstances of her life (that is, prompted by hallucination of her parents) or they may be formulaic or, of course, both – an expected part of the ritual and an individual response. The sort of slave-girl used in such rituals may have seen all her older relatives killed.

Victims can often be persuaded that their abuse has 'something in it' for them. This slave-girl was already a victim whose experience of life was probably negative enough for her to see the allure of ten days spent as the centre of attention, wearing nice jewellery, drinking plenty of *nabidh* (whatever it was) and having handmaidens to wash her feet. Her level of self-respect cannot have been high and the prospect of social status in death must have been tempting. The slave-girl would have wanted fervently to believe that there was a 'Paradise' after death, and, whatever she may have felt about him, the chance to be married to her chief, and so become a social equal, must also have had a degree of appeal.

If the slave-girl had come from one of the Slavic tribes, then her religious understanding could easily have encompassed such an idea. She may have felt at home with the horse sacrifice as, in Slavic religion, horse deities, such as Radagast, were considered to be incarnate in specific sacred animals; they were kept at holy sites, such as Rethra and Arkona, where they were subjected to ordeals, the outcomes of which were considered prophetic.[18] If she had previously served the Bulgars, or was from a Bulgar peasant family, then she could have been – unknown to Ibn Faḍlān – a Muslim herself. In any case, in affirming the slave-girl's act of volunteering as an expression of her heartfelt desire, Morten Lund Warmind ignores both these complex realities and Ibn Faḍlān's express statement that once a slave had 'volunteered' there could be no going back.

Mexica human sacrifices required passivity, perhaps even a form of complicity, on the part of the adult victims. They were expected to queue, sometimes for hours, and then climb the terrifying, precipitous stairway to their deliberately horrid deaths, all the while witnessing the corpses of advance victims being flung down the steep, blood-caked sides of the temple pyramid. Inga Clendinnen calls the array of techniques the Mexica used 'victim management'.[19] For slave victims of the Mexica, vanity in being selected, along with flattery and pampering, was probably an important factor at the outset, when the reality of death was still some way in the future. Each victim was assigned two mature women as 'face washers', who tended them until they died – a strikingly similar arrangement to that among the Rus, where the Angel of Death's daughters attend the slave-girl.[20] More symbolically, repeated face-bathing and the donning of ritual regalia indicated the loss of the old self and the adoption of a new, sacrificial identity.

Some ritual victims were given sex partners on demand in the period leading up to their sacrifice, while the *Florentine Codex* says that slave-victims at the festival of Panquetzaliztli, were given so-called 'obsidian' wine – named after the extremely sharp, volcanic glass daggers used in the ceremony – so that they would not fear death. Towards the climax, Clendinnen says, the movement of the ritual itself imposed its own coercion, with the action so relentlessly taxing, with its swift transitions between furious effort and controlled formality and its painful delays, as to be intolerable physically and psychologically: we are told victims were finally brought to be so 'anguished in spirit [that] they looked forward only to their deaths.'[21]

Mexica 'victim management' provides some insights into the way in which the Rus slave-girl was persuaded to volunteer, why she did not flee, and why she at least attempted to play a smooth part in the ritual proceedings. Even so, it is not clear how convinced she is of the 'otherworldly' reality she is required to condone when she looks over the lintel. Part of her obviously wants to see it all and can call to mind the faces of her relatives, and the last time she saw them. In her extreme state of psychological arousal, aided by *nabidh*, she may well have begun hallucinating – a phenomenon that, within her own ritual-soaked world view, she would have considered significant and 'real'. After her three views over the door-frame the slave-girl became, by degrees, so terrified that she ultimately abandoned ritual acting altogether.

The death of the slave-girl involves a trial of faith which, it seems to me when I read Ibn Faḍlān's words, she fails. Ultimately her belief that her relations and master are waiting for her across the threshold in Paradise is weaker than her fear of death and her prior knowledge of the way it will happen. Ibn Faḍlān writes about her becoming confused and having trouble entering the tent on the ship. Despite some uncertainty with the translation at this point, the sense of what is happening is clear enough. Some part of the girl's mind knows what kind of horror awaits her and prompts her to make a final pathetic attempt to save herself by mistaking the entrance to the death pavilion.

This point in Ibn Faḍlān's account strikes me most forcefully of all. Swayed by the overall context – the self-sustaining logic of the ritual – he records the girl's movements as befuddlement (identified by Warmind as a hitch in the ceremony), when they may have represented a perfect coincidence between pure instinct and fundamentally rational action: playing for time. Behaviour of the type that Ibn Faḍlān unwittingly observed was recorded in concentration camp gas chambers, where the condemned fought to clamber to the top of the mounting pile of corpses, creating a pyramid of bodies. This was because the heavy Zyklon B gas rose through the sealed chamber from floor level. Unlike the death pit at Nitriánsky Hradok, where there was pressure to acquiesce, the action of scrabbling to the top, seemingly irrational and hopeless, represented the last possible chance of survival. It was at least conceivable that someone might have flung wide the doors at the last possible moment and granted freedom. By a similar outside chance, the funeral of the Rus chieftain could have been halted by a solar eclipse, a meteorite, or a – far from unlikely – surprise attack by enemies.

In the event, the slave-girl is irrevocably led inside and put to death amid a welter of extreme sensory experiences, screaming while the Angel of Death restrains her for the serial sexual satisfaction of the six men, semi-asphyxiated, stabbed, and then fully strangled. The techniques used in these final moments are familiar, as they are used by violent sex offenders against their victims today. They are reminiscent, too, of some of the self-inflicted, sexually driven techniques of death which forensic pathologists are, from time to time, called upon to deal with. For this sort of death to take place in public in the presence of a foreign guest suggests a society at ease with the most extreme imbalances of power between individuals. The beating on the shields is understood by Ibn Faḍlān – and more importantly, *explained* to Ibn Faḍlān – in terms of power imbalance: it is intended to keep the slave-girls and boys in the dark about what goes on at such an event. (The funeral is down at the river, presumably in an area made sacred for such purposes, well away from and probably out of sight of the settlement where the slaves were; nevertheless, sounds of screaming can carry a considerable distance.)

But we still do not know why the slave-girl was killed, still less why she was killed in the precise way that she was. 'The killing of the slave-girl by the Rus so that she might accompany her master in death is a classic example of human sacrifice,'[21] writes Mike Parker Pearson in *The Archaeology of Death and Burial*, and Warmind also calls the death a sacrifice. But a sacrifice to whom or what?

Clendinnen speculates that although the Mexica's victims – prisoners of war and victims given in tribute by various subject peoples – went quietly to their deaths because of the promise of a splendid afterlife, the promise was not sufficiently powerful or convincing for the elite Mexica themselves to volunteer and nor did they represent the sacrificial victims' fate as desirable: 'to end on the killing stone was represented in the discourses of the elders as a most bitter fate'.[22] Theologically, sacrifice is normally understood to entail the surrender of some object or possession to a deity for the purposes of propitiation or homage, and classically involves a sacrificial altar or other special place, such as a mountain top or a ritual shaft. In this kind of sacrifice the victim is, in one way or another, consumed.

In Ancient Greece, sacrifices could be made to gods, to heroes, to the dead, to solemnify oaths or ensure success; animal sacrifices were variously burned, eaten, disembowelled and used as oracles, buried alive, and so on, as appropriate.[23] The principal reason that the fate of Mexica victims was considered so bitter was not because of the physical pain of the type of death they were subjected to, but because they were given over in homage to a variety of jealous gods who were nourished by them. Rather than become part of the honoured ancestral collective, the victims were rendered into supernatural fodder.

The Rus slave-girl appears to have been ritually killed but not sacrificed. Both Ibn Faḍlān and modern commentators on his *Risala* assume that what happened was a kind of 'assisted suttee', like the suttee rituals of nineteenth- and twentieth-century India where a widow throws herself on her husband's funeral pyre in order to accompany him in death. This is not homage or sacrifice, but transportation. Ritual killing for the purposes of supernatural travel is known to take a number of forms. Herodotus records that the Thracians would deliver urgent messages directly to their gods via a volunteer, who would be thrown into the air to land, and immediately die, on upraised spear-points.[24]

Morten Lund Warmind's conclusion that 'The happy girl is sent to Odin to be with her master' contains both an incongruous statement about human emotion (this cannot be happiness in terms that either I or any of us understands it, so what does Warmind mean, precisely?) and, connected to it, the unlikely claim that both she and the Rus saw her death as a means of transportation to an afterlife, her status raised by a ceremonial marriage. Although this is what both she and Ibn Faḍlān were separately led to believe, in the terms of reference of the ritual itself there are at least three problems with the idea of supernatural transportation. Together they are insurmountable.

We cannot choose just those bits of Ibn Faḍlān's account that make sense and ignore what is difficult (even if this is what the writer himself did in places). So when we hear that both slave-girls *and* slave-boys (*jariyah* and *ghulam*) are asked which of them will die with their master, it has to be conceivable that a boy could volunteer. In this case, the whole idea of a sacred marriage breaks down. There is no hint of the possibility of same-sex marriage either in Ibn Faḍlān's account of the Rus or in the Viking sagas, and there is no archaeological data that could support the idea.[25] Nevertheless, given that the form of the Rus ritual has traditional responses, we can hardly imagine that it could have been conducted without the tent-visiting.

We have to conclude that a slave-boy could have been told he could become his master's cup-bearer in Paradise, receiving favours as he had perhaps already done in life – even, perhaps, that he would be raised to equal status with the warriors. Then he would have been used sexually in the tent-lords' tents and again later in more violent fashion just before the Angel of Death killed him. The fact that, unless Ibn Faḍlān misunderstood, a slave-boy would do as well as a slave-girl means that it was not a funeral marriage partner that was required.

The second problem is with the manner of death, which makes no sense as a means of supernatural transportation. The method of killing is unambiguously horrific: a terrified and abused slave-girl died an exposed and tragic death, alienated from her own native community, without the comfort of human love and support and, finally, without the solace of faith. Not only is this closer to the truth of her own experience than the idea of a happy volunteer, it is, quite precisely, the psychological effect that those responsible for her death wanted to induce in her. The production of visceral terror in the girl as she is finally tortured to death was a principal aim of the procedure to which she was subjected. This is not described by any commentator on Ibn Faḍlān as 'sadism', not because what occurs is not sadistic (it is) but because there seems no ritual logic in torturing to death a woman whom you may later meet in the afterlife as your hostess when your dead chief invites you to dine with him. Within the metaphysical framework of a 'suttee'-type ritual, the precise form of death that the slave-girl suffers is completely unnecessary.

It is easy to see that the slave-girl was not a human sacrifice. But saying that she was not dedicated to a god does not mean that we have to accept the 'assisted suttee' idea either. Ritual killing may be carried out for purposes other than supernatural transportation: muti, ritualized psychopathic murder, public executions, and certain types of vengeance killing are all examples of it. Even in battle, the killing of an opponent may become formalized, so that the lethal etiquette of the Samurai warrior or the medieval knight blurs the boundary between ritual form and pure combat.

The funeral rites involved neither a marriage for the slave-girl nor the idea of her transportation in comfort. Although the slave-girl either hallucinates, or is required to see, her destination as 'Paradise' over the top of the door-frame, this does not mean that the Rus believed in it. That the Rus believed in some supernatural realm, and in a process that was about to unfold there, is clear from the careful provisions of the funeral as a whole and from the fact that tent-lords give the slave-girl messages to pass on to her master.

This leads us straight to the third and most difficult problem, noted by every informed commentator on Ibn Faḍlān's text: the fact that in Norse belief there is no place equivalent to the Arabic Paradise, *al-janna*, 'beautiful and verdant'. The Vikings believed in a descent into an underworld ruled by the goddess Hel for most and an ascent to Valhalla – a feast hall of dead heroes – for a chosen few. Because of this problem in the *Risala*, some people have suggested that the Rus could not have had a Norse religion while others have suggested that Ibn Faḍlān made it all up. It is also possible that Ibn Faḍlān got this part of what the slave-girl says over the door-frame badly wrong, or that we have failed to translate his Arabic properly. But I believe none of these things. I believe that Ibn Faḍlān was deliberately misled.

The idea of misinformation opens up a whole world of interesting possibilities. We know that the Rus were happy to mask the screaming with drumming to conceal one kind of truth from the slave-girls and slave-boys. There is no reason to believe that they were not also capable of concealing another sort of truth from Ibn Faḍlān.

I believe that the rite was more complex than anyone has previously supposed, and that the killing of the slave-girl was neither a homage to a deity nor a necessary procedure for launching her into the afterlife. At what stage in the ceremony the slave-girl was expected to pass the message about love on to her master is left unclear. Ibn Faḍlān infers that she thinks that the messages will be passed on when she arrives in Paradise, and he believes, and expects his readers to accept, that this is also what the Rus themselves imagined would happen.

But there are strong reasons to suppose that the tent-lords had a very different idea about their message of love to their dead chief and that its successful transmission, curiously enough, did not depend on her at all but on the understanding – central to the entire ritual – that his soul was not yet in the world of the dead. When they had sex with her, this soul was still dangerously disembodied among the living, looking and listening. Before we can pursue this idea to its remarkable conclusion, we need to know more about the strange, not uninhabited, space that extends between the living and the dead.

CHAPTER 5

Welcome to Weirdworld

Fifty more scientists were recruited to the staff, making nearly a hundred in all. Lenin's corpse could now be photographed with special cameras, analysed in the minutest detail and, where necessary, repaired and restored ... Every scientist on the staff of the lab had a corpse at his disposal on which to carry out his own experiments; he was kept completely ignorant of its identity. Even today there is still a kind of 'secret museum' of such nameless bodies ... some have been forgotten for years in their 'balsam' baths, their hair floating like seaweed. It is a sight that can have few parallels anywhere in the world.

ILYA ZBARSKY AND SAMUEL HUTCHINSON, *Lenin's Embalmers*[1]

A dimly lit room, thick red cordons, bullet-proof glass surrounding a catafalque, and a body with pale hands resting on the black quilt. It looked mundane. I had seen the body of the former Bulgarian leader, Georgi Dimitrov, once before, on a family holiday in 1974. Bulgaria was tentatively opening up to Western package tours, and visiting the mausoleum was almost obligatory. In 1985, as a visiting research student in Sofia, I went to take a second look and felt strangely disappointed. It was not Lenin.

The face of Lenin is one of the great icons of the twentieth century. The dynamically arched eyebrows and flashing eyes, the sensual, cruel, intelligent lips, the distinctive goatee beard – Vladimir Ilyich Ulyanov would not have looked out of place in a vampire film, playing Count Dracula. But he chose to create an even bigger character, Lenin, whose form, as if undead, still lies in an open coffin. If Dimitrov had had the same kind of charisma, it is unlikely that the Russians would have gifted their embalming team to the Bulgarians. The dignified mausoleum in Sofia, far smaller than its counterpart in Moscow, was a clever double homage: of the Bulgarian people to their dead leader and, more subtly, of the Bulgarian Communist Party to the Supreme Soviet.

The decision of the 'Committee for the Immortalization of Lenin's Memory' to embalm the body of the founder of the Soviet Union was intimately connected with the politics of power. It led to the creation of the extraordinary mausoleum in Red Square complete with a penumbra of living specialists and preserved corpses in its dedicated laboratory. Unwittingly, this rite echoed events 2,500 years earlier on the steppelands north of the Black Sea.

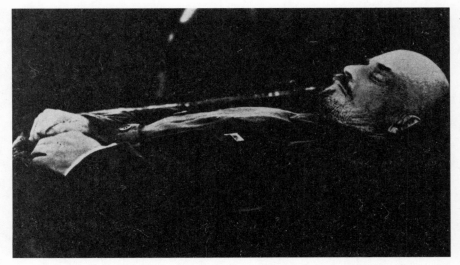

Lenin embalmed in Red Square. (Photo: © Hulton Deutsch collection/ Corbis)

Dozens of corpses, weapons drawn, sat on their dead steeds, encircling a great burial mound, facing outwards. Their hair floated in the warm steppe wind, but briefly. The wind bore huge Ukrainian vultures whose attentions swiftly reduced the dead cavalry to bony wraiths. The steppelands were ruled by the Scythians. Herodotus paints a ferocious picture of these Iron Age people, which may not do justice to their extreme violence and bloodthirstiness as revealed by archaeology. The funeral of the Scythian king, according to Herodotus, involved the embalming and display of the leader, who was entombed in an elaborate vault, and the subsequent strangulation of fifty warriors in the flower of their youth. Their corpses were given a professional taxidermic treatment so that they could be mounted on fifty stuffed horses and installed as lifelike public sculptures around the great burial mound.

It is an intriguing fact that Lenin's embalmers apparently knew nothing of the prehistoric Scythian tradition in their own country, but not deeply puzzling. In fact, the rites in both cases conform to a pattern, first observed by social anthropologists in places such as Borneo, that is recognized as universal in traditional societies.

On special occasions such as weddings, the Berewan of north Borneo put balls of boiled rice sprinkled with yeast into great sealed jars to make rice wine. Fermentation produces a liquor which collects in the bottom of the jar and the rice balls are eventually wrung out. When a person dies they are also sealed inside a rice-wine-making jar – usually one that they have themselves previously chosen and decommissioned, turning it upside down when they detect the onset of death. The 'fermentation' of the body takes between four and ten days. The decomposition fluids are siphoned off through a tube at the base of the jar until there are just bones inside, which are then removed to a little coffin and placed on a simple wooden platform in the graveyard.

Both activities, making rice wine and preparing corpses, are done ritually in preparation for a special, culminating ceremony. In the case of the corpse, this ceremony, called *nulang*, occurs no sooner than eight months after death, and may not take place for five years. When the guests have arrived for this, the coffin is transferred to a small hut constructed on the veranda of the communal longhouse and, every night for a week or so, people feast and party. Eventually the coffin is taken to a large decorated mausoleum raised up on posts, and placed next to several others.[2]

'Life itself means to separate and to be reunited, to change form and condition, to die and to be reborn. It is to act and to cease, to wait and rest, and then to begin acting again, but in a different way. And there are always new thresholds to cross . . .' wrote Arnold van Gennep, in his 1909 classic *The Rites of Passage*.[3] These thresholds (a change in marital status, the acceptance of a child into the social world, or the sending of a person into the world of the ancestors) have tangible biological correlates (having sex together, being born, or dying) but are themselves intangible unless signposted by rituals.

Rituals often involve highly tangible things (sacrificing a goat; sacrificing a human) whose impact is in direct relation to the intangibility of their purpose (having one's thanks accepted by a god; having one's entire community forgiven by a god). Van Gennep's theory that there was a distinctive class of rituals, *rites de passage*, that took the same form in all human cultures has been enormously influential both within anthropology and outside. In everyday parlance, a 'rite of passage' occurs when some unforeseen hazard tests a person's endurance to such an extent that they are afterwards seen as having changed in some way (by becoming more mature, for example). Van Gennep's central idea, distilled from case studies, was that in all traditional societies, critical events which cause deep changes in the way an individual is perceived, such as becoming a mother (having given birth), or becoming a new member of the tribe (having been born) or becoming one of the tribal ancestors (having died), do not occur naturally: biological 'rites of passage' were, wherever in the world one looked, elaborated into symbolic and cultural rites of passage, such as marriage, baptism and funerals. By comparing ceremonies observed by anthropologists around the world, van Gennep showed that a rite of passage has three stages: rites of separation (or *preliminal* rites), rites of transition (or *liminal* rites), and rites of incorporation (or *postliminal* rites).[4]

All rites of passage entail a process of removal from a previous status so that the person is free to enter a new one. But the intervening period is ambiguous. During this time the person's identity is blurred and all manner of taboos come into force. In fact they are suspended in a different sort of time – out of the normal run of the world – during which they must prepare and be prepared for the next phase. Finally comes the ceremonial welcome as the new identity is assumed. Other, more specific kinds of rite – fertility rites, divination rites, death rites, and so on – take place according to what the event is, but are slotted into the overarching, tripartite framework of the rites of passage.

In van Gennep's schema, the most dangerous and taboo state is always the transitional or liminal one, during which the person is on the threshold between worlds, separated from the past and not yet accepted into the future. The term *liminal* comes from the Latin word for 'threshold', *limen*. When the dead body enters the rice jar and is sealed, it becomes liminal. To disturb it between the state of being essentially whole, but dead, and being skeletalized, is taboo. When the jar is opened, the bones remain liminal, and can only be handled by designated people. The danger of liminality, of treading a supernatural knife edge, does not go away until the final ceremony is completed.

Similarly, among the Rus, for ten days prior to the burning the body of the chieftain was contained in a sunken, wood-lined grave chamber and covered over with earth. This was not a 'makeshift' grave to be used while the ship was prepared and the great pyre-scaffold constructed (although it did obviously allow that to happen – rituals can be functionally useful). What Ibn Faḍlān describes is a state in which the Rus chieftain is not fully dead: he has died physically but not socially. The point of social death, when he is burned on the pyre, will also be the moment of his social resurrection, but in the world of the ancestors. Robert Hertz, who studied Bornean customs in detail and who is probably the most influential and sophisticated anthropologist of death, wrote that 'For the collective consciousness, death is – in normal circumstances – a temporary exclusion of the individual from human society.'[5]

The translation of the Rus chieftain's soul to the other world was a tricky business. The man had been powerful in life. In death, his soul could be expected to want to cling on to power, opposing the disbursement and disposal of his wealth, fighting the decomposition and destruction of his body. In the period immediately following his death he was excluded from all human society, both of the living and of the dead – a condition he was unused to and could not be expected to bear with equanimity. Ritual had to take over from whatever it was that physically and tangibly killed him, in order to render him fully dead to this world.

If Rus ritual and belief wholly conformed to the patterns that van Gennep and Hertz identified, as they seem to do in many key details, then – although Ibn Faḍlān does not tell us this – we are probably right to imagine that the soul or spirit of the Rus chieftain was believed to hover near his dead body, unwilling to give up on the physical self, yet not wanting to re-enter and reanimate it because it was a cold corpse. At times he haunts the tents of the living, obsessed with revenge and the settling of old scores. The living perceive this danger and must both taboo his body – keep it in limbo and guard against its reanimation – and also prepare things that will be acceptable to the dead, so that they will welcome the chief into their realm and keep him there. Should these preparations go wrong, the soul of the chieftain will unquietly wander between worlds, wreaking havoc indefinitely. From the point of his physical death to the point at which the mound is finally raised over the ashes of the ship-pyre, the chieftain is caught up in a rite of passage, each stage of which is fraught with supernatural dangers.

The time of natural bereavement following death does not just feel weird in the colloquial sense of being strange and disjointed, but is widely conceived of as weird in its ancient, Old-English sense: imbued with a predestinating power. Because the idea of supernatural rebirth is so central to funeral ceremony, it is obvious that there will be similarities between funeral rites and birth rites. Like the chief mourner, the new mother is accorded special status. Like the newly dead corpse, the newborn baby is liminal.

The liminality of the child begins, according to van Gennep, with the recognition of an established pregnancy, at which point it is common for the prospective mother to become liminal herself, tabooed and impure, sometimes sequestered and excluded from certain activities central to the life of the community, such as food preparation. Her first pregnancy, which marks her transition into the social status of 'motherhood', involves lots of ritual, geared towards achieving that profound intangible which van Gennep terms her 'social return from childbirth'. This may not be completed until several months after the child is born.

The child 'can be born', say the Rahūna of Morocco, 'only after he has obtained the favour of those present'.[6] Adults are on the defensive, as they might be in the presence of a strange visitor. Like a stranger, the child must be separated from its previous environment (in this case the mother). The cutting of the umbilical cord has to be done properly – that is, ritually. The gender status of the instrument used to do this – an old man's knife (a male item) or a mature woman's spindle (a female item) – is often what crucially and definitively establishes the child's gender (which is both of profound importance for its life, *and* not necessarily in accordance with what we would call its biology).[7] Van Gennep says that 'Rites which involve cutting something – especially the first haircut, the shaving of the head – and the rite of putting on clothes for the first time, are generally rites of separation.' The immediate physical products of birth – the umbilical cord, the placenta, items and garments associated with parturition – are all in various ways tabooed, and require ritualized retention or disposal.

The child may not be considered to have a soul at the moment of birth, and certainly not one that is firmly resident within its physical body. The Ainu of northern Japan believe that the mother provides the child with its body, while the father provides its soul, bit by bit, over the twelve days following the birth.[8]

On the west coast of Ireland, children who die before baptism or from whom it has been, in one way or another, withheld cannot have their bodies placed in sacred ground. At least, they cannot be put into cemeteries consecrated by the Catholic Church but they can be quietly interred in 'children's cemeteries' or *ceallunaigh*. The *ceallunaigh* are not consecrated ground, although they may lie close to ground that once was. They occupy isolated, overgrown, haunting places – little, stony fields, with low walls, exposed to the wild Atlantic gales. Informal by nature, the few that are marked on Ordnance Survey maps are known only through their proximity to famous old ecclesiastical sites, like Aghatubrid and Cappanagroun. They may belong to a system of beliefs far older than Christianity. What is known for certain is that *ceallunaigh* have, since at least medieval times, served as places for the disposal of the troublesome dead, not just unbaptized children but strangers, suicides and unrepentant murderers.[9]

The babies in the *ceallunaigh* could not go through the usual rite of passage to exit the world, the funeral, because they had not completed the rite of passage to enter the world. Baptism was the rite of *incorporation* into Christian society. No baptism, no social existence. No social existence, no rite of leaving. No funeral. Never really more 'here' than 'there', they had remained liminal. The concept of a threshold, *limen*, which remained unpassed by the unbaptized was explicitly recognized in the language and dogma of the medieval Church in Europe. Priests argued long and hard about whether unbaptized infants went straight to Hell or to an indeterminate place, the *Limbus Infantus* or 'limbo'.[10]

Naming, nursing, the first tooth, baptism, and on, involve rites of incorporation which, as the Dyaks of New Guinea say, 'launch the child into the world' like a boat on to the water.[11] But if the child physically dies before its 'launching', the Dyaks, in

120

common with many Papuan groups, put the corpse into a tree. As Robert Hertz says: 'they believe humans once came from trees and must return there'. Babies who die before their rite of incorporation into society are thought to have left their tree too early or in a worrying fashion. Their death seems to be understood as the soul failing to establish itself fully within the body. Some Dyaks believe that the same soul will soon be reincarnated in the same woman's womb and make a more auspicious entry next time: 'It is as though, for the collective consciousness, there were no real death in this case.'[12]

The problem of defining the point at which a new human being can be said to exist and is thereby accorded rights under the law lies at the heart of the modern abortion debate. While the Catholic Church frowns on the act of contraception, considering that the egg becomes endowed with a soul at the moment of fertilization, many of the indigenous communities that social anthropologists have studied accept the propriety of infanticide, days or even weeks after physical birth.[13]

The motif of life as a voyage, only properly begun by a premeditated and well-thought-out ritual of launching, not precipitately started off by a mere physical event (birth), is one that seems to be present also in Ibn Faḍlān's account of the Rus funeral, in which, after many preliminaries, the chieftain is sent off in a boat to Valhalla. Funerary rites are often thought of as being like a voyage in a boat, over a river, lake or sea.

The voyage of the dead person's soul requires careful preparation and an act of cutting free. The placing of a knife in a burial, as among the Iban of Borneo, is understood to be necessary in some cases to cut the ties from the living.[14] Just as social birth follows physical birth, physical death (which must be contained by society) is followed by social death (which will be stage-managed by society). This cannot be successfully concluded until the ancestors have been properly appeased: Van Gennep said that 'those funeral rites which incorporate the deceased into the world of the dead are most extensively elaborated and assigned the greatest importance'.[15]

'The horror of death is not the same as the shock of some particular death, and neither is identical with the fear of the dead,' wrote Robert Hertz.[16] Hertz observed that the three phases of funeral rites also involve a three-way relationship between the soul, the dead body, and the living mourners. The consequence of this is that there are three distinct types of fear experienced by people in relation to death.[17]

The first of these, the 'horror of death', is felt not because corpses smell and rot but, according to Hertz, because the body 'which was in the realm of the ordinary, suddenly leaves it'.[18] The corpse is a source of natural and supernatural pollution; not of this world, it taints everything it touches.

The second kind of fear, shock at a particular death, is different. People experience fear in direct relation to the dead person's importance within the structure of society: at the death of a chief, 'a true panic sweeps over the group [while] the death of a stranger, a slave, or a child will go almost unnoticed,' says Hertz.[19] The corpse has to be dealt with in some way, but as the person is still socially living, it cannot be placed in a permanent grave or cremated; such treatment must be reserved for the moment of closure, when the dead person is accepted into the social world of the dead. A temporary holding facility, termed the 'primary' burial or funerary structure, is required.

'Fear of the dead' – Hertz's third type – is fear of disembodied souls, whether of former leaders or tiny children. This kind of fear explains why, in many societies, corpses are taken out of the house where death occurred through a specially made hole in the wall; the hole is immediately repaired, so thwarting the return of the soul. Whether disembodied or as the walking dead, it cannot retrace its route to reappear among the living.[20] People worry about whether the soul will choose to go to or subsequently be accepted in the social world of the ancestors: this fear extends nebulously beyond the actual corpse, so that land and trees owned by the deceased, the husband or wife of the deceased, their slaves and retainers and so on, are supernaturally polluted and rendered liminal by death. A recent report from a rural part of Nigeria documents that young widows are still required to keep their heads shaved and appear only naked in public for a full year after their bereavement, a state of total ignominy that they do not bear without complaint.[21]

Only a successfully completed funerary ritual can restore communal stability. It does this by creating a new status quo, not just socially, but physically and spiritually. The decomposing body needs to be treated and/or removed from people's living space; the deceased's possessions need to be distributed, or inherited, or consumed, or destroyed; and the living need to be protected from the wandering soul of the dead person. Hertz argued that what happens physically to the body after death symbolizes people's beliefs about the progress of the soul. Just as the corpse is foul and putrefying during the intermediary period in its temporary structure (the 'primary' burial), so the soul is also pitiful, existing like a ragged beggar around the fringes of the village, liable to commit acts of spite, cause illness, and so on. The living mourners have to act in ritually careful ways to avoid contamination during this liminal period, waiting for the corpse and the soul to become, simultaneously, ready for the final act.

Although the rites of passage were claimed to be human cultural universals by van Gennep, not everyone in any given society is important enough to be accorded them. The elaboration of ritual typically has a lot to do with the status of the deceased, something that Hertz realized when he spoke of the importance of 'the scale of rites'. It was a failing of much early social anthropology – including that of van Gennep and Hertz themselves – that it paid little heed to the way in which young children or slaves were disposed of when they died, part of a more general failure to notice their existence. The unstated idea of 'collective consciousness' pervades these accounts, encouraging us to believe that 'the Rahūna', 'the Ainu', 'the Berewan' or 'the Dyaks' can be considered as individual organisms.

Unsurprisingly, as Pierre Clastres' work among the Atchei demonstrated, the real individual organisms in human societies are individual humans. But individuals have different powers and statuses. Adult slaves are people who have either been stripped of their social rank or are themselves the children of slaves. They are not initiates in the social world and it is therefore unnecessary to hold funerals for them when they leave it. Among the Iron Age Scythians of the Black Sea steppe they might leave it as part of someone else's – a 'real' person's – funeral.

I wondered how I might be remembered and what would be done with my body if I fell from the vibrating oil platform. The mud-covered, corroded metal ladders had some mild steel tubing welded on the outside to grip on to, but my standard issue mittens were too large and my hand kept slipping. At the top – 59 metres (194 feet) up, as stated on the typed certificate that was presented to me afterwards – I opened my wallet and showed Leonid and Vitaly the photographs of my wife and my two daughters. Mainly, I wanted to look at them myself. Vitaly was the foreman and Leonid, who had fought on the Soviet side in Saigon, now ran this rig in the heart of Ukraine. He looked confident in his fine Siberian fur hat, and it was only after descending, drinking some vodka and eating roast goose, that I learned that two people had died on the rig, one of them by falling from the top.

The reason I risked the rig was that I was visiting one of the largest archaeological sites in Europe and I wanted to photograph it. Even from the top, only a small portion could be brought into view, the great earthworks running away and fading into the hazy distance.

In Book 4 of his *History*, Herodotus describes the thriving Graeco-Scythian town of Gelonus in the forest steppe, its wood-palisaded ramparts extending 30 *stades* in each direction. A stade is one-eighth of a Roman mile and 30 stades in modern measurement is equal to around 5.5 kilometres or 3.5 miles. Herodotus' Gelonus would, if square, have enclosed an area of 30 square kilometres or almost 12 square miles. It was long fashionable, among those who have never travelled as widely as Herodotus did, to deride him for exaggeration. But Gelonus has been plausibly identified with the archaeological site of Bielsk, where massive ditch and bank ramparts, originally surmounted by a palisade, actually enclose some 40 square kilometres. The site extends over 6 kilometres at its widest and is a full 12 kilometres from north to south, shaped like an irregular triangle.

Strategically situated on a tributary of the Dniepr, east of Kiev, Bielsk is both a vindication of the quality of Herodotus' information and a demonstration of the economic might of Scythia. The trade in slaves, iron and precious metals up and down the great River Dniepr goes back before the foundation of Kiev by the Rus, into deep prehistory. One of the golden-domed monasteries now contains a museum treasury stuffed with the fabulous silver and gold drinking vessels, quiver cases and sword scabbards of the Iron Age Scythians, overlords of the steppe in the first millennium BC. Like Ibn Faḍlān a millennium and a half later, Herodotus was a visitor. Although he may have visited Gelonus, it is more probable that he stayed in greater safety and comfort in the Greek trading centre of Olbia, near present-day Odessa, gathering and sifting information from merchants and travellers.

The Scythians were an Iron Age society based on a number of inter-competitive horse-riding military elite groups. The 'Royal Scythians' were the most powerful of these and Herodotus' description of their burial customs accords well with archaeological discoveries.[22] We can compare Herodotus' description line for line and paragraph for paragraph with what has been more recently excavated. He writes:

> The burial place of their kings is in the country of the Gerrhi, at the point up to which the River Borysthenes [the Dniepr] is navigable. Here, when a king dies, they dig a great square pit, and, when it is ready, they take up the corpse – having treated it with a coat of wax and cut open the belly and cleaned it and filled it with embalming substances: sweet-smelling sedge, parsley-seed, and anise. It is then sewn up again . . .[23]

We must thank a party of prehistoric Siberian grave robbers for allowing us to corroborate this account. Digging down they smashed through the wooden roofs of a number of freshly built Scythian-style barrows at a place now known as Pazyryk in the Altai – the 'Mountains of Gold' – at the eastern end of the Eurasian steppe. Then the robbers lowered rough-hewn tree-trunk ladders into the darkness. They found more treasure than they could easily carry, for they had to remove the tops of several of the little wooden tables placed in the graves for the use of the dead, so that they could serve as trays for carrying up the gold, silver and bronze jewellery and weaponry. The reason we know this with such certainty is that the ladders and detachable table legs survived. Opening the grave chambers allowed frozen air to percolate downwards, freeze-drying the tomb contents. So, although everything of value to the grave robbers was taken by them, their actions preserved items of immense value to archaeologists.

The 'frozen tombs' of Pazyryk, excavated in the 1950s, caused a sensation. The permafrost had preserved marvellous wall hangings, saddle blankets and the sacrificed horses that had worn them, felt toys, imported Chinese silk, leather artworks, and coffins with the bodies still in them. The corpses had been carefully prepared, cleaned out and sewn up again in precisely the manner Herodotus describes even though his information came from the western rather than the eastern end of the steppe. The Pazyryk embalmers used many of the same herbs, and also others, such as imported coriander seed.[24]

Herodotus' phrase 'and, when it is ready, they take up the corpse' tells us that the Scythian king had been in the ground some time already, interred in a classic Hertzian 'primary burial'. But the body is not supposed to rot down to bone to symbolize the process of freeing the soul. Instead, the decomposition processes are arrested to make the body more attractive to the soul, encouraging it to stay close to its own corpse during the supernaturally dangerous intermediary period. Unlike Egyptian mummification, Scythian embalming was not designed to preserve the corpse in perpetuity. It was more like modern Western mortuary practice, a temporary and cosmetic stabilization. Without the fluke conditions in the ice tombs of Pazyryk we would only have had Herodotus' word that this is what was done.

We have a fair idea of what sort of golden treasures the Pazyryk robbers carried out on the table-top trays, because graves in the western steppe were less systematically robbed. The most spectacular Scythian burial mounds or *kurgans* have been excavated to the north of the Black Sea. The difficulty and danger of working illicitly inside these massive structures was far greater than in the smaller Pazyryk *kurgans* and, although the climate has not favoured frozen preservation, many more of the precious metal grave goods survived.

The largest *kurgans* are found just south of the Dniepr rapids, in the great right-bank bend in the river, an area referred to by Herodotus as the burial place of the Scythian kings. These are the final, secondary burials, of course, and it is not clear from Herodotus' account whether the primary treatment of fresh corpses occurred in the same location as the permanent burial mounds or not. It would make practical sense if the primary rites were conducted close to the location of death, either in the steppe or beyond it, but temporary burial pits from this period have never been plausibly identified archaeologically.

Herodotus' description of the funeral ceremony continues:

– In this condition the corpse is processed in a wagon to the country of the tributary people who live nearest, and then on to the next, visiting each subordinate tribe in turn. In the course of its progress, those who successively receive it, do what the Royal Scythians do: they cut off a piece from their ear, shave their hair, make circular incisions on their arms, gash forehead and nose, and drive arrows through their left hand. At each stage of the journey, those who are visited join the procession, until they have conveyed the corpse through all the Scythian dominions and end up at

127

the place of burial, which is among the Gerrhi, who live furthest distant of all –

This procession concludes the rite of separation. The cutting and stabbing symbolize the severing of bonds with the living. The level of self-administered violence fits with Hertz' observation that at the death of a chief 'a true panic sweeps over the group'. While the 'primary burial' was in a pit that would have been dug close to where the king died, the location of secondary burial is the traditional burial ground. Until the point at which the mound is raised his body and soul remain dangerously liminal. In common with many Scythian burials, one of the frozen tombs at Pazyryk contained a dismantled wagon that would have been eminently suitable for such a rite, with big spoked wheels and a tall superstructure so that the embalmed body could be set up high to be seen by the crowds.

– Afterwards, when they put the dead man in his grave on a bed, they fix spears on either side of the corpse and set poles horizontally over them to support a roof of plaited rushes. Around this in the burial pit they bury one of his concubines, after strangling her, and his wine-bearer, cook, groom, steward, and his message-bearer. Horses are buried too, and other offerings, and his golden cups.

The rite of transition is pervaded by a great sense of danger. In a liminal period, normal rules are suspended and it is only in this special ritual time that the strangling of the king's closest servants can be legitimately accomplished. As personal servants, they do not receive any elaborate separation rite: their fate is wholly subordinate to that of the king. The killing of many of these people may have a double ritual purpose, providing the king with people to serve, defend and entertain him in death, and removing people perceived as supernaturally 'polluted' because of their close association with the dead man. Politically speaking, the killing of the king's closest retainers emphasizes the power of the institution of kingship. The cultural belief that the king's death causes profound and pervasive pollution that requires many people to die at his funeral reinforces the status of the king.

The restatement of the dead king's superior social position at his funeral also makes a statement on behalf of his successor. People do not bury themselves, and there is *realpolitik* behind the rites. The funeral provides an ideal opportunity for the incumbent to assert his new powers. As part of the reverential funerary rights of the man he replaces, the new king can, with complete legitimacy, conduct a lethal purge of suspected rivals.

It was not just retainers who accompanied the dead king. Analysis of the way that *kurgans* were constructed shows that they were principally made up of upside-down turfs of prime steppe pasture. The amount involved represents the stripping of a large ground area. Inverting the turf was probably symbolic of an allocation of pasture in the other life. The burial chambers at one of the largest of the Dniepr-bend *kurgans*, Chertomlyk, were cut down 10 metres below the ground surface. The mound was then erected, in at least four separate phases, to reach 20 metres above ground level, with a stone-packed revetment around the base. Between the layers of inverted turfs is super-compacted clay, making the mound harder to rob. Tests have shown that it would have been possible to construct such a mound in the forty days Herodotus specifies for the duration of this part of the ritual (the rite of separation), given a workforce of 400.[25]

The bodies of two young men were found inside the complex system of chambers beneath the *kurgan* at Chertomlyk, each holding the reins of his own team of horses. Other buried retainers included a pair of elaborately arrayed male warriors. A rich female, buried with her own young servant, may have been a queen, a high-status 'companion', or some kind of priestess: the outstandingly wealthy and elaborate jewellery and its symbolism remain open to interpretation.

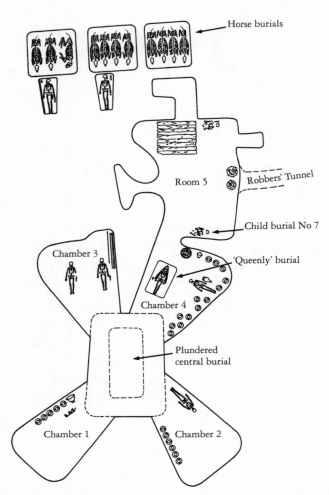

Chertomlyk, Ukraine: plan of the Scythian Iron Age burial with attendant retainer sacrifice. (After Zabelin in Rolle et al. 1998)

– This done, the people start raising a huge mound of earth, enthusiastically challenging each other to make it as big as possible –

This concludes the rite of transition and begins the process, but not the rite, of incorporation. The body is sealed into its chamber under a huge mound of earth. Equipped with servants

Chertomlyk, Ukraine: Burial No. 7 (child). (Photo: author)

and food, wealth and horses, the dead king is made a potential player in the society of the dead, but his position is by no means assured. The king has left the society of the living yet has not so far been accepted into the society of the dead. The system of rooms under the mound at Chertomlyk, overarched by the inverted pasture, forms a kind of photographic negative of life on the outside where the king's soul is provided with all that it can possibly need to keep it happy and away from the affairs of the living. He is like an astronaut in a capsule on his way to another planet, provided with a little of everything, in a self-sustaining 'limbo' society which will serve him between worlds.

– When a year has come round in its cycle, they do something else. Of the king's remaining servants they take those most suitable for their purposes (and these are native-born Scythians, for the servants of the king are those he bids serve him; he has no bought slaves), and they strangle fifty of them, and fifty of his finest horses, and they gut them, and stuff them with chaff, and sew them up –

This is the beginning of the rite of incorporation. The king's soul is now accepted into the society of the dead, and the form of this ritual emphasizes his reborn kingly status. The bodies are turned into something resembling human 'Beanie Babies'. The choice of chaff for the stuffing was functional (allowing the corpses to be easily posed), and had a symbolic association with spent grain. These men are now human husks stripped away from their souls. Any doubts about the scale of this killing of men and horses are swept aside by archaeological evidence. Although Chertomlyk contained only the skeletons of eleven horses, at Ulski Aul the excavator, Veselovsky, recorded 360, tethered in groups of eighteen to posts and rails in an elaborate layout.

Many more horses were subsequently killed when the mound had been half raised, but there were so many in this distinctive layer that Veselovsky – who had sliced straight to the centre of the mound at ground level and only began to look at what was crumbling out of the upper layers later – gave up counting them.[26] In both Herodotus' account and here at Ulski Aul, the greatest act of mass killing occurred well after the point at which the noble was first placed in his grave. He could initially have been buried with more servants. That he was not underlines his status between worlds: he only required a trusty few for his journey. It is not until he arrives in the ancestral world that he takes command of an army again.

– Then the half of a wheel is fixed, rim downwards, on two posts, and the other half-wheel on two more posts; then stout poles are driven lengthways through each horse, from tail to neck, and, by means of these the horses are mounted on the wheels, in such a way that the front half-wheel supports the shoulders and the rear the belly between the thighs. The legs hang loose to either side. They put bits and reins in the horses' mouths and stretch these to the front and fasten them from pegs. Each one of the fifty young men who were strangled they then mount on a horse. They contrive the mounting of the horsemen by driving an upright stake, parallel with the spine, up to the neck; the lower, protruding stake-ends can be fitted into the horizontal poles running through the horses. They set these, horses and riders, in a circle around the burial, and, having done so, they ride off themselves –

This ends the rite of incorporation. From the perspective of cold, hard politics, the ceremony a full year later has coercively and effectively empowered the new king. It is highly significant that these are not 'bought slaves', as this is not a ceremony of simple conspicuous consumption. The chance to serve the dead Scythian king in the next world may not have been much of an incentive to young steppe warriors with plenty of opportunities for self-aggrandizement in the living world ahead of them. The procedures of choice – whose horses, whose men – must have provided the chance for score-settling and jockeying for position.

– That is how they bury their kings. But as to the rest of the Scythians, when they die, their nearest relatives lay the corpse in a wagon and take it round to visit their friends. The various families in turn entertain their guests with a meal and offer a share of the food to the dead man, just as to everyone else. For forty days all those people who are not kings are carried round in this way, and then they are buried. After a burial, the Scythians purify themselves as follows: they anoint and wash their heads; as to their bodies, they set up three poles, leaning them against one another, and cover the structure with overlapped carpets until it is well sealed, and inside this little tent they place a bowl with red-hot stones in it. Now they have cannabis growing in that country that is very like flax, except that is thicker and taller. This plant grows both wild and under cultivation. . . . The Scythians then take the seed of this cannabis and cast it on to the hot stones. At once it begins to smoke, giving off a vapour unsurpassed in any vapour-bath one might find in Greece. The Scythians in their pleasure, howl loudly –

This describes how a lesser person – but still one of the ruling group and, probably, an adult male – is dealt with. Conforming to Hertz' observation, the dead body 'pollutes everything it touches'. And the mourners themselves require decontamination. At Pazyryk, the remains of a six-legged hemp tent were found, along with two braziers containing stones which had been heated, their handles heat-insulated with wraps of birch bark; a cheetah-fur bag contained seeds of *cannabis sativa*.[27]

The *scale* of the rites accords with what Hertz predicts: the death of an 'ordinary' man leaves far less of a rift in the social fabric than the death of a king. No one else is put to death. No rite of incorporation is mentioned, but it may not have been elaborate (for example, animal sacrifices after a year) – nothing that Herodotus found exceptional enough to be worth telling us.

When Darius the Great of Persia launched an ill-fated land and sea invasion of Scythia around 513 BC, first subjugating Thrace and then building a pontoon bridge across the Danube, he could not bring the Scythians, under their king Idanthyrsus, to battle. Part of the Scythian strategy was to tempt the Persians to over-extend their supply lines, and attempt to sever the Danube bridge. Herodotus describes Darius' increasing frustration:[28]

As this was proving a long and endless matter, Darius dispatched a rider with a message for Idanthyrsus, the Scythian king: 'Your behaviour is strange. Why do you keep running from me? You have, surely, to choose a course of action, either, if you think yourself strong enough to oppose my power, to stop wandering to and fro and give battle, or, if your mind tells you that you are the weaker, then also stop wandering and give gifts – earth and water – to the one who is your master, and come to terms with me.'

To this the Scythian king, Idanthyrsus, replied, 'Persian, matters are thus with me. I have never yet run from any man in fear; and I am not doing so now from you. There is, for me, nothing unusual in what I have been doing. This is the life that I lead, even in peace time. I will also tell you why I will not fight you just now. In our country there are no settled towns or cultivated land, the fear of losing which, or seeing it all ravaged, might indeed provoke us to immediate battle. If, however, you are determined upon bloodshed with the least possible delay, there *are* our fathers' tombs. Find them, and try to desecrate them, and you will soon find out whether we are prepared to fight you – for the tombs. Before that, we will not fight, unless some argument of our own takes possession of us. That is all I have to say to you about battle. But, as for my masters, I count them to be Zeus who is my ancestor, and Hestia queen of the Scythians. These only. I will send you such gifts as are fit to come your way. Your claim to be my master is something you will regret.' That is the speech Darius got from the Scythians.[29]

The Scythians then sent the demoralized Persians a bird, a mouse, a frog and five arrows. The precise meaning of this remained as obscure to the Persians and to Herodotus as it does to us. The Persian general, Gobryas, may have been closest in suggesting it was a hint to fly, burrow, and hop, or to face more Scythian arrows.

The Scythians were a tribally organized society not unlike those that van Gennep and Hertz studied at first hand, so it is not surprising that Herodotus' account of Scythian funerary practices fits well with the standard anthropological model of funeral rites. The fit with Lenin's funeral is rather more surprising. Yet van Gennep's triple structure is peculiarly clear in Ilya Zbarsky's account of the preservation of the communist leader's body (in which both he and his father were personally involved). Zbarsky, a research chemist, was unaware of van Gennep or Hertz, yet he describes a series of rituals which could have been written to an anthropological script. Although no one spoke of rites of separation, transition and incorporation, Lenin's corpse was undoubtedly accorded them – by a society that suppressed all religion as a central tenet of its state ideology. Even more strangely, by following van Gennep's logic we reach the remarkable conclusion that the three canonical rites were subtly and deliberately subverted by Stalin in an act of ritual magic.

After a debilitating illness (officially arteriosclerosis, although unofficial claims have been made that it was syphilitic paralysis), Lenin died on the Gorky estate, just outside Moscow, on 21 January 1924. Born Vladimir Ilyich Ulyanov in 1870, he had been a student agitator in an underground populist movement and, in line with contemporary radical chic, changed his name. His eldest brother was hanged for his part in a plot to assassinate Emperor Aleksandr III, but Lenin survived to finally emerge from a period of revolution and civil war as the leader of a communist version of the Russian empire – the Soviet Union.[30] An immensely gifted control freak, he died without having appointed a successor from among his co-revolutionaries, who included Trotsky and Stalin (not their real names).

Following Lenin's death, an anatomical pathologist, Professor Abrikosov, conducted an autopsy and then embalmed him. This was a temporary, undertaker's measure, so that the body did not smell too much or rot before the funeral. Lenin was dressed in a formal, dark suit and composed neatly on his deathbed. A photograph was taken showing him reclining on pillows, in the presence of his widow, Nadezhda Krupskaya, and various estate workers.

Lenin's corpse was then quickly taken into the centre of Moscow and put on display in an open casket, surrounded by flowers, in the Hall of Pillars of the House of Trade Unions. Massive queues formed outside, snaking over the snow-packed streets. People filed in and out over a four-day period, paying their last respects. On Sunday, 27 January the funeral service was held, and the coffin was taken from the Hall of Pillars into Red Square. Over the previous three days, Red Army engineers had blasted a three-metre-deep pit into the minus-30 degrees centigrade permafrosted ground, and topped it with a grey-painted wooden mausoleum with LENIN on it, in big relief capitals. The pall bearers were Stalin, Bukharin, Kamenev and Zinoviev – politicians striving for supremacy in the still nascent USSR. In carrying Lenin's coffin, they probably became, at that moment, the four most powerful men, for Lenin's corpse was about to metamorphose into the most potent of all symbols of the Soviet Union. Through Stalin's careful machinations Trotsky, perhaps his chief rival for the Soviet leadership, was kept away from the funeral. This marked a crucial turning point: Trotsky became detached from the emerging insignia of power and never regained significant authority. Graphs of rising economic output were placed in front of the temporary mausoleum, alongside wreaths and slogans. Access to the corpse was now highly restricted.

The activities and movements of this phase can be seen as constituting the rites of separation, beginning in the domestic sphere (the deathbed at Gorky), progressing to the public rite of separation (The Hall of Pillars), and concluding with the political rite. This involved the lid being placed on the coffin, Lenin vanishing from sight, and his transfer to Red Square. The lowering of the casket into the freezing pit marked the end of the rite of separation and the start of the rite of transition, with the pit being the primary burial, liminal and surrounded by danger.

There was no precise precedent for what happened next, although Trotsky knew what to expect. The previous October, with Lenin already terminally ill, Stalin had told the Politburo that party rank and file throughout the Soviet Union wanted

Lenin's body preserved; as Zbarsky and Hutchinson note, 'Stalin ... was careful not to name the "comrades in the provinces" who wanted to embalm Lenin, for the simple reason that this had been his own idea: he saw it as a good way of harnessing the religious sentiment of the ignorant masses'. To this, Trotsky had responded: 'If I understand comrade Stalin correctly, he proposes to replace the relics of Saint Sergei Radonezhsky and Saint Serafim Sarovsky with the remains of Vladimir Ilyich.'

Against the express wishes of Nadezhda Krupskaya, who wanted her husband properly interred, a makeshift laboratory was set up in the pit, next to the corpse, which had started to decompose quite badly. On 26 March 1924, the body was stripped and the process of permanent embalming, principally by chemical immersion, began, along with an ongoing programme of cosmetic restoration. In mid-June, Krupskaya was visited by Dzerzhinsky, the head of the OGPU (the forerunner of the KGB), and required to produce Lenin's khaki, military-style tunic. Lenin was re-dressed, and Krupskaya, along with Lenin's brother, was invited to a private view. The brother is reported to have said, 'I'm very moved. It takes my breath away. He looks as he did when we saw him a few hours after he died – perhaps even better.' What else he could have said in Dzerzhinsky's presence is unclear, but it may, nevertheless, have been true. Instead of being allowed to rot during this period, or even simply being stabilized, the body had, in a visual sense, been improved. The private view marked the end of the transitional rite or liminal phase.

The new mausoleum, a squat, stepped pyramid built of dark-painted wood, with a parade-viewing platform, was completed in mid-July 1924 and Lenin's tomb was inaugurated. Although on the same physical site as the temporary mausoleum, the wholesale change in superstructure, coffin, clothing, furnishings, and so on, allows us to consider this as essentially a different place, the site of 'secondary burial'. The inauguration was the rite of incorporation. Lenin reappeared, reclothed and physically enhanced, projecting quiet – literally unarguable – authority.

Stalin symbolized his consolidated power when, at the same time as the gulag system of forced labour camps was brought into being in Siberia and the mass killing of agricultural smallholders was taking place across the countryside,[31] the wooden mausoleum, with its resonances of Russian provincial church architecture, was swept away and Red Square became a vast, screened-off building site again. The opening, in 1930, of the imposing polished edifice of the third and final mausoleum – black granite surmounted by red – effectively signalled the beginning of the terror.

When Stalin took the May Day salute from the rostrum of the mausoleum, and the military hardware rolled past, rank after rank, line after line, emblazoned with the red star, he must have felt secure. Every watcher knew that the polished granite surface hid a granite authority. Lenin lay calm and strong, radiating his confidence in the unchallengeable new leader who stood above him, taking the applause.

The mausoleum, rather than the Kremlin, the red flag or the hammer and sickle, was the essential backdrop to the cult of personal adulation that Stalin encouraged. After Lenin's death, divining the political situation from the order in which particular dignitaries took their places on the mausoleum became a parlour game – a grim one.[32] In an unexpected and sinister conjunction of architectural symbolism and practical convenience, the simple and austere geometric design turned out also to be an ideal illusionist prop. It was the perfect photographic backdrop against which to 'erase' people. Those who fell from favour, such as Vlas Chubar', the finance supremo who was sentenced to death in 1939, had their faces scratched out from May Day negatives. It was then a simple matter to montage the uniform tones of the unadorned stone into the gap and remaster the official negative.[33] The monument to Lenin's rite of incorporation in death served to incorporate Stalin as the paramount leader in life. The other three pall bearers were shot and erased: Kamenev and Zinoviev in 1936 and Bukharin in 1938. Stalin became Lenin's sole surviving, and therefore symbolically true, heir.

The new mausoleum was designed to have more room inside, and it had room for one more name on the outside and, by my reckoning, no more than one. In 1953 Stalin, on the verge of a new lethal purge of his closest lieutenants, died, ostensibly of a brain haemorrhage, in circumstances that remain obscure. His body was embalmed and placed in a glass coffin next to Lenin. His name appeared in identically sized capitals below Lenin's until 1961 when, at Khrushchev's instigation, he was demoted and his body removed and interred among other honoured dead leaders in the lee of the mausoleum.

The close match with van Gennep's classic scheme should not surprise us. Soviet politics grew out of folk roots. Stalin, or Iosif Vissarionovich Dzhugashvili as he had once been, was the son of a pious Georgian peasant woman who had sent him to an Orthodox elementary school in Gori and then on to a seminary in Tbilisi. At the height of his power, she was reported to have expressed regret that he had not become a priest. Stalin understood the forms of religious life so well that he became a master of ritual theatre. It is not likely that he explicitly designed rites of separation, transition and incorporation for Lenin. All the baptisms, funerals and clerical translations he had witnessed had followed this archetypical pattern. It was a pattern that he absorbed, and whose psychological effects he understood. He also understood the power of holy relics, and of pilgrimage.

Lenin's muscles, fat and skin were preserved on the bones by periodic immersion in a heavy-duty rubber bath filled with 'balsam' – a cocktail of formalin, alcohol, glycerine, potassium acetate and quinine chloride. In the early days, patches of brown discoloration had to be bleached from the skin with acetic acid and hydrogen peroxide. Improvements to the techniques and the mixtures used were continually being sought, giving the laboratory with its floating corpses its *raison d'être*. Zbarsky and Hutchinson say that 'The mausoleum laboratory had in 1939 employed four scientists; after 1945 there were 35: histologists, anatomists, biochemists, physical chemists, and opticians, working on composition of skin and subcutaneous cellular tissue, as well as decomposition.'[34] By 1970, the centenary of Lenin's birth, this had grown to nearly a hundred, each of whom had a human body for personal experimentation.

The unidentified floating corpses in their individual rubber baths in the mausoleum laboratory quietly and effectively under-lined the state's absolute control of life and death. These were people whose fate was unknown to their closest relatives, who had not had funerals for themselves but were sacrificed to Lenin. Although the scientists' work was 'secret', they had families who wondered what they did in the mausoleum, and some perhaps found out. Ripples of partial knowledge spread outward, encour-aging obeisance and breeding paranoia and fear – things that the state, pre-*glasnost*, was addicted to. They were what made it work.

The experimental corpses are the modern world's closest equivalent to the stuffed warriors around the Scythian king's *kurgan*. States maintain their power through a demonstration of control of death – both individual deaths and death as a phenom-enon. The preservation of Lenin's body was heralded as a tri-umph of Soviet science.

Professor Abrikosov, who did the original autopsy and had become one of the mausoleum scientists, declaimed in the state newspaper, *Izvestiya*, in 1940 that 'This experiment, unique in all the world, has made it possible to preserve a man's corpse after his death in a state like that of a living body.'[35] Members of the team were sent to do other leaders of less powerful com-munist states – Georgi Dimitrov, Ho Chi Minh, Kim Il Sung, and several others (excluding Mao, who had to be embalmed by the Chinese).

Lenin was a biological façade: his lungs, liver, spleen, intestines and so on had all been removed and, although Zbarsky does not comment on it, it is probable that Lenin's brain is not in his cranium. So 'Lenin' was both in perfect health (for a corpse) and a semblance only. In 1928, four years after Lenin's death, the Soviet Brain Institute was founded to pursue research that included defining the minds of criminals and geniuses through

141

a study of apparently characteristic folding on their cerebral cortex.[36] The 'brain of Lenin' subsequently became a byword for supreme genius. Firm proof that it was removed for study is, as far as I know, lacking. Stalin, like all despots, was a past master at using misinformation to create mutual suspicion among his rivals. Rather than discredit the state, it lent it mystique. States not only need secrets, they like to be known to have secrets.

The uncertainty over Lenin's brain was, I am sure, deliberately generated to create the sense that he was somehow, intangibly, everywhere – a perfect cipher for the state itself. Like the mystery of the Trinity in Christianity, it was not only possible but necessary at one and the same time to imagine Lenin's corpse preserved as if alive in Red Square and to hold the contradictory belief that his actual brain was being deciphered and his wishes for the future translated by Soviet science.

His mind and his teachings were still active, his expression remained on his face and, through slogans and iconic portraiture, his presence was everywhere. All that was missing was movement, and that had been transformed into the onward movement of the USSR itself: Lenin was not really dead, he was in a new and more pervasive phase of existence. Spiritually speaking, in a country where *Elektrifikatsiya* ('Electrification') had become a desirable first-name, it is hard not to feel that Lenin's soul was also electrified by the revolution – harnessed as a supernatural power source. Lenin was technologically empowered by his corpse's own laboratory, with operatives working tirelessly on every conceivable enhancement of his appearance.

Russian theologians seem to recognize this view of a soul held in limbo by a never-rotting body, forced to keep working for this world, never allowed peace. Since the collapse of communism it is clear that, for the Russian Orthodox Church, Lenin is not incorporated at all: his body and soul remain quite explicitly *liminal*. While Bulgarian liberals 'freed' Georgi Dimitrov's soul in 1990, when his corpse was finally buried beside his Protestant parents in a Christian rite of incorporation, this has not yet

142

happened for Lenin. Pressures are building: the Patriarch of Moscow, Alexis II, recently stated that, if Lenin's body was not buried, 'his malign soul would go on hovering over the country, to its great detriment'.[37] The contrast with the relics of Christian saints (who outwardly appear to be venerated in the same way as Lenin's corpse) resides in the fact that their souls are believed to have been translated into proximity with God. Stalin, as Trotsky immediately grasped, was making a play to replace the Orthodox Church's relics with those of the Communist Party.

Lenin's corpse generates a sense of posthumous ubiquity, the state of the body serving as a symbolic equation for the imagined state of the soul. Stalin's subtle ritual magic was to neither let Lenin rot, freeing his soul, nor preserve his corpse and wall it up like the ancient Egyptians in their pyramids, constraining it, nor to allow parts of him to be kissed or touched, like a saint's relics. The myth was created that he was intact, complete, spiritually omnipresent, and untouchable. But symbols can be inverted. The same techniques, applied positively to Lenin to keep him present as a force in the material world, can be applied negatively, to prevent those who dishonour the living from exiting the material world to dishonour the dead.

CHAPTER 6

Vexed Ghosts

But I did not start to shoot him. I did not in any way owe him a shooting, and only began to drag him upstairs and into the drawing room ... And then I began to trample on my master, Nikitinsky. I trampled on him for an hour or more than an hour, and during this time I knew life fully. With shooting, I suggest, you can only get rid of a person; shooting is a let out for him, and vilely easy for you; with shooting, you don't get through to the soul, to where it is in a human being and how it manifests itself. But I am inclined not to spare myself. I am inclined to trample the enemy for an hour or more than an hour. I want to know life fully, the way it is with us.

ISAAC BABEL, *The Life of Matvei Rodeonych Pavlichenko*[1]

————

You notice the stubble first, before the noose around the neck. The two are connected, for the millimetre-long beard growth occurred after death – its beautiful evenness the result of a recent shave. His fingernails are clean and unbroken and his hands uncalloused. Yet his hair has been hacked off short with a studied lack of care and he is naked apart from a leather hat and belt. The lips are slightly pursed, as if he is concentrating.

Of the Tollund Man, discovered in 1950 in Jutland, Denmark, the poet Seamus Heaney wrote: 'Some day I will go to Aarhus/

To see his peat-brown head,/The mild pods of his eyelids,/His pointed skin cap.'[2] He looks as if he had just fallen asleep in the bog, but the assaults he suffered before death are nearly inconceivable. Looking back from the noose to the pursed lips and then to the slight frown, the sense that he is concentrating does not evaporate, but the uncomfortable thought dawns that this is the enduring concentration of a man determined not to be broken by his tormentors.

In 1984, the top half of a man's body, 20–30 years old, naked except for a fox-fur armband, was found, along with a right lower leg, in commercial peat cuttings just south of the city of Manchester. The corpse had lain undisturbed for nearly 2,000 years, the flesh and innards cured like meat and tanned like leather by the special chemistry of Lindow Moss, the peat bog in which it had been sealed.[3] The discovery caused a sensation. Not only was he ancient but he had been put to death in a grotesque manner.

'Lindow Man' is the most recently discovered and one of the best analysed of what are known collectively as the 'bog bodies'. He and Tollund Man are joined by many others, each named after the bog in which it was discovered: Grauballe Man, the two Borromose women and their child, Windeby Girl and Windeby Man, the disabled Yde Girl, Huldremose Woman, Dätgen Man, the Damendorf Girl, Elling Woman, the Röst Girl (a baby), Kayhausen Boy, Zweeloo Woman, partial bodies like Lindow III (a hand with six fingers) and Worsley Man (a garrotted head). In all there are over 100 peat-preserved corpses and parts of corpses dating predominantly to the later Iron Age and early medieval period. Many were pinned down into their bogs with stakes and some of them seem to have been screaming openly at the end.

Rather than a series of funerary rites, designed to help the soul on its journey to the social world of the ancestors, the bog bodies of Atlantic Europe were subjected to a sequence of ritual acts of ferocious, controlled violence. Their purpose is a long-standing enigma, but there is now enough evidence to conclude that, in a reversal of normal ritual logic, the killings were designed to vex the ghost and prevent the progress of the soul.

There have been many attempts to explain the bog bodies, the most notorious of them by Heinrich Himmler, the head of Hitler's SS. Himmler was an enthusiastic amateur archaeologist who knew something both of the bog bodies and of the Roman historian Tacitus' description of life among the peoples of the barbarian north. On 18 February 1937, Himmler gave a pep talk to officers of the Waffen SS, in which he applauded the legal and religious customs of the ancient Germans: 'Homosexuals were drowned in swamps. The worthy professors who find these bodies in peat do not realize that in ninety out of a hundred cases they are looking at the remains of a homosexual who was drowned in a swamp . . . That was not a punishment, but simply the termination of such an abnormal life.'[4] While obnoxiously formulated and partial (apparently focusing only on adult male bodies) there may be a germ of truth in this. To decide, we need to turn to the detailed evidence from the known cases.

More bits of Lindow Man came to light in 1988: the lower abdomen, the right thigh and most of the left leg (minus the left foot), along with additional bits of a second body, which probably go together with a previously discovered skull. This skull may have become defleshed through exposure to the open air after some recent disturbance. Certainly the second set of remains seems to have been shredded by the peat-cutting machine and ended up distributed throughout a number of bags of peat. However, we can tell that this body – 'Lindow III' – belonged to a male, aged around 22 years, who had six fingers on each hand. Although only the right hand survives, it displays a rare deformity, pre-axial polydactyly of the thumb which would usually develop on both hands. His fingernails, like those of the better preserved Lindow Man, were carefully manicured, suggesting that neither of the men had engaged in manual labour. Both seem to have been painted with a clay-based, greeny-blue, copper paint; this is consistent with Caesar's remark that 'All the Britons paint themselves with *vitrum*, which produces a dark blue colour.'[5] The carbon-14 date estimates for the two Lindow bodies agree closely, and it is possible that they died together, around the year AD 100.[6] (Technically speaking, their deaths could be separated by as much as 150 years, but their close proximity suggest that a single event accounts for their presence in the bog.)

The forensic examination of Lindow Man allows the sequence of physical assaults he suffered before death to be reconstructed with some certainty. First he was knocked to the ground by a heavy blow from behind, causing a rib to fracture. He was probably already on his knees when he was hit again, this time by an axe blow to the head. This was done violently enough to stun him and send shards of skull into his brain, but not violently enough to kill him outright (the sides of the 3.5-centimetre-long wound were slightly swollen, displaying a 'vital reaction' which indicates continuing life). Next, a carefully knotted animal-sinew garrotte was placed around his neck, and with this in place, his throat was cut with a knife. The garrotte was then tightened, fracturing his neck and causing the blood to spurt from the severed arteries with great force. He then fell or was thrust forward into the bog. Fragments of sphagnum moss in his stomach suggest that he may have made one last gasp for air as he lay face down in the mire.

His stomach contains cereal remains, unpleasantly rich in chaff and bran and heavily infected with smut mould, along with animal hair and a surprising number of weeds, including red shank (*Persicara maculosa*), fat hen (*Chenopodium album*), and small traces (three pollen grains) of mistletoe (*Viscum album*). This could have been part of a dirty porridge-gruel, but carbonized remains suggest that at least some of the grains had been baked into a cake or bannock which had been burnt black.[7]

What could be salvaged and identified of the Lindow III body shows that there were hazelnuts in his intestine, again with poor-quality or contaminated cereal: lots of husk, mixed with fat hen and red shank (*P. maculosa*)[8]. The large amount of bog moss (leaves and stems) suggests that he died by drowning.

147

The ancient bodies preserved in the peat bogs of northern Europe are typically naked or dressed in clothing that exposes more than it hides, with the occasional blindfold or restraint. Some have shaven heads, some had stomachs overflowing with rotten food. They are men, women and children, individually and in various combinations. Most, if not all, seem to have been killed with breathtaking viciousness – with fractured legs and ribs, blows to the skull, nooses or hazel branches twisted round their necks, and slashed throats.

A few centuries after Herodotus, the Greeks had been over-taken by the Romans as the principal colonial force and the barbarian tribes of Europe had changed their names. To the east, the Scythians of the Black Sea steppe had been replaced by the Sarmatians, and in the north a number of interrelated tribes known collectively as the Germani, neighbours of the Celts, emerged and were described by Roman historians, especially Tacitus who devoted an entire work, the *Germania*, to them.[9] These changing configurations of dominant tribes did not bring wholesale alterations in the way people lived or what they believed in. The coming and going of named elites not only altered things little, but ensured that little could be altered.

Slavery and slaving remained as endemic as warfare. With no permanent peace, people clung on to the lives they knew, just as they clung on to their beliefs. For most inhabitants of Europe the first millennia BC and AD were no time for religious tolerance. Religious beliefs were resilient, going back to the time of the first farmers, and extending in space through the steppelands and Anatolia to the borders of India.[10]

In the Iron Age, certain ideas were shared right across Eurasia, among the Indo-European speaking peoples. Many of the Eurasian god names have Indo-European linguistic roots. *Zeus* in Greek equals *dyaus* in Sanskrit, both meaning the *sky* god. *Dyaus-pita*, 'sky father', in Sanskrit is, in Latin, *Ju-piter*.[11] The ancient Celts, Scythians, Thracians and Germans worshipped many similar gods, who were later taken over by the Vikings, the Anglo-Saxons, the Slavs and the Balts.

There was also a concept of nature spirits who aided divination, local in manifestation but all variations on the same theme: *deva* in Sanskrit, *divus* in Latin, *diva* in Slavic, *devas* in Baltic, and so on.[12] Among the Germanic and Norse peoples, living individuals were thought to have a *fylgia* (a helper spirit or guardian angel) as well as a shared, family *hamingiur*, who could take the form of a maiden, and (probably among all the Iron Age and early medieval pagan communities of Eurasia), the revered dead themselves became minor gods – spirits who could be consulted, using proper rituals, in their green mounds. The place of burial was a permanent doorway to the beyond where one could commune, by various ritual means, with the ancestors.

Minor spirits included the dwarfs in mines and caves, and, by forest and stream, elves (*ylfe* in Anglo-Saxon). Elves were a persistent part of folk belief over a period of at least 2,000 years, and probably far longer. In the world of the Romans they were known as *genii locorum*, or spirits of place. Streams, rocky outcrops, meres and other numinous landscape features could all have their elf complement. Given that raised bogs are such a distinctive landscape feature it is likely that whatever was done to the bog bodies was connected to belief in such spirits.

Over the past two or three centuries, as many as 1,850 bodies found in bogs, swamps and fens have been reported, but not all reports are trustworthy. The doyen of Dutch bog body specialists, Wijnand van der Sanden considers 122 cases in his remarkable book, *Through Nature to Eternity*.[13] Most of the rest have now been lost to science. In the later medieval period and through to the end of the eighteenth century, many were reburied in Christian churchyards. Until at least 1895, bog bodies were obtained by apothecaries to be pulverized into medicinal 'mumia' – a cheaper version of powdered Egyptian mummy. (Egyptian mummy, the 'real thing', was sold over the counter for human consumption as late as 1924 in Germany.)[14]

When I began to study archaeology the basic text on the bog bodies was P.V. Glob's *The Bog People*, published in English in 1969 (affectionately known as 'Glob on bogs'). The idea that the bog bodies were slaves drowned in a sacrifice to the goddess Nerthus was a strong theme in Glob. Van der Sanden's more compendious, critically minded catalogue supports some of Glob's conclusions, and takes issue with others. Glob had been unsure whether the bodies were a unitary historical phenomenon or merely a collection of unfortunates from all periods who had found their way into peat bogs in various ways, some pushed, some staked down, some accidentally. New radiocarbon date estimates show that the bog bodies are, chronologically at least, a discrete phenomenon. Ignoring some accidental deaths in historical times, which are unrelated to the ritual phenomenon, the bog bodies proper begin to appear in the Iron Age, around 600 BC and continue to AD 400 with one dated as late as AD 800. The vast majority of them belong to the last century BC and first two or three centuries AD.

The corpses have been tanned like leather in the special pre- servative conditions of raised sphagnum moss bogs. Many have retained their hair and fingernails and some have more or less intact brains and viscera. They are never found with conventional grave goods, unlike the more common fen bodies recovered from wetlands throughout northern Europe. Sometimes completely skeletonized, sometimes well preserved with their clothes still on, the fen bodies probably include the former occupants of floating funeral barges, and victims of open-water sacrifice and isolated crimes. On the other hand, the bog bodies clearly rep- resent a series of symbolically interrelated ritual killings. Van der Sanden concludes that 'Bog bodies are generally associated with violent death' and that 'These are not cases of efficient, humane termination of life, but of inordinate and unnecessary violence.'[15]

The distinctive raised bogs of Europe are found mainly in the middle of Ireland, the Drenthe region of Holland, Schleswig- Holstein, Lower Saxony and Denmark, with important isolated examples elsewhere, such as Lindow Moss. British raised bogs are known as 'mosses', which is an accurate description as they are accumulations of slow-growing sphagnum moss. The extraordinary preservative properties of raised bogs are principally due to sphagnan, a polysaccharide contained in the sphagnum moss that sets in train a chemical sequence ending in humic acid – the same reactions that cause roast meat to sweeten and brown. The bog bodies 'cook' slowly, due to their low temperature. The end result is the preservation of skin (tanned a deep brown), hair (often reddened), viscera, brain and so on, and the retention of a degree of elasticity.[16]

Raised bogs sit and swell on the landscape like vast green blisters. They are naturally dangerous, treacherous to cross unless frozen or crusted over by a long hot summer. After heavy rain they may burst, as Solway Moss, on the border of England and Scotland did in 1771, sweeping away entire houses and inundating 200 hectares of arable pasture with fluid peat to a depth of 12 metres. Van der Sanden reproduces an eighteenth-century English account of a narrow escape:

On Saturday, 28th January 1744, Pilling Moss was observed to rise to a surprising height; after a short time it sunk as much below level, and moved slowly towards the south side; in half an hour's time it covered 20 acres of land ... A man was going over the Moss when it began to move; as he was going eastward he perceived to his great astonishment that the ground under his feet moved southward. He turned back speedily and had the great good fortune to escape being swallowed up.[17]

Not everyone was as lucky. On 24 June 1450, near Bonstorf in Lower Saxony, the local priest was informed of a dead man stuck in the Bormwisch bog with only his head protruding. Asked whether they should attempt to get the dead man out for Christian burial, the priest, Magnus Lauenrod, replied that the elves had got him and would soon pull him in further. Only a man possessed by the Devil, he claimed, would venture into such a place, and he was therefore to be left. The next day the head too had disappeared. The association with elves suggests that bogs were thought of as places with magical properties. These could be a source of macabre fascination.

During the winter of 1673–4 a man and woman got caught crossing a bog near the village of Hope in Derbyshire. They were discovered the following May, only their exposed parts having decomposed. Villagers interred the partially decayed corpses in a slightly firmer patch of bog near at hand and then returned on many occasions over the next thirty years to open the grave and marvel at the lack of decomposition. Eventually, the local vicar, Thomas Wormald, stepped in to stop the show and have the couple properly buried, but even he was forced to admit 'I had the curiosity myself to go to the place & see 'em taken up, & at the same time took hold of the Man's great Toe & do affirm that it was solid & firm & So were all those parts of the Body which were never expos'd to the Air by being gaz'd upon.'[18]

Tollund Man, carbon-dated to the period 350–50 BC,[19] was found in a grave that had been dug into the peat, with the plaited leather slip-knotted rope used to hang him still around his neck. But he would have died anyway because he had been poisoned.

Like Lindow Man's, Tollund Man's stomach contained the remains of a weed-infested gruel. Various species were identified alongside barley and oats, including gold of pleasure (*Camelina sativa*), red shank, fat hen, knot grass (*Polygonum aviculare*) and corn spurry (*Spergula arvensis*). Although these are all known 'weeds of cultivation', occurring in and among the main crop, their percentage representation was unusually high, indicating deliberate addition. Large numbers of smut spores (*Ustilago* Sp.), along with sand and animal hairs, suggest that the cereal component was not only deliberately packed with weeds, but was rotten and dirty. The similarities with Lindow and Lindow III are impossible to ignore.

The stomach contents of the Grauballe Man contained ergot (*Claviceps purpurea*), an easily recognizable purple fungal infection of cereals that produces a series of highly toxic LSD-like alkaloids. Ingested, it causes the painful and lethal condition

152

known as St Anthony's Fire.[20] Van der Sanden considers that 'Grauballe Man had ingested such large quantities of these substances that he must have been hallucinating and suffering convulsions and burning sensations in his mouth, hands, and feet ... The man was probably in a coma.'[21] Despite all this, it had been thought necessary to fracture his left tibia, administer a powerful blow to his right temple, and slash his throat from ear to ear, severing the oesophagus.

The Worsley Man received blows to his head, was garrotted with a knotted cord, and then beheaded (we do not know what food he had been forced to eat as only his head and neck have ever been found). Dätgen Man had been stabbed and beaten, decapitated from behind, and then staked down into the peat. The naked Borromose Man had eaten a meal consisting of nothing but weeds, had been beaten around the head and then strangled with a plaited hemp rope. The Windeby Man had been strangled with a finger-thick hazel branch before being anchored into the peat with wooden posts.

A mother and baby were found in the bog at Borromose with a cloak thrown over them. There was a second woman in the bog too, who had been scalped and (uniquely for a bog body) had received a violent blow to her face. A girl of around 13, blindfolded with her own beautifully woven wool waistband (her *sprangband*, a sign of status)[22] was found, held down with a stone and a branch, in the bog at Windeby, not far from the man. The left side of her head was shaven, but the right side showed a growth of 2 to 2.5 centimetres, suggesting that an earlier, overall head-shaving had taken place a few weeks before her killing.

A similar fate had met the Yde Girl, who was about 16 years old and disabled (she suffered from a scoliosis, which would have given her an erratic gait). The right half of her head was shaven, while the hair on the left side was a good 20 centimetres long. There was a knife wound near her left collarbone, and a careful slip-knot had been tied in her *sprangband* so that it could be wrapped around her neck three times and then tightened; the

153

The 'Windeby Girl', a 13-year-old female body from Windeby bog, Denmark. (Photo: Archaeological Museum, Schleswig)

pressure impression of the knot can be seen under her left ear. The Huldremose Woman, who had eaten a weed known as corn spurry, was covered with deep cut wounds and had had her right arm completely hacked off before death. The Damendorf Girl, aged around 14, had been pegged down. The Elling Woman was conventionally hanged, using a leather belt.

The Zweeloo Woman, like the Yde Girl, was disabled: she

suffered from an adolescent syndrome which produced body asymmetry and short legs. She had eaten a very rough, unde-husked millet gruel in which the remains of a beetle infestation could be identified, along with burnt elements and blackberry seeds. Sphagnum moss leaves in her stomach could, again, have been from drinking bog water, suggesting final drowning. Her soft tissues were not well recovered by the peat cutters who found her, nor was she subsequently carefully preserved, so the precise cause of her death remains a mystery.

Forensic analysis of the body of what was once a very fit middle-aged woman from Haraldskaer, undertaken in 2000 by Miranda Green and others, has revealed traces of where a garrotte may have been tightened around the victim's neck.[23] The cause of death has not been definitely established, but it looks like a ritual killing. The radiocarbon date of *c.* 490 BC shows that she was pinned down in the bog with a hurdle at a time when crem-ation was the usual funerary rite. She was naked and her clothes were found nearby.

Finally, there are the rare cases of younger people in bogs: the Kayhausen Boy and the Röst Girl. The boy is estimated to have been between 8 and 14 when he was killed; he may have had a deformed right femur, but the X-ray image is ambiguous.[24] He was stabbed three times in the throat, then had a length of cloth wound round his neck, stretched down between his legs and pulled taut up his back to be tied back at the neck; his arms were bent up sharply behind his back and tied with a woollen strip; his ankles were tied together with a cape. The youngest of all bog bodies is the Röst Girl, date unknown. She was two to three years old and was placed in the bog naked, legs apart and flexed, arms bent and upraised, covered over with a woollen cloak and then with peat turfs.

The bog bodies present a difficult challenge, and they have not lacked interpreters. Supporters of the 'undead' theory, on the basis of inferences from German folklore, argue that the bodies represent people such as summarily executed criminals, suicides or accident victims who were maltreated *after* death in order to incapacitate them and stop them coming back to haunt the living.[25] According to this theory, after the corpses had been maimed, they were excluded from burial in the cemetery and dumped in the poorest and least usable land – mires, bogs and fens. If this 'fear of the walking dead' theory were correct, we should expect the corpses to be uniformly blinded or hamstrung, in order that they could not walk back. While many of the bodies were staked down in the bog, their faces were left relatively undamaged. More compellingly, careful forensic work has shown that Lindow Man was killed out in the bog itself.

Lindow Man has been interpreted as a druid, on the basis of his carefully manicured fingernails and the mistletoe in his stomach.[26] The *druides* were described by various Roman authors as being equally priests, diviners and judges – ritual specialists and arbiters of disputes. Julius Caesar tells us that they took upwards of twenty years to learn the oral druidic tradition that qualified them as priests,[27] and that they made studies of the natural world as well as religion. They taught the transmigration of souls. According to Tacitus, they examined the viscera of sacrificial victims in order to prophesy.[28] Pliny wrote that the druids held a moon festival when they cut mistletoe in sacred groves with golden sickles, and it is this that the British scholar Ann Ross seized upon to suggest that Lindow Man could himself have been one of their number – a druid sacrificed by druids.

Her theory is interesting but not compelling. Ross argues that Lindow Man was sacrificed simultaneously to three different Celtic deities, Teutates, Esus and Taranis. This she bases on a statement by the Roman writer, Lucan, to the effect that Teutates received drowned sacrifices (in this case, the bog);[29] human sacrifices to Esus were stabbed and hung in trees to bleed to death (the axe blow and the strangulation); and Taranis received burnt victims. Ross asks us to believe that the latter was symbolized by the fact that Lindow Man seems to have eaten burnt cereal grains. She connects this with a folk tradition of a 'burnt bannock' in Perthshire, Scotland, where, in an eighteenth-century continuation of the pagan Celtic spring festival of Beltane, the person who took the burnt bannock was called the 'devoted', and had to act out being sacrificed by burning. But, although the motif of triple killing is known in Celtic folklore, where the king was killed by wounding, burning and drowning, this took place at the great autumn festival of Samhain (All Hallow's Eve or Hallowe'en).[30]

The idea that Lindow Man suffered exactly three symbolic 'deaths' does not quite fit. There is poisoning, drowning, beating, stabbing, an axe to the head, hanging or garrotting, and, via the charred cake, burning to be accounted for – a series of deliberately different, potentially lethal assaults. In any case, there is no real ritual logic to being sacrificed to three deities at once. To try and propitiate Teutates, Esus and Taranis together might easily lead to divine dissatisfaction, whatever the roots of the Irish Samhain myth.

Van der Sanden, in common with most archaeologists, remains unconvinced by Ross' interesting speculation and he disregards the three grains of mistletoe pollen in the stomach as too few to have significance beyond a potential medicinal use in the period before the killing. Even if Ross is wrong about a triple sacrifice, the mistletoe may still be significant. We know that it was considered magical at this time, as we have the testimony of people like Tacitus and Caesar, who, while not themselves 'insiders', observed the cultures in question at first hand. The three grains of mistletoe pollen should not be underestimated: infusions of mistletoe are made with the leaves and stem, so the amount of pollen is no indicator of the power of a draught.

Mistletoe leaves contain powerful bioactive ingredients – viscotoxin (a cardioactive polypeptide) and traces of an alkaloid. The effects of these, if ingested, include a slowing of the heart rate, sedation, and dilation of the arteries. The white berries are highly toxic.[31] What was found in Lindow Man's stomach proves that he had been in recent contact with mistletoe or mistletoe derivatives and hints at the possibility that he may have been in as bad a state of toxic shock as some of the other bog victims were from ergot poisoning.

Tacitus says that, among the Germans, 'indolents (*ignavos*), cowards (*imbelles*), and those with disreputable lusts (*corpore infames*), were drowned in mire and swamp with a hurdle placed over them'. This was the source of Heinrich Himmler's brutal judgement, but the translation is tricky: *imbelles* could mean deserters. *Ignave et imbelles* is a stock phrase in Livy, meaning men who were untrustworthy in war. *Corpore infames* is often translated as 'sodomite' or 'homosexual'. Tacitus' claims have attracted great interest because the bog bodies, in addition to the horrible injuries they had sustained, were often discovered by peat cutters pinned down into the bogs with hazel and willow staples. Pairs of naked men have been preserved in other European peat bogs besides Lindow Moss. Two were found in 1904, lying side by side at Weerdinge in the Drenthe region of the Netherlands; one of them had been stabbed in the heart, and it seems that his intestines were deliberately pulled out through the wound,[32] reminding us of Tacitus' description of the examination of viscera for prophetic purposes. Another two, naked and curled round each other, but covered by a cape, were found in 1938 at Hunteberg near Osnabrück in Germany; how they died is unknown. The radiocarbon dates for Weerdinge agree with Lindow, while the Hunteberg bodies date from around AD 400.

A number of the people who ended up as bog bodies suffered, in van der Sanden's words, 'multiple deaths'. One could go further and say that these people were put to death with minute attention to detail. To keep Lindow Man alive for each cumulative assault required amazing skill and precision: a little more infected gruel and he would have been terminally poisoned; a slightly harder axe blow and he would have been dead and incapable of being garrotted; a more systematic cutting of the throat and he would have died almost instantaneously. Yet, even after throat-cutting and garrotting, he may have remained alive long enough to take a last drowning gulp in the bog.

It seems that those who brought these people to their death tried to inflict as many insults as possible to their living bodies, short of denying them their recognizable identity. Humiliated by hair-shaving and lack of clothes, made to eat dirt, poisoned, drugged, beaten, stabbed, strangled, drowned – the list goes on. As many kinds of death as possible were symbolically inflicted. It stopped short, in nearly every case, of obliterating personal features (one of the two Borromose women is a potential exception but even so her face could have been pulped and was not). This stopping short, coupled with the extreme prejudice of the rest of the mode of termination, is highly significant. The souls of these bog people, even those who were decapitated, could still know their own faces, and could see what had been done to them, personally.

Van der Sanden firmly rejects the concept of punished homosexual transgression, writing that 'Our chances of discovering the relationship between the two Hunteberg men or the two Weerdinge men – were they relatives or perhaps blood brothers? – are as slim as those of finding out why they were selected for sacrifice. All that can be said is that the evident care with which these men were deposited in the bog makes it hard to believe that they were *corpore infames*',[33] but the logic of this conclusion is uncertain. In view of what these societies were capable of, there is no reason to rule out macabre ritual theatre in the punishment of two transgressive male lovers.

Van der Sanden himself believes that some of the bog bodies can be explained in terms of 'sacrificial punishment' theory (*Strafopferthese*): people who were ritually sacrificed to the gods because they were offenders who had, through their crimes, incurred divine wrath. But we should not be thinking of punishment for 'common criminals': among the most striking features of the bog bodies in general, from the two at Lindow to Tollund and Haraldskaer, are the well manicured fingernails and the lack of evidence for a life of manual labour. All the indications are that the victims had lived more or less privileged lives for some time prior to death. Van der Sanden argues that various mechanisms resulted in people being preserved in bogs:

It could be that the children and adults who were lovingly deposited in a bog were innocent individuals, that the persons whose hands were tied were prisoners of war and that the individuals who were severely maltreated had violated social rules. And if it is true that socially imperfect individuals were sacrificed, it is possible that physically imperfect individuals also qualified.[34]

Because the majority of the bog bodies date to between 100 BC and AD 400, a period coinciding with the expansion of the Roman empire, with all the attendant migrations, wars and population displacements, van der Sanden believes that 'social stress may have led to an intensification of sacrificial practices'.[35] Rather than viewing bogs as inferior bits of marginal land that no one wanted, he says that they 'were particularly suitable for establishing contacts with gods, spirits and ancestors. That seems to make the sacrifice theory most plausible.'[36]

Van der Sanden's explanation of the bog bodies falls short of incorporating his own key contribution to the debate: the recognition of a widespread ritual of 'multiple death'. He implies only that multiple death was in some sense appropriate to the type of sacrifice he envisions, but he does not say precisely why. Nor does he account for the lack of obviously low-born individuals who, on the 'prisoners of war' and 'violators of social rules' criteria, should have been well represented. And, finally, there is the problem of why anyone would have 'lovingly' deposited innocents in the same environment as brutally killed outcasts.

Although the 'punished sodomites' argument is not sufficient or convincing to explain the entire range of social personae so far discovered among the bog bodies, there is no reason to believe that male homosexuals did not comprise one of the classes of cultural transgressor punished in this way. The meaning of *corpore infames* – 'those with disreputable lusts' – in Tacitus is not wholly clear, but could have been broadly extended, even to include children. We need to enter another mind-set to understand this – a mind-set preserved in fragments of medieval law codes and commentaries on social behaviour, such as the *Lupi sermo ad Anglos* written by Wulfstan, the Archbishop of York, in AD 1014.

In a famous passage, Wulfstan describes the plight of an Anglo-Saxon man forced to stand by as his wife is raped by Vikings. Rather than empathize with the ordeal of the woman, Wulfstan focuses only on the husband's shame. The problem for Wulfstan is that the man is dishonoured.[37] Essentially, as in some countries where fundamentalist religious laws hold sway (as, until recently, in Afghanistan), the distinction between rape and adultery as we now understand them was not made. In fact, modern rape law grew out of a desire to uphold the rights not of the victim but of the victim's sexual proprietor, to ensure that a man's 'ownership' of his wife was not alienated.

Tacitus echoes Wulfstan. Writing of the Germans in the first century, he says 'adultery in that populous nation is rare in the extreme, and punishment is summary and left to the husband. He shaves off his wife's hair, strips her in the presence of kinsmen, thrusts her from his house and flogs her through the whole village.' The woman embodied the man's shame. Whether she had consented to sex or not was irrelevant. Tacitus does not say – specifically – what happens after the woman has been flogged through the village but we cannot exclude the possibility that she is deemed to have joined the ranks of the *corpore infames*. The early medieval Burgundian law, *Lex Gundobada*, states, 'a wife who rejects the man she is legitimately married to, shall be put to death in mud',[38] and King Harald Bluetooth had his prospective queen, Gunnhild, former wife of Erik Bloodaxe, drowned in a bog following an episode with Harald's servants, interpreted as adultery but which may have been rape.[39]

Despite the extensive theorizing about how sexual behaviour might have been linked to the deaths of some at least of the bog bodies, there have been no truly complete forensic reports on any of them, even Lindow Man. The presence or absence of evidence of sexual activity, forced or voluntary, has not been remarked on. As with the publications on many other archaeologically preserved bodies, the state of the genital and anal areas is not commented on, nor documented photographically in publication, and in most cases even the basic biological sex determination has to be taken on trust. This approach is particularly unfortunate in the case of the bog bodies.

I believe that the category *corpore infames* and the type of punishment, rather than indicating the existence of a rational law (however unfair) prohibiting specified types of sexual expression, essentially signalled an offence against Teutonic male honour. Gender categories among the Germans were not, of course, precisely like those in recent times in Afghanistan nor like those of Tacitus' Rome. Tacitus, writing of the Germanic Naharvarli tribe, whose priests worshipped in sacred groves, observed, with some disapproval, that 'the presiding priest dresses like a woman'.[40] But this does not mean that the Germans necessarily approved of men having sex with one another.

Tacitus' phrase *corpore infames* may indicate the existence of two sorts of sex crime among the Germans: first, two males, having sex *as* males, and, secondly, illegitimate sex with a female (rape/adultery), which brings dishonour on the house of a reputable husband or father, and results in the female's punishment. Tacitus' indolents (*ignavos*) and cowards (*imbelles*) may also represent concepts connected to honour. The well-kept hands of Lindow Man, Lindow III, Tollund Man and Grauballe Man suggest that these people were not common felons, runaway bondsmen or unfortunate vagrants. Physical abnormality or disability (Lindow III, Zweeloo Woman, the Yde Girl and, possibly, the Kayhausen Boy) could have marked people out as having special powers at the same time as stigmatizing them as imperfect and afflicted. It is possible that four-thumbed Lindow III was thought to have magic powers, while, for those who could not walk or bend properly, divination and prophecy might have been the only available social role – a dangerous profession if things do not actually turn out as one predicts.

Assessing the idea that the bog bodies had been transgressors or malefactors is hard. The condition of the hands, feet and fingernails of many of the bodies suggests that they were untroubled by hard manual work. If they were members of the elite, their treatment may have been connected to breaches of honour, to personal affronts and intrigues – social crimes that ordinary peasant folk were incapable of committing. But this does not explain why they were killed in the way that they were.

To understand the bog body phenomenon, we have to understand what van der Sanden has termed 'multiple death'. This is not a version of Ross' idea of simultaneous sacrifice to several deities, nor does it simply mean that excessive violence was a feature of those sacrifices where the people to be killed were van der Sanden's 'violators of social rules'. Neither explains the deliberately, symbolically 'multiple' nature of the deaths, which were excessive in one way but stopped carefully short of excess in other ways. We are talking here not of post-mortem dismemberment nor of a frenzied, no-holds-barred assault, but a calculated ritual killing.

Ritual killing, but not sacrifice. My interpretation begins with the premise that the preservative qualities of sphagnum moss bogs were deliberately sought out. Despite documenting these remarkable powers, van der Sanden, like Glob before him, does not really believe that the bodies represent anything other than a fortuitously preserved subset of all those people who were executed, sacrificed or buried in wet environments. I do not think that this is the case.

The raised bogs are 'liminal' environments. Just as the liminal phase in a rite of passage is the dangerous threshold between two fundamentally different states, so natural environments can be symbolically perceived in a similar way.[41] By being watery, like a pond, yet raised up above the level of the dry land, the sphagnum bogs break basic rules. Unlike earth, air, water or fire the bog could arrest rotting in perpetuity – essentially stop time. This made it an exceptionally special environment, as symbolically inappropriate a place for a rite of incorporation into the world of the ancestors as it is possible to find but one into which certain bodies were deliberately inserted.

We know from the survival of prehistoric wooden roads and trackways across peat marsh and fen that our ancestors had a detailed knowledge of wetland environments. Druids were keen students of nature as well as religion and there is no reason to suppose that they would not have known at least as much as Thomas Wormald about the properties of raised bogs – almost certainly far more. Put another way, it would take some peculiarly strong arguments to demonstrate how the killers of Tollund Man, Windeby Girl and the rest could *not* have known what the physical effects on their corpses would be.

The degree of damage done to the bog bodies stopped short of the deliberate disfigurement of faces. The physical comfort of the victims was of no consequence, so in theory, teeth could have been pulled, eyes could have been gouged out, noses broken, cheeks slashed. But the perpetrators wanted the bog victims to be recognizable. And by placing them in the bogs they wanted them recognizable in perpetuity (which, to an unusual degree, they are). This seems paradoxical, if no one was to see them again, and there is no evidence that the bog bodies were subsequently disturbed in antiquity – at least, not deliberately. Unlike the Derbyshire couple that Wormald describes, there is nothing to suggest that the bog bodies were continually voyeuristically disinterred.

Assuming that the people who became bog bodies were 'transgressors' of various kinds, as Tacitus categorically states, then they needed to be killed in such a way that their souls could not bother the living – or the dead. As Hertz points out, death is, in normal circumstances, only a temporary exclusion from society. These were not normal circumstances, and the transgressors required ostracism both from the contemporary social world and from the world of the ancestors. This presented a problem.

The obvious solution might seem to be to sacrifice such people to the gods. But as they were unwanted, they could not easily be sacrificed without provoking supernatural ire. The gods do not want damaged goods. It is either the innocent who are sacrificed, because they are pure, or warriors, because they are noble, or slaves, because they are costly. Satisfactory sacrifice is never viewed as wholly in a society's practical interests, it must always involve the perception of a supernatural exchange of value. Sacrifice and punishment are at opposite ends of a symbolic spectrum.

If transgressors judged guilty of capital crimes could not be sacrificed, why not execute them in a straightforward way? The problem again lies with the soul. If they were executed and given proper rites of burial, their punishment would be brief, as they would be reborn in the world of the dead; if they were not given proper burial, their souls would stay on earth, wandering and plaguing the living. The only solution was to place transgressors permanently in the liminal zone.

If this theory about liminality is correct – that the bog bodies were sent, not to another world, but into limbo – then we should expect a rite of separation to be followed by a dramatic transitional rite with no subsequent incorporation. The former would have been envisioned as a severing or cutting off from society, and would fit with the hair-cutting and shaving observed on some of the bog bodies. The key element must be a symbolically interminable transitional rite, for which the practice of multiple killing and insertion into the timeless world of a raised bog is grimly appropriate. There is no evidence that any bog body underwent a rite of incorporation. There are no grave goods and no grave markers.

As King Lear lies dying, Edgar asks him to 'Look up', but is restrained by Kent: 'Vex not his ghost: O! let him pass; he hates him that would upon the rack of this tough world stretch him out longer.'[42] This is an image of two worlds: the mortal, corporeal one; and that other one to which the ghost, or soul, must travel when the body fails. Most human societies believe that the soul must be actively helped and encouraged, sometimes cajoled (and in hard cases, bullied), to leave this world and establish itself in the next. But not always.

It is a common thread, running through the anthropological

study of death, and prominent in theological philosophy too, that a death is owned. In ordinary circumstances, a person should be able to compose themselves in the face of death, utter dying words and know how they are dying. Symbolic multiple death was cruelly vexing. Bringing the victim to the point of death in several different ways simultaneously was designed to confuse the soul to such an extent that it did not know when or where to leave the body. The process of multiple death was designed to remove ownership, to keep the soul, still physically incarnate, guessing about the body's death, until it was too late.

So, for whom was the identity of the body preserved? Certainly not for later generations of archaeologists or the museum-going public. The identity of the body was preserved *for itself*, for the benefit of the body's own ghost. The maintenance of identity, through the retention of facial features and then through the polysaccharide cold-cooking of the bog, helped ensure that the soul remained firmly attached to the body it had grown up with. And, as the body did not rot, the soul was in limbo.

Grauballe Man, with the purple ergot spores in his stomach, was – agonizingly – out of his mind. Lindow Man was expertly kept on the threshold of life, so that as many 'deaths' as could be devised could be inflicted on him. Finally, his body disappeared into the moving mire, not to decay but to be held imprisoned. The fact that not all the bog bodies show multiple death fits well with Hertz's idea of the 'scale of rites': not all transgressors were equally dangerous in a ritual sense. A tiny child, like the Röst Girl, would not need more than to have a cloak thrown over her and then be weighed down by peat turfs, for her soul to be effectively limboed. A powerful and high-status individual, like Lindow Man or Tollund Man, could not be as easily contained, and required more thorough measures.

Something else, beyond drugged confusion, multiple assaults and being pinned down with pegs, kept body and soul entrapped. Bogs were dangerous, frightening and mysterious: spiritually powerful places. While I agree with van der Sanden that bogs were perceived as liminal in themselves, I do not think they were portals linking the everyday world with the world of the gods. With their potential sudden movement, their swelling, sinking and unpredictable flowing and bursting, bogs were obvious candidates to be the sites of *genii locorum*, spirits of place. These minor spirits were often indistinguishable in Teutonic metaphysics from *álfar*, or elves. The fifteenth-century priest, Magnus Lauenrod, certainly did not want to risk contact with elves in order to extract the man from Bormwisch bog. He knew they would soon pull the body in out of sight and out of mind, and they did.

The transgressor, symbolically outcast from human society and made liminal, was taken to a liminal place, vexed beyond belief, and then thrust, body and soul at once, through into another world. The final piece of the limbo theory now falls into place, for this was not the grand world of the dead, but the mysterious, twilight world of the elves. Beneath the skin of the wet, green, mossy blisters, the victims were first trapped and then enchanted and beguiled, with elfish music ringing, for ever, in the ears which they had been so pointedly allowed to keep. Elves are not major players in grand cosmic schemes and that was crucial. They, and only they, could guarantee exclusion from all that was socially important, living or dead.

Because of their wilful exclusion to the periphery, the bog bodies have survived as a facet of prehistoric life for archaeologists to wonder at. They are, in this interpretation, not a central facet, when viewed from the perspective of ancient Germanic society as a whole. But they are important in other ways. Their widespread occurrence, peppered through bogs from Ireland to Saxony, reveals the existence of shared conduct, of a known way of dealing with people deemed to be a problem to society. In their specifics, they reveal individual capacities for well-honed violence, and an almost scientific understanding of the precise control of trauma. We may deduce from this that death, and the dead, were greatly feared. Power was fragile, and consequently it was wielded brutally.

Archaeology suffers from the mirage of survival. Perhaps

naturally, we assume that what we find most of represents what there was most of in the past. This is rarely true, and the most massive social and ritual phenomena may be almost entirely hidden from us because their direct archaeological 'footprint' is so insignificant. But where direct methods fail, acute observation of indirect and anomalous data may lead us to uncover truth.

There is a fascinating comparison to be made between the swift, compelling script of bog limboing, done in quiet isolation, in the presence of a chosen few, and the Aztec or Mexica sacrifices, which were conducted *en masse*, in full public view, at the top of towering, blood-drenched temple pyramids, following days of festivity, procession and ceremony. Archaeologically, the first survives, and the second does not. As Clendinnen says of sacrifice in the imperial capital, Tenochtitlan:

Surprisingly, the mode of the disposal of the bodies remains mysterious. We are usually told that skulls were spitted on the skull racks, limbs apportioned for ritual cannibalism, and the trunks fed to the flesh-eating birds and beasts in Moctezoma's menagerie, but such disposal techniques would clearly be inadequate. The bodies were perhaps burnt, although during their stay in the city Cortés and his men make no mention of any pyres or corpse-laden canoes, the detritus of human killings being confined, in their accounts, to the temple precincts. The land-locked lakes, precious sources of water and aquatic foods, offered no solution, so this large empirical matter remains unresolved.[43]

The remains of the Aztec sacrificial victims fail to survive archaeologically to any great extent, not despite the mass scale of the killing, but because of it. A few little spalls of bone and a handful of worked pieces are all that remain of hundreds of thousands of sacrificial victims, who were cannibalized, rendered into animal feed, and displayed as trophy skulls to be shattered by wind and rain. The more organized and energetic a process is, the more organized and energetic its patterns of disposal and reuse.

If we did not have the historical accounts to disabuse us and point us in the direction of what few skeletal remains survive, we might assume that the great temples of Tenochtitlan were the centrepieces of some peace-loving, contemplative religion.[44] Similar biases in the preserved data have allowed the revisionist historian David Irving to claim that the gas chambers of Auschwitz were not used for genocide, since very little remains in a physical sense to prove that six million Jews, homosexuals, gypsies, transvestites and others whom the Nazis hated were exterminated.

The temples of the Germans and Celts were in woods and groves. Few permanent or really durable altars existed, although some Roman-influenced ones, carved in stone, have survived. The victims, sacrificed to various deities by hanging, drowning, burning and so on, are hard to trace. The intensity of such giftgiving to the gods is evidence of greedy appetites and did not produce much in the way of permanent physical residue.

The bog bodies, on the other hand, like so much in the archaeological record, survived because they were deliberately removed from the turning cosmos, abstracted from the chain of being and becoming. They belong to the same species of symbolic phenomenon as Lenin's body, yet absolutely inverted in the scales of power. While Lenin's corpse was harnessed at the heart of the state, preserved and on display, their corpses were condemned to the periphery, preserved in order to be consciously lost. By keeping their faces, the bog people were effaced from society, but not from history.

CHAPTER 7

Annihilation

Thus – I hurl the burning brand into Valhalla's resplendent citadel!

BRÜNNHILDE IN WAGNER'S *Die Götterdämmerung*[1]

———

The ground stayed warm for hours after the longship was gone. No one who attended the pyre remained unmoved as the wind was sucked past them into the central conflagration and the waves of heat made their eyes smart. They would not see their chief again in this life and nor would they see the slave-girl, whose last hours had held their absolute attention. Finally there was only, as Ibn Faḍlān says, 'ashes, and then dust of ashes.'

Physically, two people were now in the same state – dead. Metaphysically, in the realms of belief, imagination and assumption, something more complex had taken place. Reconstructing what it was is not an easy task. The Rus rite is thought to have been Odinic: part of the elite cult of Odin, the most powerful and contradictory of the gods. It was designed to make the chieftain one of the *Einherjar*, the chosen warriors of Valhalla.

The religion of the Vikings is known mainly through the Norse writings of the medieval period, which date to some 300 years after the funeral on the Volga. The most important sources are the thirteenth-century manuscript known as the *Poetic* or

170

Elder Edda, containing much older myths and legends, and the *Prose Edda*, written by Snorri Sturluson around AD 1215, which draws heavily upon it, but also on other information since lost. The picture they paint is a complex one of rival gods and heroes, competing dominions of power, alternative forms of afterlife, and an unfolding cosmic history, originating in chaos – *Ginnungagap* – and ending with the 'Twilight of the Gods', *Ragnarok*, when Odin would die.

The world of humans, *Midgard*, was also the world of gods and its roof, the sky, was held up by the world-tree, *Yggdrasil* – a word meaning 'horse of Odin' and a grim epithet for the gallows.[2] Odin was a gallows rider and gallows swinger, hanging himself for nine days with a noose around his neck from Yggdrasil to win the wisdom that, in equal measure with fate, watered its roots. The tree rose from Asgard, the home of the gods in the middle of the world, where Odin entertained the illustrious dead who had perished on the battlefield. His wayward servants are the minor female deities of death known as the Valkyries, the 'Choosers of the Slain', who are individually named – like Brünnhilde – for battle and conflict (*hildr* means battle).[3] The Valkyries welcome fallen warriors to Valhalla (*Valhöll*, the 'Hall of the Slain'), where they feast them on pork and mead with Odin every night.

'Odin made it a law that all dead men should be burnt . . . He said that in this way every man would come to Valhalla with whatever riches had been laid with him on the pyre,' wrote Snorri Sturluson. For those who were poor, or who died of old age or disease, there was a simple burial: *Niflheim* awaited, a dark, cold, cheerless place, presided over by the decaying, corpse-like goddess, Hel, who became increasingly identified with her realm (it was eventually known as Hell).[4] A dead slave received even less care: 'they leave him there as food for the dogs and birds,' says Ibn Faḍlān.

The ideas of Valhalla and Niflheim overlay, and competed with, more ancient ideas of the afterlife. Odin, and his more populist and bluff companion god, Thor, belonged to the *Æsir*, a divine dynasty now in the ascendant over the older *Vanir*, among whom the brother and sister pairing (or alternatively bisexual dual deity) of Frey and Freyja were pre-eminent. The Vanir were less concerned with war than with prosperity and fertility. Ideologically connected to the period before the brutal raiding began, the funeral rites of Frey/Freyja required burial in Mother Earth.

Whatever afterlife was believed in, it involved a journey, and for the rich that meant a voyage on a ship. Archaeology indicates that many ship graves belonged to high-status women, who were sometimes buried with ritually killed retainers. Interring the ship, rather than burning it in an Odinic rite, identified it with *Skíð-bladnir*, the magic ship of Freyja and Frey,[5] and was probably part of their prosperity cult.

It is not surprising that, with such a wealth of deities to choose from, in a culture in which epic verse and song were central elements, the Vikings should – like the ancient Egyptians – believe a range of sometimes mutually contradictory things about death and the soul. A man who had gone to Valhalla was also believed to be able to ride away at night to his burial mound to visit his bride.[6] Belief seems to have been unchallenged by any dogmatic priesthood, and many scholars have noted the absence of priests of any sort in the descriptions that have survived, which suggests instead that it was local leaders or chieftains who were the principal intermediaries between the realms of humans and gods, communicating mainly through human or animal sacrifice.[7]

In fact, there is good evidence for the existence of shamans – charismatic medicine-men and women who could enter trances, cure illness, solve puzzles and foretell the future. Ibn Rusta, who described the Rus a few years before Ibn Faḍlān, writes of *atibbā'* which, translated literally, means 'doctors'. He says that they

> have authority over their [the Rus'] property and are like lords over them, ordering them to sacrifice to their Creator such women, men and livestock as they (the doctors) please.

When the doctors exercise their authority, they [the Rus] have no other option than to comply with the command. The doctor takes a man or an animal, throws a rope around his neck and hangs him from a piece of wood until he relinquishes his soul. He then says, 'This is a sacrifice to the God.'[8]

This ritualized hanging echoed Odin's self-hanging, with a spear in his side, from the world-tree/gallows of Yggdrasil. Parallels have been drawn between this myth and Christ's passion, but as the noted scholar of Norse literature, Gwyn Jones, has written, Odin's suffering 'had more to do with shamanism than Christianity'. It is better seen as an extreme act, with transcendent and erotic aspects, of a sort documented among shamans in circumpolar regions and elsewhere in more recent times.[9]

The Rus were an atomized, entrepreneurial society. The men are described as living together in communal houses, having sex with slave-girls, but some at least also had wives. We do not know all the details of these types of domestic relationship, whether they were mutually compatible or age-graded (young men living more communally and older men establishing families, for example). Wives were walking advertisements for their husbands' wealth: 'around their necks they wear bands of gold and silver. Whenever a man's wealth reaches ten thousand dirhams, he has a band made for his wife . . . sometimes a woman may wear many bands.'

Violence towards women is documented in many of the sagas and telling attitudes are contained in *Yngvar's Saga*, which records Yngvar's adventures while exploring Russia. His behaviour is presented without demur as heroic: 'The lady of the highest rank chose to sleep with Yngvar, which so enraged him, he drew out a knife and stabbed her in the private parts. When the other men saw what he had done, some began chasing these loose women away, but there were others who slept with them, unable to resist their seductive charms and devilish witchcraft.'[10] The subsequent death of eighteen of his men from sickness, perhaps sexually transmitted, is attributed to this.

It is unlikely that a man of wealth and power like the Rus chief would not have had a wife but, in contrast to most of the funeral rites studied by social anthropologists, she is not named as his 'closest relative' in her widowhood. That person is the one who lights the pyre – a man. At their core, the Rus were a *Männerbunde* society – a mobile, military and male elite owing a kind of allegiance only to one another through the cult of Odin, which they entered by taking a secret ring oath. In this they were no different to warrior classes the world over, associations which cross-cut family ties, have secret initiation rites and recognize things such as 'blood brotherhood'. There was little stability and less security. Ibn Rusta says at one point that 'They are virile and brave: when they descend on a tribe's dwelling, they do not leave unless they have destroyed them, seized their women and enslaved them', but he also says that they habitually wore swords 'because there is so little trust among them and because of the treachery which exists among them: even when a man has only a little property, his brother and his companion who accompanies him wish to kill him and seize it.'[11]

Neither Odin nor Valhalla is mentioned in Ibn Faḍlān's account, and these omissions have been seized on by scholars to cast doubt on Ibn Faḍlān's ability to transcend his own Arabic view of the world. Norse religion has no concept of Paradise (*al-janna*). Although the goddess Hel is a woman, there appears at first sight to be no precise parallel in the Icelandic sagas or any other piece of surviving Norse mythology, written or oral, for the so-called Angel of Death, the *Malak al Maut*. In the light of this, Morten Lund Warmind suggests that the *Malak al Maut* and *al-janna* are both 'Arab conventions'.[12] Of course, Ibn Faḍlān had little or no knowledge of the Norse pantheon so the standard explanation of the inconsistencies in his account is that he made unwarranted assumptions. But it seems more likely that he provided a faithful record that is partial for other reasons, limited by his interpreter, and by what the Rus chose to tell his interpreter.

Taken as a whole, Ibn Faḍlān's account of the funeral contains a compelling ritual logic, which he may not have recognized himself. The small details add up, while parts of the structure of the ritual, which he described but did not explain, suddenly make sense once we know about the universal structures identified by van Gennep and Hertz.

Ibn Faḍlān's frustration during the early stage of the ritual is evident. He has been invited to the funeral of an important chieftain, whom he never met in life, and the body is missing. By the time Ibn Faḍlān, Takīn al-Turkī and their Baghdad entourage arrive, the Rus chief is already sealed in a grave chamber, earthed over to form a primary burial mound. None of the visitors can see the body and not everything the Rus do is explained: 'They advanced, going to and fro [around the boat] uttering words which I did not understand, while he was still in his grave and had not been exhumed.' There is no hint that Ibn Faḍlān knows that this grave is anything more than a makeshift morgue to contain the body until the complex preparations for the pyre are complete. He has to reconstruct what has already transpired, learning that the chief has been provided with a musical instrument, fruits and *nabidh*. He does not record how the chief died and perhaps he is not told or does not think to ask (for an Odinic rite, he must have been slain, either in battle or as a result of the kind of plotting and treachery Ibn Rusta alludes to).

The exact composition of *nabidh* remains a mystery, but Ibn Faḍlān tells us nearly all that we need to know in order to understand its place in the ritual. It prompted visions, undermined physical coordination and sometimes killed revellers. It was probably based on alcohol and may have been infused with other things, in variable proportion. These could have included henbane, a hallucinogenic and potentially lethal wild herb which, as archaeological analysis shows, was used in some ancient northern European ritual beverages. Cannabis is another possibility: it can be infused as well as inhaled, grew wild on the steppes and had been deliberately cultivated since the time of the first farmers in northern Europe. Opium is a third, already an important product in Neolithic cultures as far afield as Switzerland

and Denmark, and persisting for 6,000 years as a legitimate part of European culture until some time after the death of the poet Coleridge in 1834.[13]

The funerary *nabidh* was brewed during the ten days that elapsed between the slave-girl 'volunteering' and the day of the cremation, and was paid for by the disbursement of a full third of the chieftain's property. It must have been a costly drink, made only on special occasions. The fact that some had been placed in the primary burial suggests that the Rus chief had been interred at the end of a previous series of rites which Ibn Faḍlān did not witness. These were the rites of separation, involving the construction of the timber and earth mound, the brewing of the first batch of *nabidh* and the initial treatment of the corpse.

Ibn Faḍlān remarks that the corpse is 'black' because of the cold, but we know the funeral did not take place in winter because the river was not frozen (the ship was brought up out of it). Ibn Faḍlān travelled for many months in the north, and his *Risala* comments in different places both on the extreme brevity of the nights (the northern summer) and strange light effects before sunrise (possibly the Aurora Borealis and thus one of the two times of high auroral activity, March and late September/early October). He says it is 'cold' simply because he is unused to the climate: it could have been spring, but was most likely autumn as 'fruits' were available to place in the grave chamber. Autumn would also have been the end of the fighting season, when those slain in battle would most often be received by Odin. The northern lights were understood by the Vikings to be the visible manifestation of the Valkyries as they arrived to choose those destined for Valhalla.[14]

An untreated corpse would be in a much worse state than the one Ibn Faḍlān describes, winter or not. Low temperature in itself (as Stalin found out while consulting chemists about the dead Lenin) speeds up some types of decomposition. The stench would have hung heavy in the air, decompositional gases would have bloated the belly to bursting and rotten juices would have run freely from the body as it was lifted. Instead, Ibn Faḍlān says 'Surprisingly, he had not begun to stink and only his colour had deteriorated.' Ibn Faḍlān has no way to judge the effects of temperature on the corpse not only because he was unused to the climate, but because the tradition in the Islamic world, then as today, involved swift burial after death. His description is good even though he was ignorant of what is clear to us in retrospect: the fact that the body had been treated – cleaned, steeped and stuffed with embalming herbs and waxed to keep its decomposition at bay. The procedure for stabilization may have had historical connections with the treatment Herodotus describes among the Scythians, 1,500 years before.

By the time Ibn Faḍlān arrived, the corpse was nearing the end of its transitional rites, the most liminal and ritually danger-ous phase. The main concern during this period had been to keep the dead man's soul, which had not yet been accepted into the realm of the dead, away from the living. The grave was dark and sealed to disorientate and contain the soul as it hovered near the body. The *nabidh* was there to intoxicate and confuse. A pandora (ṭunbūr) was provided to produce sweet and beguiling music, although presumably the chief would have to play it him-self in some supernatural sense.

The ship is hauled up on to the fuel pile and the chanting begins. This is the signal that the rite of incorporation is about to commence. All that is lacking is the chieftain on board. He is lifted from the opened mound, like a baby coming into the world in a caul. He is taken out of his old clothes and immedi-ately reclothed in new garments, specially prepared and never before worn. His soul is at first dazzled by the light, and then allured by the spectacular clothes (gold brocade, sable), by the sight of the ship made ready, and by the gorgeous couch, ostenta-tiously made up and large enough for two.

The mound-raising that followed the cooling of the pyre was part of Hertzian 'secondary' burial (as well as being a territorial statement). The chief could have been embalmed on board ship, ready for the burning. But the physical distance between his primary burial in the underground chamber and his secondary funeral rite, in which his body was reduced to ashes which were then buried under the earth, is a metaphor for the journey his soul takes from the point of death to the threshold of Valhalla. In order for the overall rite to succeed it is important that his body is not foul and rotting before its cremation.

But once the primary grave had been opened the chieftain's potentially malevolent soul could escape. It had to be kept, at all costs, close to his corpse as it was moved from the dug-out primary grave chamber to the ship-borne couch, and then it had to be persuaded to re-enter the body for the supernatural launch to Valhalla. With his corpse propped up in bed, more *nabidh* and fruit was brought, along with sweet basil, and bread, meat and onions.

The *rayhān* – sweet basil – was, I believe, crucial. It has strong erotic associations in an Arabic love poem of the sixth century,[15] and the two best-known types, *Ocimum viride* and *Ocimum sanctum*, are traditionally used in the treatment of impotence and low libido.[16] In the grave, the chieftain had been denied meat, onions or bread – starved of solid energy that might have enabled his possessed corpse to break out. Now, sitting up in bed dressed in finery, his physical body receives renewal and revitalization so that his soul will be encouraged to become corporeal again. All that is needed for the repossession process to be completed is the delivery of his favourite sexual partner, the slave-girl who – in Morten Lund Warmind's view – is to become his bride in death.

But having sex with the bridegroom's best friends seems an odd way to kick off a marriage ceremony, even a posthumous one. The apparent incongruity prompts Warmind to write: 'Ibn Faḍlān says that the girl has sex with the different tent-owners, who profess to participate not for fun but out of love for the dead master. To me, this rite as described is only half-understandable. Is it only with well-established relatives that sex takes place? Or is it the lords of the whole trading community who perform some sort of incorporative rite?' – that is, a ritual that would make the slave-girl into a Rus kinswoman and thus eligible for marriage. Puzzled, Warmind wonders whether the description is trustworthy,[17] but this seems unfair. Although we can speculate about what Ibn Faḍlān may have missed before he arrived, we have to try to make sense of what he saw, heard and was told.

Leaving aside the marriage symbolism for a while, the sequential possession of the slave-girl by the tent-lords is designed to make the chieftain jealous. Ibn Faḍlān is told what is going on but it is not clear that he understands it as she 'entering one pavilion after another. The owner of the pavilion would have intercourse with her and say to her "Tell your master that I have done this purely out of love for you"' – the 'you' here most probably being addressed to the dead man, although, 'you, the slave-girl' is possible.[18] The Arabic grammar is ambiguous, but any reasonable translation preserves the sense that she is to tell the dead chieftain that she has had sex with a person who is careful to justify on what grounds it occurs. The tent-lords arouse the chieftain's jealousy because it is only this jealousy, capped by the final affront of half a dozen more men having sex with her on his own couch, right next to him, that will compel his soul to re-enter his body. This is why the tent-lords make abundantly clear the circumstances in which they have sex with their chieftain's favourite bed-partner. However the Arabic is translated at this point, the 'purely' is unambiguously defensive and self-justificatory. It is their duty to sting the chief back into wholeness, body and soul, reanimating him at the moment of conflagration.

The fear of the soul reanimating the body and haunting the living in the form of the walking dead is matched by a fear of it failing to re-enter the body and remaining behind as a disembodied ghost after the body is burned. This seems strange until we realize that it is about losing control. The soul is wayward and dangerous and the corpse it belongs to is at once repulsive and a source of nostalgic fascination. Like a rogue animal, the soul requires both carrot and stick to make it compliant. Its invisibility means that ensuring that it is in the right place during every stage of the death rituals requires immense attention to detail.

I think that the tent-lords believed themselves to be in the twilight world with their dead chief. Van Gennep says that 'During mourning, the living mourners and the deceased constitute a special group, situated between the world of the living and the world of the dead.'[19] The tent-lords are bound by their ring oath, sworn to Odin. The Rus chief, bound by the same oath, is believed to be able to both hear and see the tent-lords: their actions are within the hazy orbit of liminal existence. By having sex with the tent-lords in sequence, the slave-girl enters under the same grey veil. She is required to go from tent to tent herself and although, as an enslaved concubine, none of the sex she has had while the property of the Rus can be considered consensual, at this point she may have persuaded herself to believe that she has entered a bargain with some tangible life and afterlife benefits.

There is a danger of over-intellectualizing the sex that occurs during the funeral. Sex and death have been shown to go together in many societies, an association that may have an evolutionary logic in terms of replenishing group numbers: pregnancy in many cultures seems to be more common following bereavement than at other times. Nevertheless, whatever the underlying reproductive imperatives and however these connect to opportunistic hedonistic indulgence, it is a fact that complex religious and metaphysical ideas can become connected to sexual activity during funeral rites.

The Bara of Madagascar, studied by Richard Huntington, have wild sex at funerals. They say that bawdy songs, sexual liaisons and drunken revelry during the transitional period are important to entertain the ghost, who feels lonely and isolated, separated from the living and not yet at home with the dead. But there is a deeper symbolism. Death is an expression of absolute order – totally male – in opposition to the female womb and birth, which are expressions of absolute vitality. Life is thought of as a tight-rope walk from one state to the other, requiring balance at every point. Because of this, a funeral without vitality-providing sex would be dangerous. Fundamentally and unsurprisingly, death reminds the Bara of the value of life; but the experience is elaborated in mythological and ritual details.[20]

Unlike ritual sex during Bara funerals, the sex that the slave-girl has during the Rus funeral is obviously not reproductive (she is killed afterwards). Indeed, it is possible that her killing is in some way anti-reproductive and that the sex, perversely, is designed to deflect attention from this. The death of the chieftain is an opportunity for a political struggle over the legitimate succession of leadership and the possibility that the slave-girl, if she was the chief's favourite, coerced and cajoled to put herself forward as his wife-to-be in Paradise, might already be pregnant with a child whose existence could threaten the authority of the new chief, has to be considered.

We do not know if the slave-girl could have conceived. Although it is not specified by Ibn Faḍlān, there are reasons to suppose she may have been around 14. In early medieval society, the transition from girlhood to womanhood was earlier than today: marriage at 12 was not uncommon. What Ibn Faḍlān thought of as a *jariyah* was probably someone no older than 16, and the Rus raids inevitably produced child slaves. There is no reason to suppose that sex would not have constituted an element in the misuse to which slave children were subjected, bereft of all rights in an aggressive and violent society. Nevertheless, although she did not need to be be post-pubescent to be raped, it seems unlikely that the slave-girl could have carried through her part at a psychological level, especially the 'volunteering' aspect, had she been only, say, eight or nine. Her reaction to her situation may indicate her age in some ways – an impetuous, potentially self-destructive lack of judgement.

What happens on board ship, after the slave-girl has given her jewellery away, was unambiguously physically violent rape, instigated by the six men while their victim screams. Ibn Faḍlān implies that the screaming begins just after the *Malak al Maut* has led her into the death-pavilion – which is when the drumming

181

begins. Her screams may continue until she dies, which is not such a short time, because six men have sex with her beforehand. Sudden and dramatic silence would have signalled the completion of this phase of the ritual to the funeral guests, if they could not see the proceedings within.

The two types of rape occur within the context of different rituals, because there are, for the slave-girl, two small yet significant personal rites of passage within the overarching ritual of the chieftain's funeral. The first is completed but the second is – crucially – left incomplete.

The first rite of passage begins at the time of the chieftain's death when she 'volunteers' to go with him. She is immediately separated from her slave status and quickly incorporated into the elite and receives the two daughters of the Angel of Death as personal servants, who have to wash her feet. It is in this new status, as a prospective social equal, that the slave-girl visits the tent-lords and has sex with them. She does not wear a neck ring as this is a sign of married status, but she does wear rings on her wrists and ankles which probably symbolize eligibility for marriage – a kind of maidenhood that would be unrecognized for a slave.

There is a deliberate tension between her new status and her continuing slave-like promiscuity at this point. It is precisely because the slave-girl's status has been raised to that of prospective bride that the tent-lords' sexual activity with her is so enraging for the soul of the dead chieftain. This powerful enragement is the effect that the tent-lords want to induce.

The slave-girl has apparently gone through a rite of passage which has taken her out of slavery into the circles of the elite. She is excited and apprehensive about the next rite which will, as she believes, consolidate this new position in a remarkable way by transporting her with her lord to Valhalla. Although obviously intoxicated and disoriented by the *nabidh*, it is hard to guess at her precise mental state and we would do best to think of it as fluid and riven by paradoxes – anticipation coupled with confusion and moments of lucid misgiving. The ritual's

182

own coercive logic sweeps her along like a river in spate, rushing towards the point where it bends out of sight. There is a horror she does not expect: she loses all composure and starts up her intense, terrified screaming. The Rus, of course, knew. It was their ritual, and they had made special shield-drumming provision for it.

The retainers in Queen Puabi's grave at Ur apparently died quietly, like the kneeling submissives buried alive in the death pit at Nitriánsky Hradok. The evidence suggests that people ritually killed do not necessarily lose their composure at the end (and this is one reason why these deaths are sometimes described as 'willing'). There is plentiful evidence of composure in the Indian suttee ritual, where the wife of the dead man ascends his pyre and is burned with him.[21]

Herodotus describes an Iron Age ritual, similar to suttee, among one group of Thracians (neighbours of the Scythians, in what is now Bulgaria):

> Those of the Thracians who live above the Crestonaeans do the following: each man of them has many wives, and when a man among them dies, there is a great judging of the wives, and much earnestness among his friends in this respect: as to which he had loved the most. She that is so adjudged to be best loved, and is so honoured, is greatly praised by men and women and then has her throat cut over his grave by her closest family. Being so slaughtered she is then buried with her man. The other wives feel this as a great calamity, for it is for them the greatest of reproaches.[22]

There are important differences between this and the Rus ritual. The Thracian women do not have ritual sex with anyone at the funeral. The group of women from among whom one is selected are already wives, so their suttee-like ritual killing is not, and cannot be, a ceremonial marriage in death. The woman who dies is not drugged, and is dispatched quickly so that death is not deliberately drawn-out.

The slave-girl ultimately does not behave in a composed fashion, and the Rus do not expect her to. Their explanation to her, as recorded by Ibn Faḍlān (and the one that he himself believes that the Rus believe) does not make sense. Her second rite of passage, which, if it is to be a marriage, should end in her incorporation as a bride in death is rendered incomplete by the fact that she dies in terror. There is no known rite of incorporation where this would be appropriate. What occurred was a deliberately incomplete rite, which renders the slave-girl liminal and forces her to die in that state.

After visiting the tent-lords, the slave-girl is taken to the enigmatic door-frame structure and, looking over it, 'sees' her father and mother. She may have been told that, because she has now been socially raised, her relatives, whom she thought ignominiously killed or enslaved, have been translated into Paradise and will become the in-laws of the chieftain, her master. This is the beginning of her new rite of separation. She gives up her rings of maidenhood in the expectation that she will shortly be given a neck ring to replace them, symbolizing married status. She then takes leave of her girlfriends – status-less, sister slave-girls fancifully conceptualized as unmarried maidens and brides-maids – as she sings over, and then drinks, the first cup of *nabidh*. Ring-giving was a Viking sign of elite status. But having given away all her rings the slave-girl again becomes status-less and liminal, and it is while she is in this state that the second sequence of more violent rapes occurs.

The gold and silver neck rings worn by married Viking women were part of a long tradition. In the preceding Iron Age period, the elite among the Celts wore heavy torcs made of twisted gold and silver to distinguish themselves from those whom they traded south to the classical world wearing the twisted hemp ropes and iron neck shackles of gang chains. Precious metal neck rings indicated that, as aristocrats, they served the gods rather than mortals. Meanwhile, the slaves lived and died mining the silver that their replacements were bought with.[23] In the Rus ritual the slave-girl does not receive a silver or gold neck ring to symbolize her incorporation as the wife of the chief. She does finally receive a ring around her neck, but not of the sort she may have hoped for. It is made of rope.

'The happy girl is sent to Odin to be with her master': Warmind's judgement is both emotionally implausible and theologically mysterious. Even assuming for a dizzy moment that the slave-girl was 'happy' about it, there is no way that she could have been allowed into Valhalla. Odin's heroic hall was for men only. The Valkyries were female, but they did not themselves belong to the human slain.[24] All along, Warmind assumes that the difficulties in the account are due to Ibn Faḍlān's use of Arabic conventions as a way of translating native religious concepts, but Warmind's approach fails here. If the Rus believed in Paradise, then Ibn Faḍlān's account would work, because the slave-girl could go there, but if it is – as Warmind and most other Norse scholars believe – an Odinic ritual, then the whole explanation of marriage collapses.

Warmind falls into the trap – one that has plagued social anthropology – of assuming that 'native' or 'tribal' people will tell the truth to outsiders who ask them about their sacred ceremonies. People commonly lie, particularly about those aspects of life which are focuses of taboo (actual sexual practices, for example, or information about the dead). There are inconsistencies in what Ibn Faḍlān says he was told which may indicate that he was deliberately misled by the Rus. He was, to them, 'a heathen'.[25] And he had not taken the ring oath required for initiation into the warrior society of Odin. The secret rites of the group were not revealed to outsiders. We only know that the Vikings' ring oath existed; we do not know what it was.[26]

A cast bronze statuette of the Buddha seated on a lotus throne, found 5,000 miles from its north Indian origin on an early medieval site at Helgö in Sweden, shows that the Vikings were exposed to a wide range of religious influences.[27] The little figure shows that the Rus could have had just as much knowledge about Ibn Faḍlān's religion as he had about theirs, if not more. Neither Islam, Buddhism, Judaism nor Christianity is a secret religion. They were evangelized, and the Rus could have learned as much or as little as they wanted about them.

Ibn Faḍlān was not mistranslating a foreign concept when he recorded what he was told, several times, about the slave-girl volunteering to join her master in Paradise. Setting aside the fact that the slave-girl could herself have been Muslim, the Vikings had already visited Baghdad in AD 846, and could have learned about the Arabic concept of *al-janna* for themselves.[28] They showed an aptitude for lying then too: the earliest Arabic account of the Rus, written by Ibn Khurradadhbih, notes that they claimed to be Christians in order to avoid paying Baghdad's *jizya* or poll tax on people who did not belong to a religion of the book (Islam, Judaism or Christianity).[29]

On the banks of the Volga, the Rus could have told Ibn Faḍlān that the funeral rite was all about 'Paradise' and used the Arabic word to allay any doubt. Indeed, they may have had to, given that they had no such concept in their own cosmology. Their true beliefs were something that they could not reveal to him on principle. The secret was also kept from the other slave-girls but may finally have been revealed to the one who died. The Angel of Death informs the slave-girl that she is not going anywhere, that there is no Paradise (so her parents and relatives are not in it), and that her master, whose soul has been tempted back into his body by her presence, is going, as he must, to Valhalla without her. There has already been a hint of this perhaps, understood only by initiates, when the slave-girl looks over the door-frame for the third time to see her master 'accompanied by his men and his male-slaves'. The door-frame surely symbolized *Grindr*, the gate that separates the living from the dead in the *Elder Edda*, but each of the slave-girl's glances over it is understood to reveal a different scene, reinforcing the idea that the fates of the dead are different; the final time it reveals a supernatural vista in which females are absent.

If Odinism, as we think, had things in common with shamanism, then we should expect that during its rituals protagonists may have become spirit-possessed, personifying or 'channelling' particular deities. The Angel of Death, the 'gloomy, corpulent woman, neither young nor old', may have had a special ceremonial identity. It seems possible that, for the duration of the rite, she personified a giantess who appears in the *Elder Edda*: Hyrrokin, whose name probably means 'withered by fire', is central to the great funeral of Balder, launching the ship on which he is burned.[30] Balder is the virtuous son of Odin, and a fit cipher for the Rus chief himself.

The manner of the slave-girl's death is, in van der Sanden's terminology, 'multiple'. She is given a second cup of *nabidh*, which the Angel of Death has to urge her to drink, although she has previously drunk freely. She may suspect from the smell that something is different in this drink, and that its added ingredients – henbane? ergot derivatives? mistletoe juices? – will bring more pain than pleasure. The herbal knowledge of the period was well honed, and a poisoned draught may have combined with the Angel of Death's revelation of deception, to cause her screaming – agonized as much as terrified – which continues for the duration of her multiple rape, up until the point where the noose is tightened, shortly before her death. As with Lindow Man and the Windeby Girl, the trauma of 'multiple death' is designed to keep the soul within the body, so confused about which exit from life to take that it finally takes none.

Theatrical revelling in death is a behaviour displayed by some modern-day criminal psychopaths, once their victims have been rendered helpless; not toying with death, but a slow savouring of control over the final moment. The multiple sexual assault, coupled with the tightening noose, could well have been carefully managed by the *Malak al Maut* in order to force an involuntary orgasm at the moment of her stabbing – a procedure that would have had appropriately Odinic associations.

In many cultures the soul is conceptualized as leaving the body in an exhalation. It is not pedantic to say that the final garrotting cut short the slave-girl's screams and thereby stopped them from being, technically speaking, 'her dying screams'. Her terrified screaming as the six men have sex with her one after the other may have been encouraged, not just as part and parcel of the ritual theatre and as the mark and embodiment of extreme distress in themselves, but in order to terminally fatigue her soul. The final disablement of her voice is both the ultimate mechanism and the outward sign of her soul's trapped subjection to the tortured body that it will never leave.

At the end, Ibn Faḍlān is almost taunted by the Rus man who tells him, through his interpreter, that the chieftain enters 'Paradise' at once. The Rus man then 'laughed loud and long' and adds: 'Because of the love which my Lord feels for him. He has sent the wind to take him away within an hour.' There is no mention of 'them'. The slave-girl does not die a suttee-like death, ritually killed ostensibly to benefit from rebirth as the wife of her master. Nor is she sacrificed to a particular god – offered for example to Odin, to be his servant. The slave-girl is ritually murdered at the physical level as a prologue to the murder of her soul.

After the slave-girl is killed, the whole ship becomes an object of immense danger. From the Rus perspective it now contains two souls, both on the threshold of the living world: one must leave it and be reborn, and one must stay to be burned. The chieftain's soul has re-entered his body in order to ravish his slave-girl, whose soul, in its turn, must now be held inside her body as she is finally and totally annihilated. The ship is fraught with such profound metaphysical danger that only one man in the world can now approach it, and then only with the most extreme care.

Naked, carrying a burning brand, and walking backwards with his free hand guarding his anus, the man described as the chieftain's closest relative leaves the crowd and moves towards the ship on its great pyre. Reversals of everyday practice are a common part of funeral ritual but, just as going into battle naked can be a sign of lack of fear, the Rus man's nakedness may signal his defiance of the supernatural dangers he is approaching. It is a special precaution to ensure that – paradoxically – he is not too exposed.

The soul was conceived of as like breath, wind, exhalation,

188

and this man, closest to the chieftain, shares his liminal, between-worlds state most closely. He is exposed to the specific supernatural danger that his soul may involuntarily exit his body through one of its 'gates' (Chinese jade funeral suits were provided with jade plugs for every single body orifice precisely to contain the soul). His mouth he could keep shut but the soul could escape through the 'gate of his anus' (as Ibn Faḍlān's Arabic text tautologously names it). It might be sucked out of him by the divine force, the wind of God, that was about to carry his closest relative to Valhalla.

Once he sets his brand to the pyre, the taboo surrounding the ship is relaxed and the funeral becomes a communal rite, with mourners contributing their own brands. Then comes the supernatural wind, a fierce updraught physically caused by the carefully planned structure of the pyre. It is likely that after the pyre is lit, and while Ibn Faḍlān watches as everything is 'burnt to ashes, and then dust of ashes', the naked man is already involved in a purification ritual.

Archaeologists have constructed experimental pyres to calculate the duration of a cremation ceremony and the types of bone evidence that might be expected to remain. The cremations take six or more hours and the bones are left in quite large pieces at the end. However, these tests have been conducted on a small scale, with fresh animal carcasses (rather than a corpse some weeks old), and without seasoned wood.[31] Nothing experimental has ever been attempted on the scale of the Rus ship pyre. The Arabic word *anābir* means something like a wooden barn or warehouse. Ibn Faḍlān saw an unusual, scaffolded structure which was much more than a big pile of firewood. Timber was abundant in the great forest region of the upper Volga.

The structure would have been so large and stable that, at the point in the ceremony when the rape and ritual killing took place, it could easily support the weight of the ship itself, nine people (the chieftain, slave-girl, Angel of Death, and six men), the furnishings, the carcasses of two oxen, two horses, and a dog. The ship needed to be raised high enough for the heat to build beneath it. The communal brand-setting ensured that the structure was lit simultaneously at a large number of points around the base. As the fire took hold on all sides, oxygen was sucked in ever faster, rapidly creating an extremely high temperature in the core. In a few minutes the pyre would have been quite unapproachable, and the mourners and guests must have withdrawn to a comfortable distance. The hour taken to produce a residue of fine ash may not be exaggerated.

The means by which the chieftain's soul crossed the threshold he was already standing on, into the Hall of the Slain itself to take his seat, involved tricking the slave-girl. Her presence was needed for his rite of incorporation to be successful, but she could not progress with him. The Rus lie both to the slave-girl and to Ibn Faḍlān, allowing them both, in different ways, to believe that the purpose of her killing is to allow her to enter the afterlife with her master. The tent-lords who have sex with the slave-girl in her raised status know what is to befall her; she does not.

Deception was perhaps the highest of all Odinic values. The personality of Odin has been described as 'strange and many-sided, demonic and frightening . . . violent, fickle and treacherous . . . aristocratic, perilous, incalculable . . . no god for the ordinary man to meddle with'.[32] He had violated his own ring oath for personal benefit and his popular epithets included 'Ill-doer', 'Terrifier' and 'Lord of the Gallows'. Viking warriors are known to have revelled in lies and deceit, and equated this with wisdom (Odin was also 'Wisdom's Friend'). As one of the world experts on runic inscriptions and Norse mythology, Ray Page, writes: 'faithlessness is part of Odin's general nature, as it is part of the way of life of the Vikings, many of whom must have taken Odin as their personal god'. He quotes from one of the poems in the Edda, *Hávamál*: 'men's minds are treacherous to women./When our intent is most false, we speak most fairly;/That deceives the wisest hearts.'[33] Brünnhilde, in the Long Lay of Sigurthur, found herself married to the king of the Burgundians as a result of deceit.

To the Rus, the slave-girl is dispensable. She may be thought of as a concubine who knows too much. She may have been precipitated into 'volunteering' by the suspicion that she would not be allowed to live anyway. As the tent-lords have sex with her, they feel that their chief's spirit is hovering over them, listening as they instruct her to carry their message about love to him. It is a message he can already hear, while relishing the tent-lords' deception of the helpless girl. Both things amuse him and whet his appetite for the pleasures of the flesh, so that he is compelled to re-enter his body on the couch that has been prepared for it.

The behaviour of the Rus is all of a piece. The final revelation of the non-existence of Paradise is part of the thrill for the initiates at the ceremony, who hear the sudden onset of the girl's screaming. It works with, not against, their beliefs as it further ensures the confusion of her soul, uncertain both as to its physical exit from the body and to its otherworldly destination. Symbolically, it concretely emphasizes Valhalla's men-only status by way of a dramatic rite, one not of incorporation but of exclusion.

The Rus funeral rites were permeated with fear. The destructive attitude towards the slave-girl may have been born in part of their tenuous position as an aspiring power in a land of warring foreigners. The Vikings inflicted torture and death to shield their own psyches from the horror of mortality. There was a real feeling that the chieftain's spirit could do them harm but they may have been more afraid of the supernatural revenge of the abused girl, were her spirit to be left in existence. For those whose greatest desire is control, annihilation is the greatest fear. So it was a rite of annihilation that the slave-girl was subjected to.

The rite was thoroughly Odinic. But leaving it at that is to fall into the same trap as Morten Lund Warmind, to over-intellectualize and see what actually happened as superficial in comparison to the metaphysical ideas that it embodied.

The Rus funeral appears to have been constrained by traditional rules of communal conduct. As under Stalin's rule,

191

individual opportunities for acting in accordance with personal conscience were distinctly limited. Open dissent from the procedures that Ibn Faḍlān describes is hard to imagine but, as in concentration camps, there must have been scope for individual acts of compassion and kindness by those who were otherwise compelled to operate within the overall framework. The fact that none took place raises an uncomfortable thought: that, as with muti, the ritual killing of the slave-girl was felt to be beneficial for the community as a whole.

'The death of somebody close gives you a good excuse to go a bit crazy for a while and do things that would otherwise be inexcusable,' according to Frank, the central character in Iain Banks' novel, *The Wasp Factory*.[34] The conduct of the principal actors in the funerary ritual was underlain by complex and mixed motives: some participated for the sex, some for the ritual grandeur, some for the exhilaration of witnessing terror, some in order to conform. But these diverse motives came together in a single purpose. By scapegoating the slave-girl, the community refreshed itself.

We have all been misled, not just Ibn Faḍlān. The rite was not, principally, a funeral at all. It was an act of ritual killing for which the earlier slaying of the chieftain – in circumstances that may have precipitated little genuine grief – was the pretext. The highly ritualized death of the slave-girl required complicity. The multiple rapes and the fire-setting by the whole gathering communalized her killing. Like execution by firing squad, responsibility was taken by everyone and no one. It was an assertion of human power in the face of disempowerment by death in general, and it served to create group solidarity. Groups are defined by what they exclude.

The slave-girl remained a slave. By brutally dashing her aspiration to belong, the Rus defined their society.

CHAPTER 8

Beyond the Pavlov Hills

Even from a distance, it was obvious that she was dead.
Not ill or asleep. It was something to do with the way
she lay. The angle of her limbs. Something to do with
Death's authority. Its terrible stillness.

ARUNDHATI ROY, *The God of Small Things*[1]

———

B en Steed died on 30 December 2000. He was diabetic and
his blood sugar fell too low while he was out shopping. He
was a few days short of his 25th birthday. I saw Ben quite
often because his father, Neville, is the godfather of one of my
daughters and one of my closest friends.

On 9 January I drove Ben's mother, Jean, and his sister, Kirsty,
to see him. Neville wanted to remember Ben as he had seen him
last, at the hospital where he had been taken after he collapsed
and died. A smartly dressed woman with steel-blue eyes led us
to a garage-like building with churchy features, the Chapel of
Rest. She was at once sympathetic and formal, her manner perfectly balanced between distance and intimacy. She extracted
keys from her bag and began to speak about the post-mortem:
she said that although there had been a bit of 'leakage', she had
done her best.

Damp weather had swollen the door of the Chapel of Rest so
that it stuck a little as we were ushered through into the main

room, with its rows of chairs. Off this was an anteroom where, raised on table-high trestles beneath a small stained glass window, we found the open coffin.

Ben lay, hands loosely folded together, chin on his chest. The initial impression was very shocking, because I wanted his expression to change, something to happen, and it did not. He looked like a horrific wax deception. The lady, who – as I now realized with a jolt – was the embalmer, said that she hoped Jean liked how he looked. At first I did not understand what she meant when she added 'I didn't know, because I haven't seen him'. Then it made sense: she meant that because she had never seen Ben in life, she was worried that she might have got his appearance wrong. Jean said that she was very happy with it, and he looked just like he had the last time they had seen him.

We were left with him. Ben's expression was unchanging. But my initial shock wore off and it felt like a practical visit. Jean remarked that he looked at peace; she later said that we should look at his eyes (which were set only just shut), and that he was only sleeping. Kirsty cried. They both kissed him and they said how soft his hair was, and ruffled it. I went to stand by the coffin and it seemed natural for me to rest my left hand on his head too (or, perhaps, it would have seemed unnatural if I had avoided touching him). I had to overcome an inner feeling that was accusing me of being prurient, wanting to touch a corpse. I also wondered if Jean and Kirsty would mind if I touched him. It soon became apparent, however, that my instincts were correct – they wanted me to touch him too, and not recoil: this was a son and brother and I would have distressed them if I had shunned him. I rested my hand on his hair, which was soft, and the leaden heaviness of his great cold head was apparent too. I said something stupid, and quiet, like 'It's all right, Ben'.

There was quite a lot of such inconsequential chat around him from Kirsty and Jean, smiles and then tears again. Jean had brought a bag with things in it: tissues, and two items for the coffin. I helped Kirsty decide where to put the picture frame containing a photo of Brandy as a puppy on the sofa: a cast metal frame with the words 'Spoilt Rotten' on it and little dog-bone motifs (even in a thousand years' time one would be able to infer that it had once had a pet dog picture in it). Kirsty was at a loss where to place the picture, so I moved Ben's right arm so she could rest it in the crook; it crossed my mind that it could have been put in his hands, but that might have looked macabre. She then put his favourite mug in the crook of his other arm. There was amusement over his Simpsons socks; I pulled a bit of his left jeans leg up to see if it was Bart or Homer (it was Homer).

Kirsty wanted my opinion on some staining on the collar of the deep red patterned shirt she had bought Ben for Christmas, visible above his beige turtle-neck; I said it was leakage from the post-mortem because they would have opened up his chest. I felt that it was a bit of a cover-up in a way: this was Kirsty's brother and I think she was genuinely curious and concerned to see what had been done to him, but she recomposed herself and said nothing. Jean said she had been warned by the lady on the phone that she must prepare for the fact that he had been post-mortemed. She told me that she hadn't known what to expect, and had been apprehensive: now she was relieved he looked so peaceful. She wanted to have some of his hair. She asked me if I thought that was an OK thing to want, and when I said I thought it was, she asked me if it would be all right to ask, and would I go. I went to find the embalmer; she was not in the chapel, but I found her by her house, which was adjoining. She was supportive, went off and brought back scissors and, saying that Jean probably had not got anything to put the hair into, she had found a small pale yellow plastic earring box. She gave them both to me.

I re-entered the chapel; there was the same unobtrusive male-voice sacred music playing; rows of churchy chairs and a wooden cross on a table at the front with an electrically illuminated stained glass image of the Recording Angel holding a great green quill. Ben was through a door, to the right at the back, under a window, his coffin lid (with a brass plate – full name, dates) propped against the wall. I offered the scissors and box to Jean, but she and Kirsty stood back a little and Jean asked if I could do it. It was clear she knew her mind on this, so I said that of course I would.

Kirsty had last cut his hair when he was alive and it was a short crew cut – it was hard to know where to remove a lock. I went for the back, above and behind his right ear. I didn't want to move his head too much. I joked with Ben that we didn't want to make him prematurely bald like his dad. The place where I had cut the hair was unobtrusive once I had rearranged the blue drape. Kirsty and Jean kissed him again and said that they could have spent all day there. We were in fact under forty minutes with him but it seemed longer. They asked me again about his rosy colour, which looked very natural: was it make-up? I said it was something injected to give him a better colour. It did look good. Although I didn't mention it, he had obviously been shaved. The face contrasted a lot, however, with his candle-wax pale hands and fingers, on which two or three livid red scabby sores were visible. The tips of the fingers had shrivelled a bit (as they do when one has been in the bath a long time). Jean and Kirsty were amused by the appearance of a double chin (caused by the lack of muscle tone and the head pressing back on to the neck). Jean said he looked well fed.

They both touched his lips and wondered at their softness, inviting me to feel them too. I wasn't sure Ben would have liked me feeling his lips but I obliged by just pressing the middle of his bottom lip with my index finger: it was just like a lip, but cold. Jean said that they had better go. I said they should come whenever they were ready and I moved through into the main chapel to give them some privacy. I realized then that I hadn't actually said goodbye to him but then I thought: Well, I will be at his funeral tomorrow.

Jean and Kirsty came out, and then Jean returned to check for her bag, but she had it with her already. They started to walk down the 'aisle' and I ducked my head back through the door, to check whether we really did have everything and with half a mind to say 'Goodbye Ben'. But I was shocked all over again: I realized that while we had been with him we had projected emotion on to his features, and that we had felt comfortable in the presence of his relaxed, peaceful face, despite its immobility. Looking back at him, the unchanged expression seemed a horrid joke again – he had looked like this all last night and would look like this in his coffin tomorrow; no one looking at him could change his expression, because it wasn't an expression at all, there was no intention behind it.

We came out of the chapel and the embalmer met us. Anxious to know whether Jean and Kirsty felt that he was all right, again she told us that she had done her best but as she had never seen him, she had been a bit in the dark. She seemed genuinely relieved that Kirsty and Jean approved of Ben's appearance.

Ben was extremely popular and the church was packed with his friends on the day of the funeral. The strangest thing was that Ben had recently spoken to his girlfriend about dying. He was worried about his diabetes and did not believe he would make it to 30. He had specified what music should be played at his funeral. So the coffin was carried in by his closest male friends, and later carried out again, to the sound of the rap artists Sweetbox who, over the powerful and insistent cadences of a fragment of J.S. Bach, had set the fading, haunting, repeating phrase 'Everything's gonna be alright'. I cannot begin to describe the effect. Nothing else that was said made the same impact, because this was his choice, for that occasion, and it made his presence known.

Later, at the graveside, and before the funeral tea and speeches, people threw their little shovels of earth down on the coffin lid. Now the earth is well settled and Ben is on his own. His headstone has gone up, hard Yorkshire sandstone with deeply cut, dark blue letters.

A few months after Ben's funeral, I was holding a red-stained skull in my hands. The person to whom it once belonged was only a few years younger than Ben when she died, but her name has been forgotten, along with the meanings of the things that she was found with. Known as DV 15, her burial took place some 26,600 years ago, in the Ice Age, near to the little village of Dolní Věstonice in the Czech Republic.

Looking at the sockets where the eyes of the person known as DV 15 had once been, I was tempted to imagine her life and death, the grieving of her family and friends, and the ceremonies that surrounded her corpse, through the emotional filter of the present. The sort of ceremony that surrounded Ben's death is at once so powerful and so familiar that it is hard not to interpret all prehistoric burials in its likeness.

DV 15 was buried between two other young people, 17- or 18-year-old youths, whose skeletons betrayed no obvious cause of death, and who had been posed, somewhat grotesquely, as if to tell a story. A stake had been driven into the pelvis of the young male to the left and his hands were stretching out into the pubic area of the female. A scatter of red ochre was found between her legs, either remains of a red-ochre object of some sort, or the residue of ochre plastering in that region, or simply a heavy scattering of the powdered material (red ochre – hydrated iron oxide – keeps its colour but its consistency can vary according to how it is processed and what it is exposed to). A small flint blade was also found in her pubic region, but whether this was a deliberate inclusion or something that became incorporated by accident is also uncertain.[2] The male to the right lay partially over the female, on his front with his head turned away as if shunning her. All three had worn thick masks of red ochre, broken now like dark crusts of bread, and once variously decorated with drilled fox teeth.

Dolní Věstonice lies on the northern flank of the Pavlov Hills, outside the town of Mikulov. As the glaciers of the last Ice Age built to their last maximum, mammoth hunters of the Pavlovian culture lived here, eight to ten people per dwelling, keeping themselves warm by burning locally gathered coal. There were maybe 100 people in the community at any one time. They had vibrant and flourishing arts, carving ivory objects and moulding

The Pavlov Hills and the excavation site of Dolní Věstonice, Czech Republic. (Photo: author)

The Ice Age triple burial at Dolní Věstonice. (Photo: Jiří Svoboda)

small clay figurines which they then fired. They maintained contacts across a wide area, and over 180 kilos (400 pounds) of high-quality south Polish flint has been found at the site.

When I first discussed the triple burial (in *The Prehistory of Sex*), the sex of the central skeleton was in doubt, but further analysis has strengthened the supposition that she was female. Her bones are locked in a metal safe in the village schoolhouse, now an archaeological base, and one glance shows that all was not well. Her left and right arm and leg bones do not match up, and her pelvis is so deformed that she would have walked with difficulty. She suffered from a congenital condition that would also have caused balding (alopecia), cataracts and reddened, scaly skin. She was around 20 years old when she died.

The two 17- or 18-year-old males who flank DV 15 appear to have been healthy at the time of death. There is a small healed trauma on the cranium of one of them, but neither displays evidence of chronic disease or any lethally violent attack. Although their skulls have a curiously lopsided appearance, this is probably due to post-mortem distortion, caused by pressure bearing down on them during their long burial. There are clear similarities in tooth-eruption patterns, jaw shape and so on which indicate that all three individuals were closely related. The two males could even have been twins. The way that the bodies of these three young Pavlovians are posed in death suggests a theatrical ritual – designed to distinguish the dead from the living, and perhaps to distinguish something else too.

At some point, most children ask 'What happens to you when you die?', expecting that adults know. They have already seen dead things – a frog on the road, fish in the supermarket – and their question expresses a puzzle which we cannot solve: the feeling that we cannot personally ever *be* dead. Children sense that time somehow turns people into things – a strange realization that is played around with at Hallowe'en, when skull masks and skeleton toys create squeals of mock panic and practice terror. When my younger daughter was five, I asked her whether her teddy bear, which was lying on the floor, could be dead. My question was met with disdain: 'I'll show you that teddy isn't dead, because he can't talk – because he's never been able to talk, and he's never been able to die.'

Between three and two million years ago, in a cave mouth at a place since named Makapansgat in South Africa, an australopithecine toyed with a small pebble. Made of jasperite, it must have been brought to the site from at least 5 kilometres away (the nearest outcrop) and perhaps from 300 kilometres (a bigger and more obvious outcrop). The reason for its presence was not that it was a suitable stone for making a chipped stone tool (the very earliest of which date to this period) but that it had two symmetrical round indents with a long gouge below them. These natural features give the impression of a simple face, with eyes and mouth.[3]

The Makapansgat pebble is a piece of 'found art', a pure freak of nature. The australopithecines could not have avoided seeing the face: the basic recognition is hard-wired into both human and

The Makapansgat pebble. (Drawing: George Taylor)

chimpanzee brains.[4] We know that when chimpanzees glimpse themselves in a still pool or (under laboratory conditions) in a mirror, a process of self-recognition occurs. But the Makapansgat pebble is not a reflection: its apparent expression is, in terms of intention, illusory. The australopithecines communicated in many ways, including vocalization (as chimpanzees do) but they lacked the ability to speak. They could not talk about the pebble, or 'make' it talk back to them.

The Makapansgat pebble was brought to the site and treasured because, presumably, of the funny inner feeling it produced.[5] The australopithecines, without spoken language, could not have been aware of the inevitability of personal death. And such knowledge did not come about naturally even after language developed.

The inevitability of personal death is still not something we 'know' in the same way as we know other things. The biologist, Richard Cutler, in a specialist paper on the 'Evolutionary Biology of Senescence' makes the standard assumption when he writes of our 'cognitive abilities, knowledge that death is inevitable, and our unwillingness to grow senile' as though all of these emerged as natural aspects of our evolution.[6] Yet in small hunter-gatherer groups, with changing personnel and no mechanism of permanent memorialization such as formal burial, which might demonstrate that everyone who previously existed had in fact died, it is quite possible to imagine that death may have been viewed as just one among many events that might or might not happen.

With the gradual emergence of grammatical language, which began around two million years ago, some version of the utterance 'it's dead' must have come into existence. In English, being able to say that someone has died is different from saying that they are dead. One indicates a historical process, the other an objective state. The state can be taken to imply an intangible community of 'the dead' to whom a person might eventually belong. But the creation of this 'place', like the recognition of inevitable personal mortality, took more than just language. In the beginning, 'it's dead' was an empirical observation without metaphysical resonance. To extend meaning beyond stark, non-breathing fact, required the transformation of Makapansgat pebble-play into a ceremonial ritual. At the heart of this ritual, the conflicting ideas of corpses as being at once things *and* people could somehow generate communal identities for both living and dead.

It is fascinating to read that Pierre Clastres initially thought that the Guayaki community he was invited to live among, the Atchei Gatu, were not cannibals because they seemed to bury their dead in such a familiar way. He only found out by accident that he was wrong (as he says, 'you can't walk right up to them and ask: are you cannibals?'). His suspicions were first aroused by the fact that the Atchei purported to have extremely simple funerals: 'the type of burial they described was exactly the same as the one practised in the western world – a grave dug to the measure of the body, which is placed on its back – although South American Indians frequently bury their dead ... placing the body in a fetal position in a cylindrical hole'. And that was it. Body deposited, event over. Clastres comments:

> One might have assumed that the similarity between Atchei Gatu and Western burial was simply a coincidence. I was tempted to attribute the lack of complexity of the ritual to a cultural loss ... they were unanimous in their descriptions, and I felt obliged to accept what they said. I therefore had to assume that everything I had heard about the Guayakis from the Paraguayans ... and the chroniclers [people like Hans Staden and the Jesuit missionaries who came in their wake] was merely fabrication.[7]

As it turned out, the local government-appointed administrator knew about Atchei cannibalism and was outraged and embarrassed by it. It was he who had instilled in the tribe the necessity of hiding it from outsiders. Everyone knew about his interdiction – except one old woman, Jygi. No one had bothered to tell her because she was so old. One day, alone with Clastres, she wistfully and quite openly began to talk to him about one of her daughters, a three- or four-year-old who had been ritually killed, roasted and eaten. Clastres was enabled to confront his principal 'host', Tokangi, with the implication of her testimony: 'He let out nothing more than a rather calm *Teeh!*, and then said, "*Nde kwa ma, ko!* So you finally found out." He made not the slightest effort to contradict me and accepted what I said very tranquilly.' Although not everyone was ritually killed, funerary cannibalism was the norm, conservative, proper and appropriate to the cultural leaders of the Atchei whatever its absolute ethics. They had never conducted burials in the European fashion at all.

Archaeologists have fetishized the earliest evidence of burials as providing proof of the birth of spirituality. The existence of interesting animal behaviour such as the zoning of the dead and the organizing of old bones observed among elephants, for example (the 'elephants' graveyard' phenomenon, first described by Herodotus and since filmed in the wild),[8] suggested to early scholars that there must be some 'logical' evolutionary progression that led to what we have today. Thus the French archaeologists Buissonie and Borden suggested in 1908 that one should look out for a body that was flexed, in a foetal position or as in sleep, placed in an artificially excavated pit or emplacement, covered over and accompanied by flowers, personal or ritual objects. This would indicate reverential disposal of the dead.

Other behaviours in our mammalian and primate background, such as cannibalism, which, though well attested among living human communities ran counter to fondly held ideas, have long been relegated to the fringes or openly doubted, in part because they threatened the Western ideology of individualism, which extends to the maintenance of identity even after death.

Early burials, such as those of the Neanderthals from sites like Shanidar in Iraq, are generally considered to represent an almost natural evolution from the idea of someone dying to someone being dead: 'It is possible to infer from the forms of mortuary ritual assumed in the Mousterian period that by that time the dichotomy of the two worlds, that of living beings and that of the dead, had already been fully recognized. Mortuary practices had in all probability also promoted the emergence of one of the earliest and most fundamental cosmological models. It was then that man created a world of his own, a totally imaginary world of the dead, and began creating a new culture, his own mythologized history,'[9] writes Yuri Smirnov of the Institute of Archaeology in Moscow. This is current orthodoxy (Brian Fagan, in his widely used, continually updated student textbook *People of the Earth* concurs, in the section on 'The Origins of Burial and Religious Belief', that such graves are 'signs that the Neanderthals, like most living hunter-gatherers, believed in life after death'.)[10]

At least two notes of caution should be sounded. The first comes from Robert Gargett, the most recent and diligent of a line of sceptics who have pointed out that caves are unsafe shelters, with roofs that fall in, and that many of the remains recorded as burials found within them are of partial skeletons. The natural explanation favoured by Gargett for the presence of bones of both Neanderthals and anatomically modern *Homo sapiens* (AMHS) in caves such as Tabun, Skhūl and Qafzeh, is that they represent the accidental deaths of individuals who were trapped under tons of rubble.[11] The remains of an infant Neanderthal discovered at the base of a natural shaft prone to rock fall in a cave at Dederiyeh in northern Syria in 1993, and interpreted as a burial by the joint Syrian-Japanese excavation team, may from its posture be better understood as resulting from an accident.

Gargett's observations may hold good for some material, previously claimed as intentional or ceremonial burials, but his idea of a purely random, natural process producing the Neanderthal 'burial' phenomenon is stretched to breaking by the *lack* of evidence from cave shelters in Spain and Portugal. Although these caves contain Mousterian stone tools and have roofs no less dangerous than their central European and western Asian counterparts, only one skeleton has ever been found.

Alban Defleur has devoted a book to establishing firm claims for a series of Neanderthal, Mousterian-period burials.[12] Caves such as Shanidar in Iraq and La Ferrassie in France each contain whole and partial skeletons of between eight and a dozen individual Neanderthals. More than half of the best-preserved skeletons at Qafzeh are foetal or infant remains, which makes little sense from the 'accident' point of view, even if small children are more prone to accidents.[13] In many of the caves individual bodies were positioned in artificial depressions and these 'graves' are clustered in particular areas in patterns that are hard to envisage as accidental. So, despite the absence in many cases of clear grave goods, or, necessarily, of clearly dug pits, or indeed, of complete bodies, it does seem that there is something deliberate going on.

Caves are good preservative environments once things are buried in them. This suggests that not too many of these 'burials' have been destroyed over the years, and from this it follows that very few individuals from the communities of Middle Palaeolithic Neanderthals and modern humans who were around over a period of 65,000 years were placed in caves. If we look at the bones we have, and classify them by age and sex, we find that they do not match the standard demographic patterns of any known human community: taken at face value, the age, sex and mortality ratios are a nonsense unless we accept what must in fact have been the case – that the people who were chosen for burial were few, and they were not selected at random.

As happened much later with the raised bogs, caves may have been specially chosen for their preservative qualities. But if this is true, then Robert Gargett's other objection to these being 'burials' becomes pressing – why are so many of the skeletons incomplete? His argument that, on this point, the phenomenon does not look like burial *as we understand it* seems strong, 'Unless one is to imagine that they were purposefully buried in an incomplete state'.[14] Gargett does not try to imagine this, but we will. This is where the second objection to the orthodoxy espoused by Smirnov and Fagan comes in.

Before attempting to imagine why incomplete bodies might

Qafzeh 11: burial of a modern human juvenile holding deer antlers over his shoulders. (Drawing: George Taylor)

have been buried, we have to ask what happened to the remains of most of the dead and this brings us back to cannibalism. Large numbers of fragmentary human bones, both of Neanderthals and anatomically modern *Homo sapiens*, are found in deposits other than apparent burials, and many – like the infant skull from Engis in Belgium – show clear traces of having been cut. Skulls from others deposits, such as the Grotta Guattari in Italy, have an enlarged foramen magnum, indicating removal of the brain.[15] At the rock shelter of Krapina in Croatia, excavated between 1895 and 1905, systematic cut-mark patterns have been observed on the bones of eighty or so Neanderthals.

People have argued against the idea of cannibalism in all of these cases, appealing either to natural processes, such as animals scavenging for human brains, or complex cultural practices, such as ritual funerary defleshing. The biological anthropologist Mary Russell has argued that cuts on the Krapina bones were 'consistent with post-mortem processing of corpses with stone tools, probably in preparation for burial of cleaned bones'.[16] The idea, imported from social anthropology, is that white bones would be needed for the rite of incorporation, signalling the reception of the soul into the world of the ancestors. But this is certainly anachronistic thinking for the Neanderthals.

The origin of the defleshing behaviours some anthropologists have reported on (albeit partially) can only make sense, to my mind, when seen against an established background knowledge of human edibility: put bluntly, to assuage the fear that if you do not deflesh your relatives, then other humans or animals will scavenge them. The 'defleshing' hypothesis does not explain where the 60 or more kilos of prime meat ended up – an issue that Russell does not consider, even in passing. Were the Neanderthals Russell imagines minded to feed their prime cuts to cave bears? Or would they have simply let them become flyblown and rot?

The Krapina bones have been in a museum for so long, handled and varnished and labelled, that it is hard to reanalyse the cut marks on them. But recent excavation by Alban Defleur and Tim White at the 100,000-year-old French cave of Moula-Guercy has demonstrated cannibalism beyond any reasonable doubt. The site contains butchered animal remains, predominantly red deer. Among the bones are the skulls of two young Neanderthals, their masseter muscles filleted and the tongue removed from at least one of them; the cut marks on the inner face of the mandible are virtually identical with those made on the inside of the 12,500-year-old modern human mandible from Gough's (New) Cave, described in Chapter 3 (see p. 80). Crania of both deer and Neanderthals were broken open to get at brains and, Defleur observes, 'in both taxa, marrow bones were systematically broken, and bones without marrow were not damaged'. The bones show no signs of roasting, suggesting the meat was either eaten raw or cut off to be cooked. White concludes that 'No mortuary practice has ever been shown to leave these patterns on the resulting osteological assemblages.'[17]

The cannibalism at Moula-Guercy was apparently non-ritual – either survival cannibalism or, more likely because of the intermixing with deer bones, of an aggressive type in which humans were hunted for their meat. In contrast, the recently analysed complex of La Chaise de Vouthon reveals an extraordinary picture with clear ritual dimensions. Two, interlinked cave chambers contain the remains of a number of Neanderthals. In one, the Suard chamber, mainly adult Neanderthal skeletons were found, with mainly juvenile skeletons in the adjoining Bourgeois Delauney chamber; the adults' bones were uncut, while those of the juveniles displayed deliberate cut marks.[18]

It seems that there are clear patterns of Neanderthal burial and at least two kinds of Neanderthal cannibalism, as well as some evidence for other forms of misadventure or violence (Dederiyeh cave). We cannot account for all the bones, however, so we cannot exhaust all possibilities. But what the 'burials' actually mean is a more difficult question. Paola Villa, in her critical examination of Mary Russell's defleshing hypothesis, frames her argument in terms of the 'two alternative hypotheses of secondary burial and cannibalism', debated since the second half of the nineteenth century.[19] But this ties us down to choosing between categories of behaviour observed by social anthropologists among modern humans, and we can tell, just by looking, that Ice Age societies were unlike anything in existence today or in the recent past. The idea that secondary burial – a defined rite of incorporation like that described in the case of the Rus chieftain – could have come into being fully fledged is naïve.

To identify the differences between apparent ritual funerary cannibalism in some caves (Krapina, Grotta Guattari, La Chaise de Vouthon), non-ritualized cannibalism in others (Gough's, Moula-Guercy, Fontbregoua) and the often partial and shallow burial of uncut and still-articulated remains accompanied by occasional 'grave goods' (Shanidar, La Ferrassie), we must, para-doxically, seek the connections between them.

A discovery that may link all three types of behaviour comes from Combe Capelle, an Early Upper Palaeolithic site in the French Périgord excavated by Klaatsch and Hauser in 1909. The only known *in situ* photograph of this *c.* 34,000-year-old burial is from a postcard of 1910. The bones of what was probably a mature male AMHS were sold to the Royal Prussian Museum in Berlin, which was bombed in the Second World War. They were retrieved from the ruins in 1955, but the skull had already been taken by the Russians and has never been returned.

Although deemed 'lost to science', the bones from the Combe Capelle skeleton were reanalysed by Bernd Hermann. His fascin-ating conclusions, published in German in the Berlin excavation round-up for 1972, have never attracted the professional atten-tion they deserve. Here are, without doubt, the remains of a person who was violently killed with a series of brutal cuts and stabs, after which muscles were systematically removed from his long bones (interpreted by Hermann as evidence of cannibalism). No long bones were split to remove marrow and the corpse was not systematically butchered like an animal. There are resonances of Sima de los Huesos here, where, between 300,000 and 200,000 years ago, thousands of cut-marked *Homo heidelbergensis* bones were deliberately deposited in a cave shaft in the earliest death rite we know. At Combe Capelle, however, there was just one individual, formally buried.[20]

The earliest burials indicate a fetishization of a body, pointedly excluded from the normal cycle. This exclusion made the corpse special but not, as has usually been assumed, in a directly positive way. I believe it entailed ritual behaviour of the sort described in the Old Testament book of Leviticus: 'Aaron shall lay both his hands upon the head of the live goat, and confess over him all the iniquities of the children of Israel, and all their trans-gressions in all their sins ... and he shall let go the goat in the wilderness'. Scapegoating has a long history and it may have an even longer prehistory.

In his classic book, *Violence and the Sacred*, René Girard argues that scapegoating a human, and especially an innocent, can break the cycle of revenge killings that can so easily become established between two communities. It is 'an act of violence without risk of vengeance',[21] and can serve to bring a vicious circle of retaliation to an end by diverting its spirit into other channels. Among the shamanic Chukchi, reindeer hunters of north-east Siberia, people often averted feuds by killing a member of their own family. As Girard puts it, 'by offering a victim to their potential enemies they enjoin them not to seek vengeance, not to commit an act that would constitute a fresh affront and oblige the other side to seek further retribution. This expiatory procedure brings to mind the sacrificial process; the fact that the victim is someone other than the guilty party drives the resemblance home.'[22] The theologian Fergus Kerr has usefully summarized Girard's overall argument as follows:

> In wide-ranging investigations of classical and modern literature ... Girard has gradually reached the conviction that the stability of any society is maintained by the periodic expulsion of an often quite arbitrarily chosen victim. Every group suffers from internal tensions; one member of the group becomes the focus of everyone else's frustration. He becomes the alien who threatens the community, but, since expelling him restores peace and harmony, apparently, for a time, he also appears as a saviour. Anger and desire are thus equally lodged in this 'scapegoat'.[23]

I believe that the Combe Capelle individual was killed as a scapegoat. If we set this against a long-term background of cannibalism, then those deemed fit to eat were those who were either part of the community or part of someone else's. This man's violent death, the partial eating of his corpse and the separating off of his bones through burial all express degrees of emotional ambiguity: 'Because the victim is sacred, it is criminal to kill him – but the victim is sacred only because he is to be killed.'[24] But there is perhaps something else at Combe Capelle, even more atavistic than what Girard identified. The philosopher Martin Heidegger says that 'Along with the certainty of death goes the *indefiniteness* of its "when."' This uncertainty leads us into a kind of habitual, tense, unconscious denial.[25] This may provide an emotional logic for controlled killings of many kinds. By dictating its time and manner, communities relieve anxiety and domesticate death.

The idea of burying the dead can now be seen as the opposite of cannibalism. Alongside the edible dead who were absorbed were the toxic dead who were isolated. The first uneaten burials, placed in caves either whole or in bits and pieces, were ostracized. Caves, with no dawn or dusk, are a symbolic limbo. I think of these first burials of the Mousterian, with partial bodies and few grave goods, as 'isolating'. They are more characteristic of the Neanderthals than the modern humans from this same Middle Palaeolithic period, but they occur among both. They do not show cut marks, and any elaboration – flowers, antlers, and so on – is part of a magic aimed at keeping scavengers, whether people or animals, away from these bodies and body parts so that they cannot be reabsorbed, transformed and given cosmic posterity. The people may have been prototypical scapegoats. Their location after death in the timeless space of caves echoes and emphasizes their exclusion from the normal cycle of life and death.

Things as dramatic as Skhūl or Shanidar or Combe Capelle cannot, eventually be contained. They have their own material force which may in the end rebound on those who planned them. This is one of the most fascinating aspects of human material culture – it gains inertia and begins to kick back against its creators, creating unintended new realities. The reabsorbtive act of funerary cannibalism may have long kept any categorical recognition of the inevitability of death at bay. Ingestion, by whatever means and in whatever circumstances, mops up the mortal trail, leaving little material record not just for archaeologists but – more significantly – for the early human communities themselves. The move to burial began to memorialize death, even if its first candidates were victims of their community's need to maintain solidarity in the face of mundane conflicts and existential fears.

Combe Capelle combined isolation and absorption in a single choreographic rite. The man was both partially eaten and partially isolated, fulfilling Girard's idea of an alienated saviour, provoking both anger and desire, and standing on the threshold of the far more complex societies and sophisticated symbolism that were about to come.

The three people at Dolní Věstonice were not buried in a cave. The rite of interment took place in the open, in the heart of the settlement. The ceremony would have had a large audience and the place would have been marked afterwards. The completeness and articulation of the skeletons suggest that the three people died at around the same time (rather than one or more of them being stored in advance of a multiple interment). The causes of death are unknown, in the absence of any fatal skeletal traumas. A natural cause, such as a contagious disease, is possible, but takes no account of the stake in the pelvis and fails to explain the postures. An alternative possibility, taking account of their similar ages, is a social contagion – something that the killing of the three, by means such as ritual poisoning, could have been designed to combat.

The Dolní Věstonice triple burial suggests two events: the death, perhaps killing, of the three individuals, separated by an intermediary period from the dramatic burial. Elaborate care had to be taken to make sure the bodies were posable: rigor mortis, which would have moved the three out of their carefully choreographed positions must have been allowed to wear off (a variable period, but two to three days would be normal), and there is a strong possibility that the bodies were either kept for longer or deliberately vented to stop the normal gaseous post-mortem expansion of the viscera which otherwise would certainly have moved the hands of the man on the left out of their position reaching into the central female's crotch (they could not, conversely, have moved into this position because of post-mortem swelling).

The range of animal bones at Dolní Věstonice indicates that hidework was something of a speciality. One of the most striking things about the three skulls is the state of their teeth, which were strongly worn down because the people used their mouths to grip leather, pulling it taut as they used ochre to cure it and awls to sew it into clothing. If animal hide could be prepared then there is a strong chance that these techniques were used to preserve human skin. Red ochre, which arrests bacterial attack on animal hides, did not just create the dramatic decorative crusted face masks but played a part in the stabilization – effectively the embalming – of the corpses.

Only when the preparation of the corpses was complete – when the three were probably arrayed in elaborate costumes and posed in the shallow grave – could the theatrical ritual commence. The final phase seems to have involved covering of the bodies with branches which were then set alight, not so much cremating the bodies as searing them (a rite which, as we shall see in the next chapter, has close parallels in eighteenth- and nineteenth-century vampire burials in Transylvania). Here was physical death followed by social death, in two distinct events. At Dolní Věstonice we can see for the first time, I believe, the emergence of the secondary rites although – curiously enough – no need yet for primary ones or a distinct liminal period between. The killing was ceremonial, but the freshly dead bodies were not dangerous, as the spirit was not embarking on any journey to a world of ancestors.

If the three had violated some precious distinction or taboo, then chaos might have threatened the fragile body politic of the Ice Age hunters. This implies perhaps some action of their own, and I speculated in *The Prehistory of Sex* about possible sexual transgressions. The symbolic (and often linguistic) equation of beds with graves is recognized in many cultures, and the positioning of the three in their shared grave retains a symbolic power that still hints at improper relations over 25,000 years later. While it would be perverse to ignore such potent symbolism, it does not necessarily bring us any closer to understanding the specific nature of the transgression. There could have been issues of incest, adultery, reproductive dysfunction, or even all three, but the ultimate and underlying transgression may have been essentially passive.

The idea that similarity provoked the deaths at Dolní Věstonice may seem at first to be a preposterous and wild speculation, but there are grounds for believing that the three people may not have been individual enough.[26] Their similarity to one another – male twins perhaps, and a sister whose pelvis was narrow and dysfunctional, all three of similar age and stature, with closely similar facial anatomy – could have threatened the idea of distinction itself, the concept that lies at the heart of all cultural order.

One of Girard's most remarkable insights is that the existence of twins, which is often not tolerated in tribal societies, does not so much hamper logistics and social classifications (two people arriving where one was expected) as erode the concept of distinguishability and so presage chaos. Twins are thus harbingers of violence: 'the disappearance of natural differences can . . . bring to mind the dissolution of regulations pertaining to the individuals' proper place in society'. Similarity is not restricted to twins, of course, and Girard goes on to point out that phobia of physical resemblance is a fact in many societies.

The pioneer social anthropologist, Bronislaw Malinowski, caused problems in the Trobriand Islands when he pointed out the resemblance between a visitor and a man in the village where he was staying. The visitor was in fact the man's brother. Malinowski writes:

> I had commited . . . 'taputaki migila,' a technical expression referring only to this act, which might be translated: 'to-defile-by-comparing-to-a-kinsman-his-face.' What astonished me in this discussion was, that in spite of the striking resemblance between the two brothers, my informants refused to admit it . . . I made my informants quite angry by arguing the point.[27]

Similarities between children and their father were accepted, but because the father was considered to be the 'bearer of difference' the heresy of pointing out that similarity to the father implied similarity among siblings was always 'indignantly repudiated'.

It would be highly speculative to apply such ideas to the triple burial at Dolní Věstonice if it could not be shown to form part of some broader pattern. For an Ice Age society such as this to deliberately lose three precious members through an act of scapegoating or sacrifice would imply currents of belief so powerful that they should show up elsewhere.

As it happens, the Dolní Věstonice triple burial is not the only multiple burial of the period from 27,000 to 23,000 years ago. Others include a triple burial from Barma Grande in the Italian Grimaldi caves, and double burials at Sungir, north-east of Moscow and in the rock shelter of Romito in southern Italy. The three Barma Grande individuals show vertebral osteophytosis with one of them (Barma Grande 2) displaying bilateral asymmetry in the upper limbs. The Romito burial contained the male skeleton of a dramatically chondrodystrophic dwarf and an older female, possibly his mother, who, despite having normal proportions, was extremely small.

In all these burials the individuals are matched in some way. At Barma Grande, the three people look remarkably similar – and they all face east, nested one behind the other as if they had all rolled over the same way in a big bed. At Sungir the two adolescent boys are well matched for stature and their burial, head to head, could not be more neatly symmetrical if a mirror had been placed at one end of a single interment. At Romito the congenital dwarf has been matched by an adult without – in our terms – any congenital condition, who is nevertheless the same height.[28]

I do not want to say that the pretext for all Middle Upper Palaeolithic (MUP) burials was a crisis of distinction, but that they do all represent something more than isolation, a thing we might term the 'Theatre of Transgression'. Being too similar to someone else was one kind of transgression, breaking down essential cultural distinctions. Being a physical intermediate could have been another. It may be significant that the only burial from this period known from Portugal (Abrigo do Lagar Velho) is of a child who is considered to be a hybrid between modern humans and Neanderthals and so, perhaps, someone whose appearance elided an important cultural and species boundary.[29] Many other skeletons from the period show physical disfigurement, such as the histiocytosis X of one of the famous Cro Magnon skeletons and the chronic degenerative disease in the ribcage of the Ohalo 2 skeleton.[30]

Sadly, we can say nothing about the health status of two dozen burials from Pavlov II, the settlement site which forms the continuation of Dolní Věstonice. These bones were completely destroyed during the Second World War when fire broke out in the nearby museum in Mikulov Castle. Nevertheless, the high percentage of MUP burials with dramatic afflictions, coupled with the fact that, as in the preceding Mousterian, there is absolutely no reason to suppose that burial was the normal funerary rite, strongly suggests that burial was used only for a subset of people. Only around 150 burials dating to this period are known in the whole of Europe, yet 'stray' human bones are more or less abundant, scattered and fragmented in the occupation layers of settlement sites.

In the 'Theatre of Transgression' individuals may not have been 'transgressors' in any sense we can easily understand, but were singled out by virtue either of shared similarity or congenital abnormality, or for behavioural reasons, or because the circumstances of their natural deaths were deemed inauspicious or frightening. There is probably no single specific reason, yet it is clear that in death they represent a genre – a carefully filtered section of the communities to which they belonged and from which they were ultimately excluded.

For Middle Upper Palaeolithic communities to maintain population sizes of 100 or more, with an integrated system of long-distance trade and the production of virtuosic art, they may have needed not just the tension-reducing scapegoating mechanisms used by the smaller, Mousterian groups of the preceding Middle Palaeolithic period, but the beginning of a rule of law and the elaboration of convention. The Middle Upper Palaeolithic was a time of marked environmental fluctuations coupled with increased population densities and the emergence of complex networks of raw material exchange. Jiří Svoboda and his collaborators say that the novelty of the Pavlovian societies lay in their capacity to remain stable in such a rapidly changing world.[31]

It is perhaps poetic justice that these bones were caught up in the carnage of the retreating Wehrmacht during the Second World War. The baroque façades of the town of Mikulov have seen ostracism and violence in the name of cultural distinction more recently. On the surface, order and civilization. The smoothly rounded profile of the nearest hill, the Heiliger Berg or 'Holy Mountain', a small southern outlier of the Pavlov massif, forms a theatrical backdrop to the elegant little cobbled square and is surmounted by the gleaming white Byzantine church of Svatý kopeček. The church is a place of pilgrimage, reached by a processional route that winds up via sixteen chapels. The same number of synagogues once punctuated the network of backstreets in the town below. Only one remains, on Husova Street, and that is now a gallery – shut when I visited. The Jewish cemetery lies unused since the Munich agreement of 1938 saw the Nazi annexation of Czech lands.

Communities scapegoat individuals and classes of individuals, sacrificing the few, and even the many, to revitalize the solidarity of the majority in acts that have a continued resonance. The Jews were once German too, but now we say that the Germans exterminated the Jews.

To become *persona non grata* one needs first to have a *persona*. It may seem obvious that individuals such as Shanidar 1 or Combe Capelle had personalities but they did not yet belong to classes: they were not reduced to stock types as the Jews of Mikulov were, until much later. But the emergence of isolation burial led people towards a new way of creating and enforcing social rules in a pattern that extends onwards to the bog bodies and beyond. Aberrance was not exclusively physical, but predominantly social, labelled and brought into being through the Theatre of Transgression burials themselves. These not only fulfilled but created their objective.

When Ralph Solecki published *Shanidar: The First Flower People*, he thought he could detect the advent of a new society that was both religious and caring. In their standard textbook, Jurmain and Nelson caption a picture of the Shanidar 1 burial with the question; 'Does he represent Neandertal compassion for the handicapped?', which they answer by quoting the conclusion of two eminent palaeoanthropologists, Eric Trinkaus and Pat Shipman: 'a one-armed, partially blind, crippled man could have made no pretense of hunting or gathering his own food. That he survived for years after his trauma was a testament to Neandertal compassion and humanity.'[32]

The disabled Neanderthal man known as Shanidar 1 may have been kept alive following his initial debilitating injuries for reasons other than compassion. The existential 'benefits' of living mysteries – participants in freak shows, walled-up nuns or the people who sit for ever on top of high poles – cannot be lightly dismissed. As tableaux they bring home the fact that no one among us can escape either from the world or from our body, however we live. But there is comfort in conformity, and the realities of other lives can make those of the majority seem so much more attractive.

Of course, Shanidar 1 may have been required to work hard too. Today in many parts of the world disabled people are still set to routine tasks because their status is low and they lack alternatives. There is no reason to suppose that the desperate arthritis of the Shanidar 1 male would not have been exacerbated by his compulsory duties. When his end came, whether natural or not, he was singled out for special treatment, not necessarily because he was positively special but perhaps because he was negatively so. His burial enhanced solidarity by highlighting the fact that, despite their inevitable daily frictions, the other members of the Shanidar community shared something precious.

This is not the caring society of 'first flower people' that Solecki wanted it to be. It was not flaky, hippie or (necessarily) compassionate: it was ruthlessly cohesive.

Our ancestors were efficient killers. Aesthetic and deftly engineered wooden spears, found preserved at Schöningen in Germany, show that hunting was highly organized by at least 400,000 years ago. The tip-end of each spear was carved from near the base of a young spruce trunk, where the wood is hardest, and each has its centre of gravity a third of the way back, just as in a modern Olympic javelin.[33] These are interpreted as spears for hunting animals, but they could also have been used in conflicts between groups. As our human ancestors became more adept at hunting large animals with their consummately designed wooden spears, they were able to plan death in advance and unleash it at distance.

Their strategic and temporal abilities eventually found form in permanent aesthetic achievements, such as the fantastic polychrome paintings of horses, bison and deer in the cave of Altamira near Santander on the northern Spanish coast. In Jacob Bronowski's words, these express 'the power of anticipation: the forward-looking imagination' in art.[34]

At Dolní Věstonice things were organized in classes: stone tools and weapons, statues, beads. Burials were a new sort of thing – installations that mixed what had been living and was now dead with that which had been dead and, through culture, carving, painting or engraving, had been brought to life. One of the most remarkable finds from the Pavlov culture (and one of the most disconcertingly modern prehistoric artefacts I have ever seen) is an ivory marionette from Brno, comprising three anatomical elements with perforations for articulating them with sinew or nettle-twine. The puppet theatre of Prague comes to mind as one looks, amazed, at the separate head, torso, and one surviving arm, of a little man who would originally have been 30 centimetres or so high and who could have been made to dance. Dead mammoth, transformed into something human and posable has its counterpart in dead human, transformed with fox teeth into who knows what kind of entity, equally posable.

There is a sense of freezing time in all of this, and the Ice Age was, *par excellence*, a freezing environment. The people of the Pavlovian would, inevitably, have come across animals perfectly preserved but dead in glaciers. When they began to ceremonially bury their dead in such a way that, not only could they not be eaten or disaggregated, but the living would thereafter know who they were, they were extending this natural idea of cold permanence into the cultural understanding of death.

'Isolating' burials were elaborated by the Middle Upper Palaeolithic modern human populations in Europe into the Theatre of Transgression seen at Dolní Věstonice where an armoury of props was used not to ostracize and eventually forget, but to label and memorialize the transgressive in death. The community made space in their living world for those who no longer existed. But if that sounds quite like modern burial in a contemporary cemetery, we have to think again. This was not permanence for all, because they buried only some of their dead. We are not talking about a variation on a well-known theme (like the modern alternatives of burial, cremation, or burial at sea), but about the burial of an extremely small proportion of the population. The funerary rite for the majority remains a mystery, but any assumption that it was the leaders of communities who were singled out for a special place in memory does not fit the evidence (that pattern emerges much later, among the early urban civilizations).

Although, at first, burials operated in a very limited way, they had far-reaching effects. They told the living that this was how they would be if they fulfilled or, conversely, failed to meet certain conditions. At the same time, the creation of permanent emplacements, which certain people were excluded *to*, had the effect of generating a feeling that these people had not really gone. Memory of where and how they lay was what made the Theatre of Transgression effective as a form of social control, but it also conferred a more nebulous and positive sense of immortality.

The dynamic was a forced one. It was born of intense inter-group competition, as early modern humans and Neanderthals vied for access to resources in difficult, changing environments. Although bad luck could bring failure, consistent success was not down to chance. These communities needed to be cohesive. Long before laws could have been put in writing, ethics may already have been arising out of the apprehension of personal mortality: death as the ultimate limit suggested other limits. Before long, burial was adopted for more positive statements and became a luxury that everyone aspired to. Only those whom no one cared about were left to the animals and the hungry.

CHAPTER 9

An Unexpected Vampire

... not many people at his funeral knew him well enough to feel as bad as they knew they ought to. They went to be sociable. The few who wept did it out of custom and because they didn't want to pass up the opportunity.

GARRISON KEILLOR, *Lake Wobegon Days*[1]

———

Tiny shards of black volcanic glass glinted against the patches of red-brown earth as I walked across the great prehistoric settlement mound. The sharp obsidian was brought here 8–9,000 years ago, across the plain from the Hasan Dag volcano, to be worked into knives and arrowheads at Catalhöyük. I knew that everywhere beneath me were unmarked Neolithic burials, embedded in the floors of the collapsed mud-brick houses that have yet to be excavated. But I was looking for something more recent. Coming down the east side of the mound, with Turkey's Konya Plain stretching to the horizon, I saw, poking up out of the sun-baked tangle of brown grass, a pinkish gravestone.

The inscription read: HU MERHUME-HUSEYIN KIZI GULLU AYŞA RUHUNA FAT IHA 22/2/1933: 'Pray for the soul of her, the daughter of Huseyin named Ayşa, who has died 22/2/1933.' Osman, a middle-aged man from the nearby village of Küçükköy, told me Ayşa's story, via an interpreter, as it had been passed down to him.[2] Küçükköy simply means 'little village'

Catalhöyük: Ayşa's gravestone with the Neolithic mound rising in the background. (Photo: author)

and was Ayşa's home. In her time, she – as Osman phrased it – 'danced in the rooms for men and did everything', for which she earned money. As she lay dead some people wanted to take her gold teeth but she screamed at them and they recoiled.

I was told that the reason for her burial at Catalhöyük was that the village had been planning a new cemetery. Ayşa's was to be the first burial in it; but after she was buried, the abandonment and consequent demolition of a house adjacent to the old cemetery solved the space problem and left her isolated. She was not allowed to rest in peace. Not long after her interment, her grave was desecrated and her gold teeth successfully removed.

Before beginning his story, Osman had apologized for the fact that he might not be able to contain his feelings. His sentences were punctuated with short hisses which I took to be signs that he disapproved of what had been done. To understand more of what happened and the story now told about it, we have to appreciate the dramatic change in attitudes towards death that began to occur between 15,000 and 10,000 years ago. It was in this period that the Ice Age finally came to an end.

Part of the effect of the earliest burial was unexpected. Although the rite was initially understood in negative terms, as an exclusion from normal death rites, it created a physical memorial of sorts. By degrees, the idea of permanence arose – the feeling that those who had been frozen out of the cosmic cycle at the back of caves were somehow still there. The places where burials first took place gained a sense of being haunted. The uneaten, still articulated bones, suggested their counterpart – a skeletal personality, an active yet invisible being, who also remained in some way articulate. It became important that this disembodied soul should be found a place to live, and the idea of this place being a new body, magically constituted on some other plane of existence, took shape. In Europe during the Late Upper Palaeolithic or Magdalenian period – 15,000 years ago – the burial position of the few who were chosen for interment became uniformly foetal for the first time, as if the earth had become a womb from which some kind of resurrection was expected.

Some of the new Mesolithic communities who had settled into a more sedentary way of life by the sea now chose to bury their dead in small cemeteries, invoking a symbolism that went beyond the limited and negative context of the Theatre of Transgression. At Skateholm in Denmark, old men in antler head-dresses and a dead child laid out poignantly on a swan's wing are among sixty-five individuals buried over a 200-year period around 5000 BC.[3]

Each grave at Skateholm appears to represent a verdict. It seems possible even now to distinguish between those who were well thought of and those whom the others were glad to see the back of: one adult male was buried face down and arrows were fired into the earth as if to fix him there. The community owned some of the first domesticated dogs and eight have their own graves in the cemetery, with red ochre in their pelvic and head regions, just like many of the humans. Mature in years and with skeletons displaying no signs of violence, these dogs seem not to have been sacrifices but honorary members of the community, buried at the end of their natural span of years.

Further south, with the end of the Ice Age, the climate of the eastern Mediterranean became warmer and drier and the wild plants of the Levant, native wheat and barley, oak, almond and pistachio, started to colonize ever higher ground. These plants produced an abundance of highly predictable and easily stored foods (acorns are easily leached of their bitter tannins and can be ground into a palatable flour). Glacial meltwaters flooded parts of the coastal plain, dramatically reducing the extent of the richest hunting grounds. The Natufian communities, who inhabited Jordan at this time, were torn between securing access to wild cereals and tree crops as part of their seasonal movement through the landscape, and maintaining their control of the ever more valuable surviving lowlands, where they killed gazelle.

Competition and conflict grew between increasingly squeezed communities and, as population rose, the dead were deployed in the service of the living. The Natufians started to make use of the presumption of the latent power of disembodied souls, less forceful than living people in most circumstances, but invisible and unpredictable. Clusters of burials began to appear on open air sites in the lands bordering the eastern Mediterranean. They contained not the ostracized or transgressive dead, but the upstanding and reliable majority, who had completed a significant journey to arrive in their graves. Aspects of the rite of passage, so familiar from later anthropology, are detectable at this point: the Natufian culture shows unambiguous secondary burial at sites like Ain Mallaha, with the body kept for a time before permanent interment.[4]

The clearly marked graves were a territorial statement designed to ward off rival communities. No longer isolated, the soul had joined others in the collective World of Ancestors which was thought of not as a distant place but as a staked-out part of the real world – strategically situated to shield and designate the ownership of real resources (hunting lands, cereal stands and tree crops). From this time on, no group could launch an attack on another without considering that they were also assaulting the dead. To protect or attack the community would entail planning on both a material and a supernatural level.[5]

The next step occurred around 8000 BC when the hunter-gatherers at Abu Hureyra and Jericho in Jordan, who already lived in permanent year-round settlements, found that instead of striving to ring-fence the vulnerable cereal harvest of the uplands, they could gather the wild crops and sow their seed in the nearby floodplain. This unusually fertile earth sustained no permanent vegetation because it was under water for several months each year. By sowing at the start of the dry season, gathering in, and resowing seed corn as the floods subsided, the Jericho community created a reliable new source of valuable food. Their discovery ushered in the economic revolution known as the Neolithic. Farming spread first to Anatolia and later to Europe; its dramatic implications remain with us today.

There are few places in the world where an archaeologist can stand inside a Neolithic room, and probably nowhere other than Catalhöyük where the walls still rise above your head, their white lime-plaster finish almost as bright now as when it was fresh. Moving with great care on the soft, damp floor, I took in the strange subterranean feel which stemmed not from the fact that I had climbed down into a deep archaeological excavation, but from the fact that this was how the Neolithic people had experienced their houses too. Entry had always been from above: I could still make out the steep diagonal scar where the left-hand rail of the access ladder had rested against the side wall.

Catalhöyük at its height had comprised several hundred mud-brick and plaster houses, built cheek by jowl in a constant occupation lasting 1,700 years. As houses fell into disrepair, they were filled in with mud-brick rubble and old plaster. The sun-baked building materials crumbled naturally and the remains were easily levelled. New houses were constructed above them, starting a process of elevation which meant that, while the first village was at the same height as the plain, by the time the settlement

227

*Catalhöyük: the author standing within one of the excavated houses.
(Photo: Alex Hansen)*

was finally abandoned it formed an impressive artificial mound, visible from many kilometres away. The earliest archaeological excavations, in the early 1960s, revealed fourteen levels of houses, their collapsed plans superimposed one on top of another; more layers have since been discovered, the earliest and deepest dating to 7200 BC.[6]

The careful removal of soil, rubble and ancient refuse has revealed the groundplans of the Neolithic houses, each with a main room from which led off two or three small store rooms, accessed by small crawl-holes. There were never any exterior doors because the houses were built up against each other. Although there were no party walls, the gaps between buildings were almost non-existent. The flat roofs formed a near-continuous surface, strong enough to walk on, that served as a public space during the day. The interior walls of the houses were often painted with scenes in red and black and some had elaborate sculptural reliefs. The most striking fixtures are the plaster-covered *bucrania* (the actual heads and horns) of great

228

Catalhöyük: the inside of a house with bucrania, *as reconstructed in Ankara Museum. (Photo: author)*

wild aurochs, the forest cattle that were still hunted to augment a diet of the staples provided by domesticated animals and cultivated plants.

In these homes, the dead and the living shared space. After death, the bodies were first exposed. It has been suggested that they could have been picked clean by vultures, as happens today in the Zoroastrian 'Towers of Silence' in Bombay. But although vultures are depicted alongside decapitated human forms in some of the murals, they are prone to tear and carry off entire bodies and, at Catalhöyük, mostly it was intact corpses that were buried.

In what corresponds to the rite of incorporation, the dead were wrapped in mats and lowered into holes dug down into the sleeping platforms (the slightly raised sections of floor that abutted the main walls of the living rooms within each house). The living slept, had sex and gave birth over the skeletons of their dead ancestors.

Catalhöyük is a classic example of the new farming economy and the new fashion in funerary practice that went with it. Unlike in the cemetery at Skateholm, where each person was individualized in death, in the great artificial mound on the Konya Plain there were, with very few exceptions, just two types of burial. There is clear spatial segregation, with women and children under the sleeping platforms on the north-east side of the square rooms and men towards the south or south-east side.

Female burials were accompanied by polished black obsidian mirrors, part of a display of stereotyped sex differences in death which suggests that a segregated afterlife was envisaged (as we already know it was much later, in the Odinic ritual of the Rus), zoned very much like the world of the living, with activity areas

Catalhöyük: sleeping platform with the dead buried beneath it.
(Photo: author)

appropriate to women and children on the one hand, and adult men on the other. People were first representatives of their gender and only secondly individuals. This symbolic division mirrors the real-life dietary segregation suggested by a new study of skeletons. Analysis at the isotopic level shows that men had more access to wild meat while women ate more of the new domestic produce.[7]

As death so often mirrors birth in its symbolism, the placing of both male and female dead under the beds at Catalhöyük may have been as much about controlling them as revering them. Relief sculptures of birth-giving 'goddesses' are moulded on some of the walls and the most famous find from the entire site is a clay statuette of a burly woman, seated on a throne whose arm-rests are in the form of panthers, with a newborn child's head appearing from between her legs. It is unsurprising that interest in birth is expressed in stark terms in the art and symbolic architecture of the site. The power of reproduction among both humans and animals was central to the success of the new economy, but the idea that Neolithic societies were ruled over by peaceful matriarchs – widely mooted in some popular archaeological literature – can be ruled out. Birth-giving goddesses no more indicate the political power of women as a class than the much later iconography of the Virgin and Child did in Catholic Europe.

The striking symbolism of the 'vulture goddess' at Catalhöyük, which apparently extended to the modelling of clay breasts with nipples formed from vulture beaks,[8] suggests that the point of separation between mothers and children was tense. It is a typical feature of warlike societies that weaning is made into a combat which the child loses, internalizing a pool of aggression that can be drawn on in later life. If weaning involved an aggressive struggle, imposing greater independence on the unwilling child, death could have been seen in similar terms. The deceased were not expected to give up the comforts of the domestic hearth without a fight.

The death rites were a forced separation in which corpses were weighed down not just with layers of clay but with the vital and assertive bodies of the living. It is clear from the design of the houses, with their peculiar roof access, that children, and even adults, could have been easily contained against their will, either by the removal of the ladder or by closing some trapdoor. The dead were spatially (and perhaps symbolically) at an even lower level, contained not just by a roof above them, but by a floor too. Yet the position of the dead was also powerful. As each new phase of mud-brick building was physically supported by the buildings of the past, so the living were spiritually supported, or even psychically dominated, by the layered presence of the dead beneath them. At Jericho, the dead were also placed under the floors of houses: there, their skulls were coated in the fertile mud, given cowrie-shell eyes, and cached like seed corn in storage pits.

This was when the earth first began to be widely seen as 'Mother Earth', providing a womb into which the dead could be placed like seeds, awaiting a new spring. The dramatic changes in mortuary symbolism that occurred at the start of the Neolithic period expressed a deeper revolution, in metaphysical understanding. In many societies in the South Pacific, where farming was adopted in much more recent times, myths about 'man's loss of immortality' and 'how death came into the world' are intimately linked to the discovery of horticulture.[9] They hint at what I believe the prehistoric archaeology of the Near East shows us, that before the, initially accidental, memorialization that burial promoted, most human groups saw death as process rather than state – a moment in a timeless cycle of physical and spiritual renewal. The creation of a Neolithic company of ancestors was connected to investment in the earth, expanding lineages and inheritance. Where land had once been limitlessly interconnected, hedges, fences, ditches and boundaries were created to protect the fields. The planting of the dead in them was a final act of colonization – a literal and a metaphysical composting that would promote future fertility.[10]

Burial became a normal rite, and eating the dead less acceptable. The shift from direct consumption towards indirect absorption (such as burial under an apple tree, as in contemporary Montana) had begun. Burying one's own dead, in ground that had been cleared and tilled and sweated for, expressed lineage, territoriality, ownership, and the power of a World of Ancestors to guarantee a prosperous future. But the facts of vegetative germination naturally suggested an intermediary period. The dry seed, placed in the ground, would not be reborn without the powers, or 'gods' of sun and rain exerting themselves in correct measure. Similarly, the gods' approval was needed for the dead to be reborn.

This change coincided with a change in the way animals were thought about. The big game hunters of the Ice Age glorified their prey in skilful cave paintings and ivory carvings; the pursuit of particular animals could become the stuff of stories and even myth. But, at the time of the ritual killing of the man at Combe Capelle, there is no evidence that animals were sacrificed – they did not yet belong within the human community and so could not be offered up. Once farming began, animals who had been captive from birth were killed at will. Lambs and calves, which had been warmed and fed by the domestic hearth in winter, were destined to be hung in blackened sausages over the fire. The timetables of life and death were drawn up, and there were few deviations. To compensate for the loss of the drama that the hunt had previously provided, and maybe to distract the mind from the guilt attendant on the latent hypocrisy of the juxtaposed nurture and predation that maintaining a domestic herd entailed, some animals were chosen for a higher and ritual death.[11]

Farming led to civilization and large villages like Catalhöyük were succeeded by cities. In Mesopotamia, great temple ziggurats and royal storehouses were constructed. Defensive walls went up and beyond them, over the plains, irrigation systems were installed to serve vast new farmlands. In Egypt, civilization relied on the essential seasonal flooding of the Nile, around which a complex religion of cosmic death and rebirth was constructed. Some of the most elaborate provisions for a journey to the World of Ancestors were made by the Egyptians.

When he opened the tomb of the boy Pharaoh Tutankhamun in 1922, Howard Carter discovered a potent symbol of vegetative regeneration. Stowed under chests and model ships was a box that contained an 'Osiris bed' – a seed tray in the cut-out shape of the god Osiris, whose cult focused on life after death. Nearly life size, it had been filled with a thin layer of clear quartz sand from the bed of the Nile and into this barley had been sown. When Carter opened the box and unwrapped the bed he found that all of the grains had germinated in the dark and the seedlings had grown about 8 centimetres before withering.[12]

Civilization also meant specialization. Priests and bureaucrats emerged within the social divisions served by scribes. Above them was the king and below them the artisanal classes, the peasants and, at the bottom, the slaves. Food production became an industry. The first known disposable fast-food containers – single-use clay vessels that provided a meal portion for the construction workers – have been discovered in the foundation trenches of the ziggurat at Ur.[13] Meat was prepared by butchers and as these people became inured to suffering others became insulated from it: as the novelist Thomas Pynchon so memorably puts it: 'Cities begin upon the day the walls of the Shambles go up, to screen away Blood and Blood-letting, Animals' Cries, Smells and Soil, from residents already grown fragile before Country Realities'.[14]

Animal sacrifices joined human sacrifices in sanctifying and thus validating the foundation of the earliest states. Both demonstrated control of death and production. A hierarchy was projected upwards from the apex of the living – the priest-king. The royal ancestors were now transformed into the first gods in human form and were fed on the burning vapours of animal and human blood. Although the cemeteries of the first farmers had been essentially inclusive, urban civilization reasserted the human tendency towards ranking and distinction: citizenship of the necropolis – the 'city of the dead' – was as exclusive as citizenship of the city of the living. For the non-royal, the only way into the royal cemetery at Ur was as a ritually killed retainer.

The exclusionary power of cemeteries remains strong today. Outside the gates of Montparnasse cemetery in Paris, a bronze angel with outspread wings bears the legend SOUVENIR – to remember. On the surface, this is an injunction to remember the dead. But when one walks among the family vaults and the busts of famous artists, politicians, scientists and philosophers, the feeling grows that one should remember, above all, that these are Parisian dead and that they are at home. This city for the dead legitimizes a city of the living. 'Souvenir' is a reminder that one is a stranger.

The English war poet, Rupert Brooke, wrote in 1914, 'If I should die, think only this of me: / That there's some corner of a foreign field / That is for ever England.' The great war cemeteries of Belgium and France, containing mostly the bodies of British servicemen, were created at a time when cremation was rapidly gaining in popularity in Britain. There was a convenience factor: on this scale interment was probably easier to arrange. But the territorial symbolism of potentially fertile land unavailable for use by the living local inhabitants for centuries to come cannot be ignored.

Despite the massive cemeteries, by the end of the First World War over 500,000 British corpses were unidentifiable or wholly missing. These dead were commemorated by the Whitehall cenotaph in London and by 25,000 war memorials in their home towns and villages.[15] Physical disappearance in times of conflict, often deliberately achieved (as in conflicts in Chile, Northern Ireland or Iraq) so that the relatives do not know where their dead are, is not just a modern problem. The people in the mass graves recently discovered in central Europe at Talheim, Asparn/ Schletz and other sites dating to the Neolithic period (mentioned in the Introduction) appear to have been massacred. If there were any left to mourn these 'disappeared', they may have conducted funerary rites in the absence of the corpses.

Where a head would have been, crude clay masks have been modelled into the base of some of the graves at the Varna cemetery on the Black Sea in Bulgaria. There is nothing under them

– no actual body. The masks are variously adorned with golden earrings and elaborate head-dresses, and many were given a small flat, beaten gold, T-shaped face mask. These 'cenotaph' burials date to 4500 BC and are part of a spectacular cemetery of around 300 graves from the turn of the Neolithic and Bronze Ages (the short-lived 'Copper Age'). Nearly a quarter of the graves contain no bones at all.[16]

The phenomenon is seen to continue, as the Bronze Age gets into full swing around 2200 BC, at the cemetery of Nitra in south-western Slovakia. Men and women were found buried in individual graves, dug in an east–west direction, but with their heads lying in opposite directions, suggesting resurrection to different realms, women arising to face the rising sun and men to see it setting.[17] But in six graves there are only grave goods to suggest that the head would have lain to the east, the male direction: the bodies are absent. The prevalence of healed injuries among the intact skeletons in this cemetery suggests regular conflict which people often survived – a pattern consistent with slave-raiding, where the Talheim-style massacre of an entire target community would have been counter-productive. It is quite possible that the empty graves were dug to remember those who did not return.

Cenotaph graves are not for people who were necessarily physically dead, but for those deemed socially dead. In Georgi Vladimov's satire on Soviet Russia, seen through the eyes of a camp guard dog, *Faithful Ruslan*, the principal human protagonist, 'the Shabby Man' is drafted in 1940 for the Finnish War, taken prisoner by the Germans in the Second World War, imprisoned on his return to Russia in 1945, put into the gulag system of 'corrective labour camps', and finally released in the winter of 1956–7 along with eight million other prisoners.[18]

These things really happened, and while those imprisoned by Stalin for a specifically political offence were 'rehabilitated' (given the right to proper housing and reinstatement in an appropriate job), the former German POWs were given a blanket amnesty, without right of restitution. That is, they were let out of the camp gates in Siberia without money, civilian clothes, travel tickets, organized jobs or help of any sort. The Shabby Man moves in with a local woman, Stiura, and says to her 'Supposing I did go back, and I told them I'd been released under the amnesty ... They lit candles in church for us – how can we go back now? Who'll be glad to see us come back from the dead? It's a sin, after all, to light a candle in church for someone who's still alive!' Through a ritual of death, the Shabby Man has become dead to those left behind at home.

Among the Luba of western Kenya, if a body cannot be brought back from far away then an effigy of the person is made and buried. As in all communities with such mechanisms, the person is now socially dead even if the information about their physical death turns out to be wrong. There are ethnographic reports of lost people being killed on their eventual return home. Often it is more important that the physical body conform to social reality than that society be destabilized by uncertainty. Like scapegoating, the behaviour signals both the fragility of society in the face of the trauma of death, and how solidarity can, conversely, be created through death ritual.

It is not just the body that can be missing from a burial. As the use of metals broadened after 6000 BC, more and more items that were not only precious but recyclable, made of gold or bronze, found their way into graves and became a temptation for the living. Grave-robbing was commonplace during the Iron Age in Scythia, where barely any of the great *kurgan* mounds remained unrobbed. Most were despoiled in antiquity, soon after they were sealed (as at Pazyryk, where the robbers left their wooden ladders and made off with the treasure on table tops).

Burial that included real weaponry could be a liability. The famous terracotta army of life-size clay soldiers that, along with real ritually killed retainers and concubines, accompanied the first emperor of China, Qin Shi Huangdi, appear to have held real swords and composite reflex bows in their hands when the massive tomb – built by 700,000 conscripts – was sealed in 210 BC. In the rebellions that followed the funeral, it is known that at least part of the subterranean tomb was set on fire, including Pit I where 6,000 of these model troops stood. It seems very likely that their weapons were taken by the rebel Xiang Yu to assist in his (unsuccessful) struggle against Liu Bang, eventual founder of the succeeding Han dynasty. An army designed to wage war for the Qin dynasty in Heaven contributed to the chaos of its downfall on earth.[19]

Certain measures could be taken to discourage robbers: burying proxy weapons or ritually 'killing' the metalwork, bending and breaking it so that it was of no immediate use. Nevertheless, Bronze Age and early medieval grave-robbing across Europe is breathtaking in its systematic scope. At the Bronze Age cemetery of Gemeinlebarn in Lower Austria, all 250 graves were robbed at once. Parts of human bodies were thrown out from the bottom of one grave to land in adjacent graves that were already standing open as the robbers went about their systematic plunder.[20]

Graves, almost from the outset, have encouraged grave-robbing. 'World of Ancestors' type cemeteries developed as predominantly political-territorial statements or provocations. The fact that the super-wealthy burial mounds of the Iron Age were so often placed outside defended settlements was not just about zoning a realm of the dead away from the living but about giving rival groups the 'come on'. Getting rich is not the only motivation for reopening a grave. Desecration can involve robbery but it is a symbolically aggressive act in itself, still recognized in English law (as recently used against some self-defined 'Satanists' – violent cult-oriented paedophiles – in London who were convicted, among other things, of 'offering indignities to a corpse').[21]

Patchy Viking graffiti inside the Neolithic tomb of Maes Howe on Orkney suggest earlier attempts at grave robbery: 'It is surely true what I say that treasure was taken away treasure was carried off in three nights before those . . .' and '. . . is to me said that treasure is here hidden very well'. There are also inscriptions that suggest more recreational use of the tomb. Next to a picture of a leering dog's head with its long tongue drooling out is the statement 'Ingigerth is the most beautiful of women' and a further suggestion that Ingigerth had accompanied the writer.

The Vikings had a name for the valour that was required for desecration. In the Norse concept of *Haugbrod*, the decision to enter a particular grave is seen as a great and brave act, to which status will accrue. The hero who decides to enter a grave enters a liminal zone where he will have to fight with the malevolent spirit of the dead, and anything he removes – sword, chalice or neck ring – will be imbued with special power and earn him status. Real risks were interpreted in supernatural terms: in the absence of an understood aetiology of disease, generalized fear of the dead was enhanced when an especially putrid corpse caused sickness or death in the person who disturbed it.

Grave robbery (as well as the now established primary and secondary rites of burial) meant that people became very familiar both with the normal human decomposition processes and with instances of abnormal decomposition. Sometimes the opened grave revealed an unrotted corpse whose finger- and face-skin had sunk, giving the impression that the fingernails had become more claw-like and the face hairier (as the base of the stubble was revealed) with receding gums suggesting that the teeth had lengthened.

The vampire is such a potent horror-film image that the historical story of vampires is now all but forgotten, and when not forgotten, doubted in every aspect. The eighteenth-century French philosopher Jean-Jacques Rousseau wrote 'If there is in this world a well-attested account, it is that of the vampires. Nothing is lacking: official reports, affidavits of well-known people, of surgeons, of priests, of magistrates; the judicial proof is most complete. And with that, who is there who believes in vampires?'[22]

Fear of the returning dead has a long prehistory. Once burial for isolation had been superseded by burial as a positive and usual rite, new ways had to be found to mark out the excluded. Rubbish pits inside the fortified late Iron Age site of Ehrenburg in Bavaria contained various human remains, including a violently killed woman with a large stone on top of her (Pit 62) and a man thrown face down and covered with a similar large stone (Pit 19).[23] More formal than casual post-massacre dumping, these burials demonstrate both violence and fear, as if a precaution is being taken against the ghost of someone who might have a perfect right to feel aggrieved.

Murderers, women who died in childbirth, sexual deviants, prostitutes, suicides and people with strange diseases have all, in the historical period in Europe, been considered unable to die properly. They are all seen as socially transgressive. Other people become transgressive – or have their transgressiveness enhanced – *after* death. In most societies the state of the corpse is thought to mimic the state of the soul: improper decomposition indicates uncompleted acceptance in the afterlife.

Human bodies, *en masse*, alter ground acidity and the microbial life of the soil. As cemetery burial became increasingly popular in Europe, the ability of the ground to effect decomposition was in many places compromised. Over the past few centuries, cemeteries in eastern Europe have been divided into zones of primary and secondary burial. Children's bodies were typically disinterred after three years, young people after four or five years, and the old after seven years. After these intervals, if decomposition is complete, the bones are washed in water and wine and a reinterment service is held. But decomposition is not always complete and in rare cases it may not even have begun. Then it is supposed that the corpse is a vampire (*vârcolac*).[24]

The classic Slavic vampire is thought of as a creature who has managed to short-circuit decomposition by taking fresh moisture into its body. It does this either by rising from the grave under cover of darkness to drink blood, or by metamorphosing into a nocturnal animal (usually a wolf) in order to feed and so arrest the decay of the buried corpse. But the main characteristic of the vampire is the state of being undead.

Both actual corpses and living people can be declared undead. People given this label while still alive may frequent marginal places, like parish boundaries or crossroads, or be considered to have special powers (making vampirism potentially coincident with the practical circumstances of illicit activities like prostitution). The folklorist and anthropologist Agnes Murgoci writes of a woman who made such good bread that half the village ate it. The rumour spread that she knew how to take bread-making power away from other women and she was accordingly considered a vampire, sucking vitality from others. Other people considered vampiric may be thought to possess the powers of certain animals – an ability to sniff things out or to recover things that have been lost or stolen – and may even hire themselves out on this basis.[25]

Cross-cultural beliefs in shape-shifting and vampirism were described by the anthropologist J.H. Hutton in the 1920s in a useful summary of seventeenth- to nineteenth-century literature:

> The actual practice of lycanthropy is clearly associated with a form of hysteria and a pathological condition (frequently recorded in pregnant women) manifesting a depraved appetite and an irresistible desire for raw flesh, often that of human beings, frequently accompanied by a belief on the patient's part that he or she is transformed into an animal ... we find the belief in Armenia, where sinful women are punished by becoming lycanthropists at the bidding of a spirit who brings them a wolf skin.[26]

The animals that people believe they turn into vary according to the wild fauna in the countries where the shape-shifting takes place: bears in Scandinavia, wolves and dogs in Greece and Rome, tigers in Malaya, hyenas and leopards in parts of Africa, jaguars in South America, and so on. Hutton notes that the

> usual method of effecting the change in Europe was by rubbing with magic salve or by putting on a girdle of wolf- or sometimes human skin ... The wer-wolf is called *vrkolak* by Bulgars and Slovaks, and by modern Greeks βρυκολακας [*vrykolakas*] ... the body remains cataleptic while the soul

241

enters a wolf. After its return the body is exhausted and aches as after violent exercise. This form is connected in popular belief with vampires, and Serbs give the same name *vlkoslak* to both.

The folklore of shape-shifting brings to mind Lindow Man's fox-fur armband, which he wore on his otherwise naked body. Across medieval Europe, wearing such a band was a symbol of lycanthropic/vampire status, facilitating the transition to the animal state. This may be what prompted Lindow Man's grisly killing and preservation in limbo.

Scientific explanations of 'vampirism' in human subjects have often drawn attention to comas and temporary vegetative states which result in premature burial of a person supposed dead,[27] as well as to the aetiology of other medical conditions, like rabies, photophobia (sensitivity to light) and the more extreme condition of porphyria (a congenitally produced syndrome in which sensitivity to light is accompanied by skin blistering and scarring in sunlight, vomiting and various psychoses).

In the case of definitive corpses, incomplete or arrested decomposition is not the only feature attributed to vampires. Dead bodies can stay warm by producing heat anaerobically and can also give off a pale light, particularly in the temperature range of 15°–30°C. Under certain conditions they can preserve a full complement of liquid blood, stay ruddy and pink, swell, move, burst and make loud, ripping noises. The angles and lengths of teeth, hair and nails can shift in relation to skin and gum surfaces, and pulmonary oedema can cause bloodstained fluid to escape from around the mouth. All these features, observed frequently by pathologists in exhumed bodies, would obviously have lent support to folk beliefs in undead blood-suckers.[28]

Post-mortem screaming is another phenomenon known to forensic science. The shifting airs and fluids of the fresh corpse and the gases produced during certain decomposition processes can make the mouth gape open and the body produce noises which, due to the chemical and surgical armoury of modern undertakers, are no longer familiar to most of us. The possibility of such sounds would once have been more widely known, but this does not mean that it would have been interpreted in a banal, pragmatic way. Often the bereaved have understood these sounds as active communication, from the dead themselves or from demons possessing their bodies.

In communities where belief in vampires was strong, methods of dealing with them included placing amuletic protection (crosses, garlic) on the body or grave to keep the vampire's soul from reanimating the body; putting stones or incense in the corpses' orifices and under the fingernails; fumigating the grave with cannabis; placing physical restraints on the body so that in a reanimated state it could not pull free from the coffin or exit the grave; dismemberment, such as placing the head between the legs or the legs on the chest; using rocks, sealing, and closing spells; staking (which can be unpleasant as it obviously releases fluid and gases under pressure); and, finally, burning (in which the same gases can cause flames to shoot from the mouth, another feature of folk accounts dramatically confirmed in laboratory tests).[29]

When, around the year 1914, the mother of a Romanian peasant called Dinu Gheorghita died, swiftly followed by several grandchildren, she was exhumed, and because she had not decomposed at all, she was blamed for the deaths:

> They took her and carried her into the forest, and put her under a great tree in a remote part of the forest. There they disembowelled her, took out her heart, from which blood was flowing, cut it in four, put it on hot cinders and burnt it. They took the ashes and gave them to children to drink with water. They threw the body on the fire, burnt it, and buried the ashes of the body. Then the deaths ceased.[30]

There is an epidemiological logic hidden here. The vampire panics can coincide with the natural panic that 'real' disease epidemics generate. At the height of an epidemic, when a community may feel compelled to take extreme measures such as disinterring and staking 'vampires', the only people left alive to do the job may be those with a developed disease resistance. It then appears that their brave action against the undead was the crucial factor in halting the epidemic.[31]

Although cremation is supposed to be successful against vampires, communities plagued by the belief do not practise it widely, either for suspected vampires or as a normal rite. This is partly to do with cost and periods of scarcity in fuel timber. Cremation is a well-known prehistoric rite, but it is not as common as inhumation and was probably always more costly. The innovation of full cremation followed from the pyrotechnic and transformational skills of smelting and forging that first developed at the beginning of the Bronze Age. The magic of metal-making and the creation of something sharp and gleaming from something dull and rocky through the application of heat provided a new symbol for the ritual transformation of the soul after death. Like ownership of metal, cremation was typically restricted to the elites. But there are periods when it became much more common and it has been suggested that these may have been sparked by vampire epidemics – that is, by a real plague.[32]

There is clearly discretion in where a body is initially placed in a cemetery, allowing scope for the 'creation of vampires'. Clayey or waterlogged areas may be reserved for suicides, murderers, adulterous women and other transgressors precisely because they will provide poor conditions for decomposition. When these bodies are exhumed after some years, they may not have decomposed much at all, and at this stage the accusation of vampirism can be effectively made. Rather like the preservative properties of raised bogs, the variations in decomposition rates which occur with different types of soil and in the presence or absence of particular minerals will have been well known since at least the Neolithic period. It was then that horticulture, the storage and preservation of meat, using practices such as salting, and the prospection of different pottery-making clays, all became foci of intense interest.

People living close to the land continued to know about these things, as exemplified in an interview with two monks recorded in 1826 by the Serbian writer Joakim Vujić. There had been a local outbreak of vampirism that both the principality and the Church felt was getting out of hand: various corpses had been exhumed and had had hawthorn stakes driven through them.[33] This had caused a sense of panic within the community. Vujić tried to calm the monks, saying:

> in some places is found earth which is salt-sulphur [*salitro-sumporita*], that is it is such that when you put a dead body, in which there is still considerable blood to be found, in such ground, then the blood will coagulate and the body will swell and the earth will not allow the body to decompose.[34]

The creation of vampires was perhaps of benefit to many communities – a continuation of the Theatre of Transgression that allowed the rules of proper conduct to be exemplified and encouraged. This brings us full circle to Catalhöyük, the Neolithic burials incorporated as powerful ancestors in the mound and the lone burial that took place there some 7,500 years later. As I stood by Ayşa's grave, I pressed Osman concerning the account he had given me about the events in Küçükköy in the 1930s. My interpreter asked as delicately as she could about social ostracism, specifically about whether Ayşa had been isolated in order to make it harder to offer prayers for her soul. Osman firmly maintained that this was not so. But he also informed me that another prostitute had been buried alone on the other side of the village at around this time, and that prostitutes nowadays are incorporated in the village cemetery. The latter is practical, apparently, because there are now more prostitutes, and it is considered morally better, as there they can easily be prayed for when people go to pray for their own relatives.

There is much in the tale of Ayşa that is not easy for an outsider to understand. There must be much that was private to her community and is not discussed today. Osman was born some thirty years after her death and his account of her life, for all its genuine earnestness, contains a buried feature that seems to poke through into the present from an earlier time, just as her gravestone protrudes from the Neolithic mound.

Symbolic and superstitious thinking is opportunistic. It is important that Ayşa screamed *and* that she was a prostitute – an outsider category with anti-social force and untamed sexual power. She 'did everything' to sustain herself materially in life and earned enough for a set of gleaming gold teeth. These teeth, in death, remained a potent symbol of her powers of predation – at least as conceived by those who used her services, in their self-justifying inversion of the genuine dynamics of her exploitation. After her death, her image would continue to visit some of her clients in their dreams, sucking their life from beyond death. In an uneasy village ambience, Ayşa's screaming, which might have been ignored in another corpse, was taken as a sign.[35]

Burying Ayşa on her own at the mound of Catalhöyük was as deliberate as it was dramatic. Although the scientific investigation of the site did not begin until the early 1960s, the low hill must have had a prior place in local superstition. The black obsidian knives glittering in the moonlight are striking enough, but the sandy mound also attracts the sort of animals associated with the unquiet grave in lycanthropist and vampire lore. Foxes dig earths there and jackals and feral dogs retire there with their pickings, beyond stone's-throw of the village. Their grubbings bring Neolithic material to the surface, including, from time to time, human bone.

Catalhöyük was a deliberate choice for Ayşa's burial. In 1933 it was understood as a numinous pagan necropolis of the unnamed, pre-Muslim dead, rather than a prehistoric settlement site. But burial in isolation from her community was just a first stage for her. When it failed to protect the living from lustful memories and bad consciences, the same men who had apparently been too frightened to touch her when she lay freshly dead reopened her grave and removed her teeth from her stinking corpse. The conclusion that they did not do this for minor financial gain is inescapable. Her mouth was desecrated – made to return its profits – in an attempt to finally lay her ghost.

Although Montague Summers' classic book *The Vampire in Europe* claims that belief in vampires is uncharacteristic of Islam and offers no examples, recent research by a team of Greek and Canadian scholars indicates that anti-vampire remedies were (and are) not exclusive to the Christian part of the Balkan-Anatolian world. During excavation of a late eighteenth-/early nineteenth-century Ottoman cemetery on the island of Mytilene, a grave was found containing a skeleton with 20 centimetre nails driven through its neck, pelvis and ankles; spatially isolated from the main group of burials, it seems clear that this classic horror-film interment was of a person thought to be undead.[36]

Symbolically, Ayşa's burial on what became the world's most famous Neolithic settlement site incorporates elements of Isolation, Theatre of Transgression and World of Ancestors types of burials. Physically the grave was isolated from the rest, the exhumation for the gold teeth, along with the story told about it afterwards, was theatrical and stigmatizing, while the formal gravestone with the instruction to pray for her soul is doctrinally conventional. That this is a burial from the first half of the twentieth century in rural Turkey should not blind us to the presence of the 'have it all', bet-hedging spirit of modernism, where a person can find themselves at one and the same time accepted and rejected, and where apparent religious orthodoxies are underlain by folk belief and overlain by local political expediency.

But this attitude may not be that modern. The archaeologist Falko Daim has suggested that the incompleteness of the grave goods found in many early medieval burials (for example the provision of sets of decorative horse-harness without the inclusion of horses) suggests a certain empty formality – even scepticism – about the afterlife.[37] Inclusion in a world nobody can actually see, easily forgotten in the day-to-day, may generate little real passion. The popularity of the standard burial and cremation ceremonies that first clearly emerged in the Neolithic period, conducted *as if* there was a world of ancestors, may have lasted for so long because they provided a communal rite from which people could be excluded.

CHAPTER 10

The Singing Bone

But now that he had apparently made every preparation for death; now that his coffin was proved a good fit, Queequeg suddenly rallied; soon there seemed no need of the carpenter's box: and thereupon, when some expressed their delighted surprise, he, in substance, said, that the cause of his sudden convalescence was this; – at a critical moment, he had just recalled a little duty ashore, which he was leaving undone; and had therefore changed his mind about dying: he could not die yet, he averred. They asked him, then, whether to live or die was a matter of his own sovereign will and pleasure. He answered, certainly.

HERMAN MELVILLE, *Moby-Dick*[1]

The others had gone to bed when I began to cut myself. It took an hour or so to make a couple of hundred small incisions with my penknife. I avoided arteries. My ribcage and ankles were too bony to go deep. I left my face and hands so that my clothes would hide everything in the morning.

It was a warm July night in Vienna, 1982. I had returned to the city with the digging team, having finished excavating the early Christian burial in the forest meadow. I was staying in a friend's apartment and we had been drinking wine. It grew late and I remained sitting alone. The city reached that state of late-night quite in which the noises of trams and trains become distinct. The small chandelier cast an even, yellow light over the grand piano, the sideboard, the lace-covered table. There was a crucifix on the wall. I undressed, placed a bath towel on my chair to protect it, sat down and opened the smaller, sharper blade of my Swiss knife. I was calm to begin with and, as I proceeded making incisions, I became even calmer.

The blood ran from the cuts and the towel absorbed most of it. I felt nothing particular on the surface of my body, even though I winced from time to time. The pain was discrete, coming and going, while I was somewhere deep inside myself, untouchably strong. Although I had not done anything like this before, or even considered it, I felt fond of myself, perhaps for the first time. It was a miraculous feeling.

I continued to cut. Past a certain point, the body's natural painkillers, the endorphins, begin to affect the brain pleasurably. I remember a kind of peaceful floating as, having patterned every available surface with the knife, I went round again, filling in small gaps and deepening wounds that had stopped bleeding. But I had already cut further onto my hands than I intended, and this provoked the first feelings of anxiety, which then grew. My heart started pounding, my breathing quickened and I began to panic. Even though I had been wiping blood away in order to locate uncut surfaces for my blade, it was a shock to realize that I was now glistening all over. My wounds began to ache and smart. I hurt as I got up, laid the knife on the towel, and went quietly through to the bathroom.

I did not lock the door; the lock was noisy and, even though I did not want to be discovered I also did not want to cut myself off from help. I used a flannel to muffle the sound from the tap as I ran warm water into the bath. My fear had constricted the flow of blood, but the water immediately became a lurid red. All I now wanted to do was get clean and go to bed. But one of my friends had woken and her face appeared round the door. I looked back at her from over the edge of the bath, keeping as low as possible, as we engaged in a short and farcical conversation about what I was up to. Something gave me away and she came over and I heard her say my name in a whisper before she went to get help.

My friends gently cleaned me up. I felt stupid and exposed, but as dawn broke through the tall windows, bathing and warming the parquet floor with golden light, one of them took my photograph with the site-recording camera. I looked, he laughed, like one of the '*Indios*' – a tattooed and scarified native American.

In his novel *Moby-Dick*, Herman Melville describes the tattoos that covered the body of the harpooneer Queequeg. These are said to have been done by a 'departed prophet and seer of his island', so that Queequeg had no way of understanding their symbolism, 'though his own live heart beat against them'. I was at first equally ignorant of the meaning of the scars that now formed on my body. Although they had been self-inflicted, I had not followed a design. Even as I opened the blade of my knife, I had not reflected on what I was about to do.

Vienna is the spiritual home of Freud's *thanatos*, the death drive, but I was not trying to kill myself that night. It was an action in the realm of ritual. Not repetitive and formulaic, but nevertheless structured, expressive, potent and carried through during a time period that was liminal, between *time before* and *time after*. It was a once-off, unrepeatable act. A rite of passage.

Although, at the time I cut myself, I had been reading the work of the Greek historian Herodotus as part of my preparations to study the Iron Age Thracians, I had not yet paid particular attention to his description of Scythian burial practices, as discussed previously in Chapter 5:

> the [Royal] corpse is processed in a wagon to the country of the tributary people who live nearest, and then on to the next, visiting each subordinate tribe in turn. In the course of its progress, those who successively receive it, do what the Royal Scythians do: they cut off a piece from their ear, shave their hair, make circular incisions on their arms, gash forehead and nose, and drive arrows through their left hand.

251

As I nowadays realize, my behaviour was not original. It was something that medics straightforwardly term 'cutting', part of a broader catch-all category known as 'self-harming'. Done at times of stress and anxiety, cutting is a calming 'fix', one that is without doubt effective. It is also compulsive and can easily become habitual. Biochemical evidence suggests that cutting may help the brain to rewire itself in the wake of events which have had a pain-numbing effect. Trauma engenders a 'dissociation state' in which the body produces natural opium-like substances (opioids) that alleviate psychological and physical distress.

The human brain is a chemical powerhouse that lacks any master-switch to return it to 'normal' running. As the brain unfolds and enlarges in childhood, generating new neural connections by the million every day, the levels of particular chemicals set themselves in response to the perceived external environment. The chemicals are not there in order to produce any necessary feeling of well-being or happiness, but to encourage behaviours that maximize the fundamental survival chances of the organism. As time passes and circumstances change – improving, for example, as certain dangers recede – many of the settings governing basic actions and reactions remain stuck at their original levels, unless subjected to a significant jolt. Recent research concludes that 'Cutting, a common form of self-destructive behaviour associated with early trauma, may be an attempt to autoregulate out of the altered pain sensitivity associated with the elevated opioid activity of the dissociative state'[2] or, in lay terms, recalibrate the mind so that the outside world is no longer continually experienced as if through a sheet of bullet-proof glass.

The Scythian display of cutting and mutilation belongs to an equally well known class of behaviour. Associated with specific rites of passage and known as scarification or cicatrization (the formation of scars), it has been documented from Aboriginal Australia, south-east Asia, Africa and the Americas, although it is less well known in the recent history of European peoples. The founder of sociology, Emile Durkheim, recognized this kind of activity as *piacular*: 'anything that is ominous, and anything

252

that motivates feelings of disquiet or fear requires a piaculum' (atonement or the appeasement of an angry deity).[3]

Among the Warramunga of Central Australia, whose death rites were studied at the end of the nineteenth century,[4] cutting begins even before the person, having been recognized as deathly sick, has died: 'Some of the women, who had come from all directions, lay upon the body of the dying man; others stood or knelt all around it, pushing the points of their digging sticks into the tops of their heads, thereby causing wounds from which the blood ran down over their faces. They kept up a continuous wailing all the while.' Men too, join in; one of them 'rushes onto the scene, screaming with pain and brandishing a stone knife. As soon as he reaches the camp, he makes such deep incisions across his thighs, into the muscles, that, unable to hold himself up, he finally falls to the ground in the midst of a group; two or three of his female relatives pull him away and apply their lips to his gaping wounds while he lies senseless.'[5]

After the death, the tightly choreographed violence begins again. Thigh-slashing may only be done by the maternal grand-father, maternal uncle and the deceased's wife's brother. Closely related women must cut their hair, cover themselves with clay, and keep silence. They are only allowed to use sign language during the mourning period, which can last up to two years.[6] During mourning, the women use red-hot sticks to reopen the wounds they have made, and sometimes carry this to the extreme of causing their own deaths.

My cutting did not precisely fit either of the standard patterns. It was a one-off and, unlike the Scythian and Warramunga cere-monies, it was private and avoided often-seen body parts like the head and the hands, rather than explicitly focusing on them. Although what I did can be considered compulsive, it did not have any sense of harm about it beyond superficially damaging the skin. And even a clinician would have to agree that smoking cigarettes involves a greater degree of physical self-harm than what I actually did. I was not intending to maim myself, either physically or, by scarring my face, socially.[7]

Women mourning among the Warramunga.
(Photo: Baldwin Spencer/Pitt Rivers Museum, Oxford)

Although I can only appreciate such preliminary care in retrospect, in ensuring my knife was clean, avoiding major blood vessels, and managing things so that – while private enough for my purposes – I was not actually alone when I did it, I minimized risks. To explain all this – why I cut myself, and why it made me feel better, not just at that time, but ever since – I have to explain something of my circumstances on the previous day.

My plan was to travel east that summer, working on archaeological sites in Austria, Hungary, Romania and Bulgaria. I had applied for admission to the D.Phil. programme at Oxford and specified Christ Church as my college of preference, but uncertain of funding I had begun a year out, working on excavations in Britain and abroad. The choice of Christ Church was peculiarly significant in the light of my personal history because my maternal grandfather had been, until shortly before his death, its Assistant Librarian. I remembered being in Tom Quad with him, looking at the goldfish in the ornamental pond under the bronze statue of Mercury, holding his hand when he took me to the upper library to see the glass case containing the spell-binding carved and painted miniature figures from *Alice in Wonderland*. Now I wanted to make it a place to which I belonged as an adult.

While I was digging in Austria, I heard that although I had been offered a place by Christ Church, I had failed to be awarded a grant by the British Academy. I knew that my application had been weak, but I felt devastated by the outcome. For a long time afterwards I could not make sense of what then happened. The prospect of not being able to go on with my studies threatened to unhinge me. I felt helpless and out of control. I had no consoling or practical thoughts of a change of career and could see nothing ahead of me except the oblivion of insanity. Since being blamed for my grandfather's death, I had harboured an unspeakable and usually unthinkable guilt in my heart. The dam was finally breaking.

The natural psycho-biological sequence observed by counsellors and psychologists in bereaved people – shock, protest and denial, searching for the deceased, and, finally, detachment – was arrested for me at an early stage, leaving me frozen in persistent shock.[8] I still have trouble believing that I did not kill my grandfather (it was not until quite recently that I came to realize that heart conditions do not emerge from nowhere and that he must have been suffering from angina for some time).

In Vienna, the skeleton illuminated by lightning was fresh in my mind. I had always felt detached when I handled the dead, but when the horror of mortality was revealed to the footballers who fled the excavation on the lower Holzwiese, it was somehow transmitted to me. My emotions were confused. My disappointment at failure was mixed with relief that I did not have to go to Oxford.

I now began the long process of exoneration. I have never

since felt the same intense calm as in those midnight hours when by some grace I found that I had the courage to act. The moment I started to cut, I began to draw my inner mental world and the outward physical world – symbolized and most directly exemplified by my body – closer together. What was needed was a physical act, one that revealed to me the immediate possibility of my own death.

I had always known, somewhere in my heart, that I had been scapegoated. Even while guilt corroded me, I sensed that I had been accused of an unreal crime. My grandfather, after all, had joked with me as he lay in hospital, and my widowed grandmother had never pointed an accusing finger at me. I had lived with a false accusation and I now needed to replace my phantom action – killing him – with something real, the aggressive marking of my own body.

Symbolically, cutting can be understood as an assertion that a person is trying to heal. Healing was, in fact, the intended purpose of much deliberate cutting in medieval medicine. Surgeons, leeches or chirurges worked swiftly with a knife to remove ulcerated skin or to speed up healing processes under its surface; the clean quality of the scars or cicatrices then formed was taken as a token of the efficacy of the cure. Whatever the complex biochemistry entailed in altering the brain's opioid-level settings, watching wounds heal is a powerful reminder of our own restorative powers. At times of stress I still look at one of my scars, a short pale line at the base of my left thumb, and again feel relieved that a symbolic line has been drawn under everything that went before.

Cutting leaves a person vulnerable and I was lucky to have friends whose non-judgmental and respectful concern bolstered my fragile sense of self-worth. Many people who decide to cut themselves and are admitted as hospital casualties feel that they have only succeeded in making themselves into a bigger problem; bad feelings lead to repeated cutting which, in turn, provokes denigrating and increasingly negative responses in those around them. I had been damned with words: my friends' soft-spokenness and love in the crucial aftermath of my private ritual set the seal on its healing power and helped ensure that once was enough.

A week after I cut myself, the cuffs of my work-shirt discreetly buttoned over my wrists, and shielded from the scorching sun on the Great Hungarian Plain by the cool depth of a grave, I worked to clean the skeleton of an Avar woman who had died around AD 750 and I found myself again wondering what I was doing. I considered that the golden earrings I was freeing from the damp sand at her temple were not only not mine, but that, by rights, they were not the property of the museum in Kecskemét (where they now are) either.[9] They were hers. But she was not there. I felt that, just as cutting my own body was my business, moving this woman's legs and arms should have been hers.

But a feeling of care crept over me and I brushed her cheekbones with a refreshed sense of propriety. Somehow, the act of cutting myself had provided me with the confidence to take responsibility for this exhumation, not via any inner appeal to the archaeological professionalism that I was keen to develop, but directly and personally. My experience helped me to break down an academically formalized, suspiciously bourgeois view of antiquity and forced me to start thinking in an emotionally engaged way about past states of mind, my sentiments now on the trail of cold chronologies.

The acts of cutting that Herodotus describes among the Scythians can be understood as functioning psychologically – whatever their local religious rationale may have been – to underline for each participant that there was *time before* they saw with their own eyes that the king was dead, and *time after*. Scars index an event in the scarifier's life. Like my scars, they became trophies, talismans, *aides mémoires* or souvenirs of the moment of acceptance of death. The Scythian custom represents a similar kind of personal imperative to mine, culturally formalized as part of a traditional grieving ritual and directed as homage to the idea of the king. For them it was a form of closure, whereas for me it very effectively reopened unfinished business. Each type of cutting formed part of a process of mourning but my cutting was informal and private and arose, psychologically speaking, *in extremis*, many years after a normal mourning process might be expected to have finished.

The dramatic cutting and slashing which attends death in many communities was thought by Durkheim to be a theatrical expression of the destructive emotion of the dead person's soul, inhumanly angry at its disembodiment, which the living community felt had now been transferred to them. The rites are communal because they are a display of moral unity and vitality in the face of loss. Ferocious grief is collectively expected and thus collectively generated. But because every death is imputed to some magic spell, victims are required to avenge the dead person: 'a woman serves more often than a man as the passive object of the most cruel mourning rites. Because she has lower social significance, she is more readily singled out to fill the function of the scapegoat.'

My life experiences, while individual, are wholly unexceptional. Many stories have been told to me by people adversely affected by death during their childhood who had never spoken about it before: people who were told that their little sister had 'gone to heaven' and understood it in the same way as 'gone to hospital' and therefore still believed, against all odds, that their lovely playmate would one day return; people who as children witnessed the death of a parent and live forever with the image of their own helplessness and, worse, the nagging feeling that they did not do the right thing. Faced with the intolerable reality of death, those who have no one or nothing else to blame, blame themselves. Because death is an uncontrolled event, we constantly try to exert control over it. Random or accidental events are far harder to accept than deliberate or intentional acts. They lack pattern and are so meaningless that we are driven to remake them as deliberate and causal happenings. By finding someone or something to blame for a death, we can make it seem that the death could have been avoided.

In the fairy tale 'The Singing Bone', two brothers are challenged by their father to kill a troublesome boar.[10] The one who is successful will win the hand of a princess. Venturing first into the forest, the quiet and unglamorous younger brother is presented with a magic black spear by a fairy. Courageously, he confronts the ferocious creature and kills it. During this time, his arrogant elder brother is still carousing in the hall with his drinking crew, mustering his courage for a combat from which he fully expects to emerge triumphant. Eventually setting out at evening, the elder brother meets his victorious sibling. Pretending to congratulate him, he lures him to a little bridge and kills him, dumping his corpse in the water and taking the dead boar himself. He returns to a hero's marriage. But one day, a shepherd boy finds a bone in the stream under the bridge and carves it into a flute. When played, it sings the song of itself, a shocking song of fratricide and deceit. The boy comes before the old king with his singing bone and plays it. Consequently, the stream is dredged, the skeleton exposed, the elder brother confesses in its presence and is executed, and the younger brother is reburied in a beautiful grave. Justice is done.

Justice and honour coincide in the resolution to the story – not only is the truth ascertained but the murdered brother is reburied with dignity. In real life, however, these principles often come into conflict, as in the increasingly acrimonious debate between archaeologists and indigenous peoples over the control of the dead. The 'reburial' issue, which mainly but not exclusively involves pressure from native American and Australian Aboriginal groups for the return of human skeletal remains from the laboratories of university departments (including my own) in order that they should be ceremonially reinterred or placed in tribal 'keeping houses', has produced headlines around the world.

In July 1996, at Kennewick in Washington State, a skeleton was found washed out of the bank of the Columbia river and, after a short spell in the care of archaeologists is, at the time of writing, under the control of the US Army Corps of Engineers. The bones have provoked a bitter, complex and at times ridiculous controversy, well documented by the archaeologist David Hurst Thomas in *Skull Wars*. The 'Kennewick Man' bones appeared to those who first saw them to be racially 'Caucasian' (i.e. white) and were thought to perhaps be those of a murdered drifter. There were several injuries on the body, including a fractured skull, crushed chest, damaged elbow and a healed pelvic wound. But when a CAT-scan showed that there was a stone spearhead inside the right hip, it prompted the local archaeologist, James Chatters, to wonder if the bones were of historical interest, belonging perhaps to an early settler, killed by Indians.[11]

Because the spearhead was archaic in form, Chatters arranged to have the bones carbon-14 dated. The analysis suggested that the bones were 9,200–9,500 years old and prompted immediate requests and writs for their 'repatriation' by an alliance of five American Indian tribes who insisted that no more science could be done on them, because it would be sacrilegious and illegal. Armand Minthorn, an Umatilla leader, said 'Our oral history goes back 10,000 years. We know how time began and how Indian people were created.' The oral tradition did not preserve the deceased's name, however, so he was called Oyt.pa.ma.na. tit.tite, 'The Ancient One'.

As the debate became more heated, the US Army Corps of Engineers confiscated the bones. Scientists then protested that their own civil rights were being violated as they were being denied access to the bones on grounds of their race and ethnicity. Into this mess came the Californian Asatruans, a modern-day Norse religious and political group with links to the Ku Klux Klan and the 'Aryan Nations' who claimed Kennewick Man to be one of their own – a supposed Viking-American.

Reburial is not a modern phenomenon. In 1834 a peat-preserved body was found naked, pinned down under hurdles in the bog of Haraldskaer in Denmark. Thinking logically, people at the time, including the then Danish king, Frederick VI, thought that they had found the body of Erik Bloodaxe's widow, Queen Gunhild of Norway, who was said to have been drowned by her new husband, King Harald Bluetooth some time in the mid-tenth century AD.[12] The bog preserved both Harald's name and evidence of the kind of death the historians described so Frederick accorded the body a state funeral and a new resting place in an ornate carved oak coffin in the church of St Nicolai at Vejle (where it still lies).

Radiocarbon accelerator dating now shows beyond reasonable doubt that the woman found in the Haraldskaer bog died in the early fifth century BC. If the bog ever contained the real Gunhild as well, she has not been found. The politics of false Gunhild's reburial in 1834 prefigured the Kennewick incident: the initial suppositions were plausible, but the kind of firm proof which would normally be required to justify subsequent actions were lacking. They were overidden by vested interests.

Frederick VI, nearing the end of a long reign, was worried about the destabilizing effect of a number of liberal, peasant and national movements that had grown up following the end of the Napoleonic Wars. There had been revolts in Norway in 1830, and the bickering and incestuous rivalries of the Danish, Swedish and Norwegian aristocrats had alienated public goodwill. By honouring the supposed remains of the old Norwegian queen, Frederick was effectively apologizing for an act of ancient Danish summary justice. 'Gunhild's funeral' provided immediate pomp and circumstance, history and a hoped-for revitalization of royal authority and so helped pave the way for the accession of the Norwegian king, Christian VIII, to Denmark's throne five years later.

The identity of the 120 people who died in the Mountain Meadows massacre in Utah in 1857 is not in doubt. The issue is the identity of the killers. Traditional accounts say that the ill-fated Baker-Fancher wagon train was shot at by local Mormon militiamen but that the central atrocity, the massacre of almost the entire party including the women and children, was per-petrated by native American Paiutes. The politics of the period were volatile and the wagon train, on its way to California, was not welcomed by the Mormons who believed that the United States represented Babylon to their new Jerusalem. They had recently been stirred up by the suggestion of one of their 'apostles', George A. Smith, that the bodies of the US Army might best be composted: 'bones make good fertilizer ... I can think of nothing better that they could do than feed a fruit tree in Zion.'[13]

The dead lay unburied, exposed to the elements and scavenged by wolves, until, some eighteen months later, the army officer J.H. Carleton was dispatched from Los Angeles to investigate. He described what he found when he reached the massacre site:

> Women's hair, in detached locks and masses, hung to the sage brushes ... Parts of little children's dresses and of female costume dangled from shrubbery or lay scattered about; among these, here and there, on every hand, for at least a mile in the direction of the road, by two miles east and west, there gleamed, bleached white by the weather, the skulls and other bones of those who had suffered.[14]

Carleton's troops gathered up the grim remains as best they could, dug a mass grave and erected a cairn over it with a cross and the inscription 'Vengeance is mine: I will repay, saith the Lord.'

Accidental disturbance of one part of the cairn in 1999 revealed human bones and triggered full excavation and analysis under state law. A mass of human bone, including 1,400 cranial fragments, was recovered and a picture began to emerge of men shot once in the head and women and children bludgeoned to death but – significantly – a marked absence of the scalping, beheading and throat-cutting that had been attributed to native Americans in 'historical accounts'. The investigators, Shannon Novak and Derinna Kopp, tersely note, 'the bones of the victims have not been affected by self-interested rhetoric', but they were not allowed to finish their analysis. Pressure was brought by government officials, many of whom belong to the Church of Jesus Christ of Latter-day Saints, and the terms of archaeological permit were changed. All the bones were reburied at twenty-four hours' notice, under a new memorial engraved with the words: 'Mountain Meadow Massacre/Grave Site Memorial/Built and maintained by/The Church of Jesus Christ of Latter-day Saints/ Out of respect for those who died and were buried here and in the surrounding area/Following the massacre of 1857. /Dedicated 11 September 1999'.

The Haraldskaer, Kennewick and Mountain Meadows sagas belong to a long tradition of religious and political behaviour aimed at reviving the dead. David Hurst Thomas assumes that the principal interested parties in the Kennewick business are the archaeologists, the Indians and the government, who are caught up in 'a very public fight that no side feels it can afford to lose'.[15] But what originally worried Chatters was that the body might represent a crime. The fact that the estimated date of death of the person discovered at Kennewick has changed does not alter that.

The examination of the Kennewick bones clearly indicated a violent death of some sort and makes the five tribes' insistence that what washed out of the river bank was a normal, reverential burial of one of their own look blinkered. Whatever the oral histories may say, no one knew that the Kennewick skeleton was there. He does not appear to have belonged to a cemetery, but even if he had been found in a native burial ground, there would be no overriding reason not to carbon-date the bones and conduct a full forensic analysis. The interests of the relatives of all the 'missing, presumed dead' people in America, whatever line of descent they claim, oblige us to run more than a single carbon-14 date on the Kennewick bones. (Standard practice for important finds is to take several samples and split them between different laboratories so that the possibility of rogue readings is minimized.)

That this was not done as a matter of course shows how far the reburial issue has become part of the romanticized Western idea of indigenous peoples. Behind the posturing is a rather patronizing projected jealousy of the perceived greater depth of native spirituality as manifested in an apparently passionate concern for the ancient dead. But the underlying issue is disempowerment. People throughout history and prehistory have habitually tried to exert control over death. In the developed world, so much of the control of death has been ceded to the secular state that we are gripped by the reburial issue – it is a form of vicarious political combat over something that we hardly know how to begin to address for ourselves.

The Umatilla and the other Indian tribes who claim the Kennewick bones naturally want to exert more control over their own lives. Control of the past is perceived, often correctly, to lead to control of the future and for the 'people without history' – the dispossessed, oppressed and colonized – archaeology promises what the absent dead cannot themselves deliver: an absence to hang on to. Fifty years ago, no Aboriginal Australian knew that some of their ancestors had been cremated some 26,000 years ago at Lake Mungo. Burial of any sort was not a common rite in the majority of native Australian communities of the nineteenth century. Attitudes in general were like those of the Christian Church in Europe, where, after the funeral rites were completed and the soul had gone, the physical residue (except in the case of saints) had no special identity or power.

Among most Aboriginal tribes, the bones of ancestors could be handled informally after the secondary rites were completed. A mother might keep the finger bone of her dead son in her dilly bag much as we might keep a photograph of a dead family member on the mantelpiece. The primary rite in some regions involved the placing of the body on a platform up in a tree, where insects and the elements would rapidly reduce it until only the larger bones remained; these might subsequently be removed to a rock-shelter in the secondary rite. Elements which were still recognizable, like skulls, might end up being treated in fairly unreverential ways: as soon as it was considered that the spirit had permanently left, there was nothing either to fear or regard as especially sacred.[16] The central sacred aspect in native Australian belief was the landscape, which was thought of as pervaded with spirits and numinous places. There was no more idea that land could be owned than that time could be owned and the Australia that the first white settlers moved into had no fences, no fields and no cities to indicate that it belonged to anyone.

Tribes who could not protect their traditional lands from mining and development companies by asserting its inherent sacredness, found that they were listened to more seriously once they switched focus to ancient burial sites, effectively opting into the millennia-old game that connected cemeteries to claims of land ownership. The switch to the metaphysics of burial that had created a revolution in the Neolithic of the Near East occurred all over again in a modern state, and involved a wholesale opportunistic invention of tradition by urban Aboriginal property lawyers. What happened unfolded with a perfectly appropriate cultural logic.[17]

Since the scientific dating and analysis of the Lake Mungo and other excavated bones have proved their antiquity, they have been wrested back in a paradoxical process that has seen archaeological science vilified for permissionless desecration while its chronological conclusions have been incorporated into a powerful indigenous claim to prior sovereignty of an entire continent.

The new keeping houses for the memorialization of the archaeologically reactivated dead might be seen as the Aboriginal equivalent of the Lenin mausoleum, but for one thing: it was not known who the dead were. Aboriginal tribes paid little heed to bones after the secondary rites because they knew who they belonged to. But the archaeologically excavated bones were seen by some tribespeople as supernaturally dangerous because their identity was a mystery. No one knew if secondary rites had been properly completed for these ancient people. If they had not, then their unquiet souls might have been released during the process of archaeological excavation. The transfer of bones to tribal keeping houses is not just an expression of a generalized reverence towards the indigenous dead, but is seen by some as an essential rite of incorporation.

The problem of the unknown dead must have arisen many

times before. The Neolithic burial mound of Lough Crew in Ireland was re-entered 2,500 years after its original construction. The Iron Age Celtic people who have left traces of their presence there do not seem to have been interested in desecration. They reset the great slabs that held up the door.[18] Under them, on the threshold of the world of the dead, they buried little flat bone objects, pierced at one end and engraved with swirls and circles. These objects are 'bullroarers', a class of sound-producer used since the Ice Age and best known in recent times from Aboriginal Australia.

When attached to a long string and whirled round the head, bullroarers spin first one way and then the other, producing a distinctly eerie booming-whirring sound with much of the frequency generated in the 'infra-sound' range.[19] Infra-sound cannot be heard, but it vibrates in the human viscera, creating a strange feeling. Using a bullroarer while standing in the doorway of the Lough Crew mound would have amplified this effect.

The Celtic people may have used the bullroarers as 'singing bones' to invoke the spirits of the dead – not immediate ancestors, but the unknown and mysterious dead who lay inside the mound – in order to get them to prophesy. This possibility is suggested not just by the location of the bullroarers under the doorposts of the tomb, but by what we know about oracles from later Celtic literature: Bran the Blessed continued to speak to his warrior companions after he was dead, so they kept his skull with them at all times and consulted it when they wanted to know the course of future events.[20] Archaeological finds from the Rivers Thames and Walbrook in London suggest a flourishing skull cult in the later Iron Age and Roman periods. This may have been connected to a widespread belief among the barbarian tribes of Europe that part at least of a person's spirit continued to reside in the head after death (this belief has been found in parts of Borneo and Amazonia more recently).

The logic of Bran the Blessed warning his living companions of impending danger is that control of death can be achieved through control of the dead. This conceit is writ large in the ideologies of the first civilizations, with their gigantic mausoleums and their deification of ancestors. All made their gods appear in statues and paintings as commanding, human figures with an elaborate dress style that echoed the regalia of their kings. And the kings, through their ceremonial attire, could claim that they were becoming godlike, rather than that they had made gods in their own image. They came to believe not just in their indispensability to their people but, in the worst cases, in their personal immortality.

But they doubted it too. Death was the one thing that disobeyed them. It could not be subjugated by armies. To compensate for this failure, they could at least decide to whom death should happen, and when, and this appears not just to have provided a personal, psychological compensation but to have had social-structural significance.

The historian David Carrasco has argued that all early civilizations practised human sacrifice, especially when first established, in order to assert their legitimacy.[21] In ancient Egypt, Sumer, Shang China, the Aztec and the Maya empires, choreographed and public killings, often on a grand scale, demonstrated the ultimate power of the state over life and death. Not just individual life and death but cosmic life and death. If the prescribed rituals, including human sacrifice, were not undertaken, it was said that the world would collapse (how strongly or universally this was believed is hard to say).

The current leader of the most economically and militarily powerful nation on earth, George W. Bush, began his quest for the White House by signing go-aheads for the execution of death-row convicts in Texas. Bill Clinton did the same in the previous election run-up. Although framed within law rather than ritual, such behaviour has echoes of the state-organized sacrifices of earlier civilizations, and its bottom-line effect (beyond the important, complex and local issues of justice for victims and perpetrators) is to show who legitimately controls death in America. Discretion is involved in capital punishment and it is neither novel nor controversial to suggest that by demonstrating his juridical power over life and death George W. Bush sent a signal that he was fit to be the ultimate executive of America's nuclear arsenals.

Perhaps archaeology threatens the state's monopoly of death. The US Army sided with the five tribes in the Kennewick case, and pre-empted further scientific investigation not just by seizing the disputed bones but by effectively destroying the find site under 600 tonnes of boulders and an afforestation scheme.

The power of withholding the corpse from examination has been well understood by Saddam Hussein of Iraq and is expressed in the horrific treatment of some of the families of people killed by his security forces. Unlike the regimes in Chile and elsewhere, where the bodies of dissidents tortured to death were secretly disposed of (at sea for example), Saddam Hussein sanctioned the return of corpses to grieving relatives, but under escort. Families were allowed to bury their dead but not look inside the coffins. By denying people the right to see what had been done to their loved ones, Saddam was able to perpetuate a terrified obedience very similar to that which characterized Stalin's reign in the Soviet Union.

There is a basic power in denying the bereaved sight of their dead, observable even in animals. One of my friends – a psychologist and archaeologist – recently described what happened when she had to have the life of one of her two cats ended by the vet. Instead of keeping the corpse away from the surviving cat, as she had done on a previous occasion, she allowed it to be examined: 'this time the survivor looked, walked away, and seemed to check a dozen places where the dead one used to go – and did not go through any of the jumpiness we had witnessed before'.[22]

There is a general tendency to remove the dead from sight in modern Western culture. Hospitals, where most people now die, naturally want to project an image of health to their living patients. Death is zoned and controlled so that it can be given as low a profile as possible. A ward nurse in a British hospital told me that, in her experience, hospital death is as deeply frustrating and unsatisfactory for staff as it is for the immediate relatives of the dying person (and the dying person themselves).[23] She told me how she was continually brought close to the dying, who talk about their lives and fears as she holds their hands. But then, typically, after some days, she goes off shift, returning the following week not only to find that the person she had got to know has died but that their body has gone too; in its place, in the same bed, is a new person, two hours from death, needing care, who there is now no time to get to know.

Melville's Queequeg, when 'close to the very sill of the door of death', orders himself measured for his coffin. Then he recalls the 'little duty ashore', rallies, and affirms to the wonderment of all that his death is a matter of his own 'sovereign will and pleasure'. The noble harpooneer stands as the antithesis of the presumption of the state to control death, a person sufficient unto himself who believes that he can decide when to die (even if things do not turn out that way in the end). Social anthropology supports the veracity of the description in the novel, but in more negative terms: from voodoo curses to Aboriginal 'pointing the bone', there is evidence that people condemned by a shaman, witch doctor or tribunal of elders and informed that they will (for instance) die before nightfall, actually do so; the psychologist Martin Seligman has recently reviewed descriptions of such cases and believes them.[24]

In these cases people believe that they are not islands and that life is possible only as part of a society. Condemned to leave society, they become socially dead, and without a social world no worthwhile (or even practical) physical existence is possible, so they die. The contrast to modern consumer society could not be greater. Nowadays, if we do not like a social set-up, or even country, we consider leaving it. Yet we cannot avoid death. The Texan oil magnate, Miller Quarles, who put up the money for the Quarles Prize for a 'cure' to the 'disease' of ageing, did so, as he candidly admits, in order to 'save his own ass'. In the Mohave desert, George van Tassel has built what he calls an 'Integretron' in order to add 50–80 years to the mortal lifespan; it currently lacks the supply of compressed air it apparently needs to work.[25] People like Quarles and van Tassel believe that, like a consumer durable, we 'have' life, and death takes it away (obviously unfairly). But we do not have life, we live it.

The extent to which we have lost control of our personal endings is mirrored in loss of control of our personal beginnings. There is as strong a symmetry between birth and death in modern Western culture as in the traditional cultures studied by social anthropologists.

When my wife and I decided on another home birth, we were already conversant with the risk statistics. Marjory Tew's thorough analysis of figures on perinatal mortality and birth complications for twentieth-century Britain had been published shortly before the birth of our first daughter.[26] This time, with a birth pool set up in the front room of our house, and the same two midwives as before, we knew we were facing two kinds of risk, the first practical and medical, the other moral and social. We knew that planned home birth was safer in most risk categories, and we could also weigh the risk of the unknown against the clear evidence of fewer surgical and drug interventions in water births. Fewer interventions correspondingly lowers the risk of death and permanent damage. So we were as sure as the most precise science in the world could be that we were not facing a *higher* risk of death in mother or baby, but risking it in *different* ways. But the quantified and documented risks of medical statistics do not exhaust the risk possibilities. There are deep qualitative differences between home and hospital. Hospital carried many unknown short-, medium-, and long-term risks and disadvantages, physically and psychologically, for us all.

When, after many hours of labour, something happened, the look on my wife's exhausted face was briefly unfathomable. The form that broke the surface, cradled in her arms, was as grey and inanimate as wet clay. For the briefest moment I panicked, but my wife could feel and sense what I could not and within seconds our new baby daughter blossomed into glowing life. The practical and medical risks were easy to assess in comparison to the moral and social ones we faced when we took responsibility for the outcome of childbirth. Ultimately, we *wanted* to take personal responsibility for birth, but in doing so we had to face the possibility that, if things went wrong, we would be blamed for death.

The rise of civilization is a history of the emergence of specialization on a scale unknown in the animal world. Today there are thousands of discrete professions and few if any of us has a complete repertoire of skills that would allow us to hunt, kill and cook our own food, doctor our sick, assist in childbirth, construct shelters to live in and defend them against wild animals and the predations of other humans. The people who, through the complex workings of intention and chance in our increasingly complex societies end up with ultimate responsibility for controlling both birth and death – the surgeons and doctors – may easily come to feel that, through it, they somehow control life. More significantly, the majority of us who are not part of the medical colossus, can easily come to feel that we do not.

Visceral Insulation

> . . . insane simplification is refreshing, it's one of the virtues of war.
>
> ISABEL ALLENDE, *The Infinite Plan*[1]

Until you have used a sieve to find the finger bones of a newborn baby in ploughsoil it is hard to explain how small they are. The distal phalange – the smallest bone at the tip – is the size of a match-head, but recognizable to the trained eye. The fragments of the vault of the skull are like eggshell and, unless scrutinized closely, could easily be mistaken for something animal. 'Rabbit' was the emphatic verdict of the site supervisor. We had dug down only a few centimetres and he wanted me to shovel everything into a wheelbarrow so that the team could continue excavating downwards to reach the archaeological levels we were looking for. It was only because I stood my ground, pointing out the distinctive junction of the sagittal and lambdoidal sutures, where three of the main bony plates of the cranium come together, that the dig director was eventually summoned and the status of the bones established.

We do not like to think of the remains of babies lying around in shallow unmarked graves, but they do. The incident I have just described happened in Austria, when I was a student, but

Yorkshire: view towards the mouth of the narrow cave showing the rubble fill where bones were recovered. (Photo: author)

it is matched by recent experience from an excavation that I was directing in the Yorkshire Dales.

The cave had been discovered when a gamekeeper's dog chased a fox down a tiny hole among the high limestone scars and needed to be rescued by an experienced caver. He was a friend of Neville Steed, and Neville and I went with him one evening to take a look. The pothole was narrow and ran down at an angle of 30 degrees. I was not really expecting to find any archaeology the first time I went down it, or I would have brought some finds bags. As it was, there was much of interest and time was of the essence. New potholes in this region are vulnerable to illegal caving using an array of techniques including, occasionally, explosives. I took off my rubber boot – no easy job in the tiny space – so that I could fill my sock with a selection of the jumbled bones.

I found two dog skulls, fox bones, badger bones, sheep bones, and lots of small bones that I could not identify (which turned out to be water vole and toad). But what prompted me to sacrifice comfort for science was the sight of some human remains – an unmistakable piece of a human sternum and one of the cervical vertebrae (the atlas, which supports the skull directly). The external surface of the sternum, where the pectorals had once attached, was roughened in a way which indicated that it had belonged to a well-muscled adult, probably male.[2]

The caver was amazed when I showed him, telling me that he and other cavers find bones all the time and it never crosses their minds that some could be human. It is true that, once bones have been broken up into bits the size of jigsaw-puzzle pieces, technical knowledge is needed to identify them. Nevertheless, I was as taken aback by the blithe assumptions of his fraternity as he was by what I had in my wet sock. During the short trial excavation that I subsequently conducted with a small team in the mouth of the cave, a human heel bone was discovered and dated in the Oxford radiocarbon accelerator laboratory. It produced a later Bronze Age date, a period when burial in and around caves is a well-known phenomenon.

But I also found tiny fragments of foetal or neo-natal bones, mixed in with a twist of silver foil and a shotgun cartridge, among the scatter of rocks at the cave entrance. I know that most people, including many archaeologists, would have overlooked these entirely. The limestone 'pavement' of the Yorkshire Dales is covered in little bits of bleached bone: skulls of ferrets, bits of sheep and rabbit, and tiny fragments that have crumbled out of owl pellets. There are also spent cartridges all over the place, and shreds of sweet wrapper. Worms constantly move such material around so that, in the upper 5 centimetres or so of almost any landscape, the fact that things are found together can mean very little. My assumption was that the baby's bones related to the use of the cave as a funerary site during the Bronze Age. It was the simplest explanation.

When an archaeologist finds human bones there is a legal obligation to report them. For this excavation I had to obtain a Home Office licence under the terms of the Burial Act 1857. Apart from that, however, I am considered the expert. Following excavation, the bones have either to be kept under suitable conditions in a laboratory or museum environment or returned to a designated place of burial, either a crematorium or a municipal cemetery.

The two unexpected babies' skeletons I have excavated remain mysterious – just two of the many millions of unaccounted dead. But I feel increasingly unsettled by what I have found. Archaeological sites are a focus not only for archaeologists but for all sorts of people attracted to mysterious places and liminal environments (the site in Austria was well known, the one in Yorkshire unknown but close to ancient hut circles). Bones such as these may be very ancient, or they may not. They may be the result of natural deaths, or they may not. Recent reanalysis of the bones of a decapitated man, excavated over thirty years ago from one of the ditches at Stonehenge, surprised everyone. Instead of being another later Neolithic or early Bronze Age sacrifice, contemporary with the period when the monument is known to have been in use (like the man shot full of arrowheads at Stonehenge, or the baby with its skull cloven in two at the centre of nearby Woodhenge),[3] the new radiocarbon date shows that this skeleton belonged to an Anglo-Saxon.[4]

Most Anglo-Saxon criminals were hanged and then buried in special cemeteries near the gallows, so the decapitation at Stonehenge – achieved by a single powerful blow that sliced clean through from the back of the neck – is as unusual in style as location. Stonehenge was both a mysterious monument and, by Anglo-Saxon times, on the border between two parishes. Liminal in two ways, it was an ideal place for a powerful rite of exclusion. The man's head may have been removed to stop his return as the walking dead (a type of anti-vampire rite), but what is more interesting is that the prehistoric site was still a focus for death ritual some 3,000 years after its original construction.

The John Radcliffe Hospital where my grandfather died is one of thirty-eight British hospitals currently under investigation on suspicion of removing body parts, including large numbers of children's hearts, without the relatives' consent or knowledge, prior to burial or cremation. This scandal has revealed widely divergent attitudes to the dead, with largely uncomprehending and often unrepentant hospital doctors on the one hand, and traumatized and shocked relatives on the other. In the case of Marc Clynes (the baby mentioned in the Introduction), the John Radcliffe took sixteen years to admit what it had done. His shocked mother has said, 'Now I keep thinking the reason why the funeral director said it would be nice for Marc to have a hat on when we had him buried was because they had taken his brain.'[5]

It is extraordinary that a mother in modern Western society, unlike a mother in virtually any other human culture that has previously existed on the planet, *would not know* that her dead child's brain had been removed. Marc's parents remained so physically detached from his corpse that a strategically placed hat was all that was required to conceal the secret of a cranium as empty as a discarded eggshell.

Grief leaves people vulnerable in a way that often encourages greater deference towards doctors – the comforting experts. The whole set-up of modern hospitals conspires to keep death under institutional control. The body does not legally belong to the bereaved. It cannot be owned in a normal sense, a property vacuum that is filled by the structures and protocols of the state, with its interest in causes of death, potential foul play, and the aetiology of disease. The position of the bereaved parents is weak. Their access to their child's body is discretionary – a matter of custom and etiquette rather than a judicial right.

What happened in the Clynes case, and many like it, is one facet of a pervasive cultural style which I call 'visceral insulation'. This phrase describes the way in which the necessary specialization of the modern world screens or insulates people from 'visceral' things – bodies, blood, death screams, screams in childbirth, excessive grieving – all of which are compelling in their potential uncontrollability. Visceral insulation is a recoil from corporeality, as if we feel that, by coming too close to what is bodily, our inevitable mortality will somehow make itself too painfully known.

The entire history of visceral insulation will take another book to describe, but we can see its origins in the stone slingshots and chipped-stone projectile points of the Palaeolithic period. The ability to deal death at a distance made killing easier, not just technically but psychologically. The beautifully crafted 400,000-year-old throwing spears from Schöningen in Germany did the job even better, while modern guided-missile operators typically cannot see their target directly at all. The ability to kill at a distance did not mean an end to up-close killing, and the advent of farming saw the death of animals brought into the heart of communities, but screening and delegation kept some people closer to visceral realities while others became distanced from them.

The shift away from cannibalism as the default way of dealing with human bodies was crucial in the unfolding of visceral insulation. The human experience began to become more varied, so that markedly different, culturally generated psychologies could emerge, at an individual and a group level. It was this that led to the deep-rooted differences between the Greeks and the Callatians of India in the way they treated their dead – not innate in any genetic sense, but matters of settled custom (as Herodotus emphatically concluded).

Specialist morticians emerged during the period of the Old Kingdom in Egypt (2181–2163 BC), gaining enough knowledge of the human body to set down the first scientific treatises on medical anatomy and conduct a widening range of operations. But the development of surgery had been thwarted by religious sanctions by the time that the New Kingdom came into being in 1567 BC. Priests now insisted on the integrity of the body and the retention even of diseased tissue, so that painful abcesses in the jaw were often left to fester when the simple removal of teeth could easily have alleviated them.[6]

The zoning of death in ancient Egypt meant that, at least among the wealthy, there was little need to face the nitty-gritty. Freed to pursue theological and philosophical enquiries, they concentrated almost entirely on the mystery of death on a cosmological level. It is tempting to think that this was because it had become physically distant from them. In the modern world, even morticians display elements of visceral insulation: 'We instil in our staff the need to handle each body as though it were a member of their own family, though, having said that, I wouldn't want to embalm anyone I know,' as one embalmer recently admitted.[7] This is a reversal of the common practice in tribal societies, where the care of the corpse is specifically the duty of the nearest relatives and the idea of a stranger being involved would be deeply offensive.

Visceral insulation did not arise overnight. As humans spread out around the world, a vast spectrum of cultural types was brought into being: rainforest hunter-gatherers and tundra hunter-fishers, village-based rural farming societies, and great states and empires, with an extraordinary complexity of statuses, classes and professions. Within civilizations, dirty and distressing jobs were delegated to people who could become habituated to them. The viscerally immersed specializations of slaughterers, tanners, butchers, embalmers, grave-diggers, and refuse collectors freed others to become insulated enough to specialize in the arts and sciences. Without visceral insulation there would have been no Johann Sebastian Bach and no Marie Curie.

The contrast between societies who had become civilized in this sense and the many smaller-scale tribal groupings who lived closer to nature became more sharply felt as global trade developed. Maritime empires, such as those of the Portuguese and British, began to enforce uniformity of behaviour at the same time that cultural diversity was first being systematically studied by the early anthropologists. In many parts of the world, colonial administrations forcibly brought indigenous funeral ceremonies to an end, not just in societies that still practised funerary cannibalism, but in those with the full-blown tripartite rites observed by van Gennep at the turn of the nineteenth and twentieth centuries: 'Throughout Melanesia, colonial officials suppressed death rites, often involving secondary burial and exposure of corpses, because they found them repulsive, and condemned them as unhygienic,' write the anthropologists Peter Metcalf and Richard Huntington.[8]

In the Trobriand Islands these rites had vanished by 1920, so that, when a young anthropologist named Bronislaw Malinowski came to study the people, only garbled vestiges remained. Unable to see any logic in them, Malinowski dismissed death rituals in general as irrelevant to the study of belief systems. As his career took off and he became, arguably, the most influential social anthropologist of the twentieth century, the trend was set that inevitably led to the 1980s' and 1990s' blanket denial of ritual funerary cannibalism. It may even be that Malinowski was influential precisely because his studies sat comfortably with the increasingly viscerally insulated style of modernism.[9]

The banal reality of Clastres' statement that the Atchei, with whom he lived in Paraguay in the 1960s, 'do not roast very young children for the simple reason that there would not be enough to go round. But when they are boiled in water with *tangy* [hearts of young pindo palm], everyone can get a normal helping' is hard for us even to begin to conceptualize. William Arens' disbelief in custom cannibalism (discussed in Chapter 3) is an intellectual variety of visceral insulation. Du Chaillu, travelling in the mid-nineteenth century, was able to compare a Fang woman toting a human thigh with the usual way 'we' might carry a haunch of meat home from market. But the 'we' has changed. Like morticians, even some of our butchers show signs of becoming viscerally insulated: on a recent visit to the meat counter of my local supermarket, I asked for kidneys and was doubtfully proffered a large slab of liver. The person who served me was wearing the distinctive red-and-white striped apparel of the butcher's trade, but possessed talents better suited to stocking the freezer cabinets with some of the classic style statements of visceral insulation – burgers, nuggets and dippers.

Visceral insulation also pervades the contemporary debate about satanic ritual abuse (SRA). While some people accept claims concerning the ritualized sexual abuse of children and the killing

Visceral engagement: preparing food with flint blades in standard prehistoric fashion. (Photo: author)

of newborn babies by perpetrators who may remain unidentifiable to their victims behind Hallowe'en masks, others, alerted by good historical evidence of false witchcraft accusations in European history,[10] remain highly doubtful that the phenomenon is real.

Epping Forest is a large area of dense woodland on the northeast edge of London, a place where people go to indulge in a variety of activities, legitimate and illegitimate. The key witness in the Epping Forest satanic ritual abuse case, which collapsed on 19 November 1991, was a 10-year-old girl who testified to a horrific catalogue of sexual abuse but finally broke down in court, saying, 'I am not sure if it did happen or if I was just imagining it . . . the bits with the killings and that, I am not sure of'. The judge dismissed the entire case on this point, saying that her evidence was 'uncertain, inconsistent, and improbable'.[11]

The claim of 'improbability' is demonstrably suspect: in August 1989 Peter McKenzie, who operated in nearby Hertfordshire, was sentenced to fifteen years' imprisonment for raping

281

a number of young children. During the rapes, he conducted black magic rites and told the six-year-olds that they were being initiated as witches. Responses to the McKenzie case are particularly interesting as they show how doctrinal schisms within pagan groupings closely mirror those within established churches. Arguments rage (mainly on the internet) about the relationship between 'wicca', paganism, satanism and their seemingly myriad brands. McKenzie, once convicted, was effectively denounced as a heretic, because he told his child victims that there were five steps to initiation as a witch, as opposed to the three apparently recognized by aficionados of the occult.[12] What, precisely, the terms of heresy are in belief systems which, like the Odinic cult of the Rus, explicitly revel in lies and deception, is hard to say. But the police conclusion was also that McKenzie's rituals were not 'real', the ceremonies being 'purely a device that McKenzie used to abuse young girls', as Detective Chief Inspector Richard Pottinger put it.

The McKenzie case establishes a pattern that can be followed in other convictions. The law does not recognize a specific crime of SRA and so does not take account of the potential additional psychological damage that victims may suffer in a deliberately disorienting ritual context (whether subjected to the 'real thing' or an empty 'device'). Likewise, those who defend paganism as wholesome are at pains to point out the doctrinal errors of convicted perpetrators (such as misspelling spirits' names during invocation ceremonies). One historian of the occult says of Malcolm Smith, a convicted paedophile who ritually abused children, that 'there was no lineage of Satanism, no connection with any other Satanic group or Satanist' and that Smith's motive was 'perversion which would have occurred whether or not there had been any occult connection'.[13]

Researchers such as Valerie Sinason have documented how perpetrators use a variety of techniques – including masks, drugs, lies, threats, simple conjuring tricks, illusions and theatrical props – to terrify and disorient victims and render any later testimony confused.[14] This seems to be part of the sadistic kick in itself.

Yet, although nothing that has been described as taking place during satanic ritual abuse falls outside the range of known human behaviours, those who disbelieve it often designate themselves 'sceptics', as if what is at issue is too categorically bizarre to be humanly possible. The same hollow certainty of viscerally insulated inexperience pervaded William Arens' *The Man Eating Myth* of 1979 (the comforting and popular book that doubted the existence of custom cannibalism at any time in any place) and finds echoes in Jean La Fontaine's recent *Speak of the Devil: Tales of Satanic Abuse in Contemporary England*.[15]

Markus Tiedemann, in his award-winning 1996 book, '*No One Was Gassed in Auschwitz': 60 Far-right Lies and How to Counter Them*,[16] demonstrates in compelling detail how, when a particular form of human behaviour is not directly experienced or has ceased to occur, it is possible for people to begin to doubt that it ever happened. Denial of the Holocaust has produced a vast range of shifting and mutually contradictory justifications for disbelief. Lie No. 33, 'Because no one survived a gassing there is no reliable testimony that they occurred', may be compared to Lie No. 32, 'The words "gassing" or "gaschamber" do not survive in any document from the Third Reich', and Lie No. 35, 'Yes, there were gaschambers, but they were never used'. That Tiedemann, over fifty years after the event, has to reproduce the definitive documents (for example, the word *Vergassungskeller*, 'gassing-cellar', appears in the official documentation relating to the construction of the No. 2 Crematorium at Birkenau in 1943)[17] may tell us something more general about human psychology.

The things that are said about the impossibility of the Holocaust are so varied and creative that one is forced to rule out an orchestrated conspiracy of denial. Self-deception could be part of our natural psychological defence mechanism: 'Confronted with horrors, Dr Johnson said, we take refuge in incredulity. We can also go for explanation – but, sometimes at least – it is ourselves we need to understand, and, understandably, we prefer not to.'[18] Part of our own way of doing things is to accept them as right to the point where we flatly disbelieve that they could be done differently.

The Holocaust was so well organized that there are virtually no surviving human remains from the six million who were exterminated. By comparison, the killing and subsequent disposal of a few newborn babies is relatively easy to perpetrate without discovery. Hidden pregnancies happen all the time: a newborn child found in a Sheffield telephone box in March 2002 was the fourth such abandonment in three years in Yorkshire alone (all four mothers so far remain unidentified).[19] In SRA claims, a hidden pregnancy and an unregistered birth mean that there is, in legal terms, no known victim. It is not surprising that people doubt SRA. But absence of material evidence is not evidence of absence, and we must also remember that evidence does not become evidence until it is recognized as such. There are bones to be found; it is simply that we do not know who they might belong to.

A black-and-white photograph taken in Scotland in the 1960s shows a young woman posing as a witch at the grave of Maggie Walls, a woman accused of witchcraft and burned at the stake in the village of Dunning, Perthshire in 1657. The face is that of Myra Hindley, a self-styled witch who was holidaying with her lover, Ian Brady. It is not known if the pair killed in Scotland – Brady confessed to two murders there but no bodies have ever been found. What is known is that they went on to torture at least six children to death while sexually abusing them. They left a record of photographs and tape-recordings of their activities which are among the vilest pieces of evidence ever brought before an English court. But if you enter the word 'witch' and the name 'Myra Hindley' in an internet search engine you get a string of hits all decrying the 'hysterical' media 'witch hunt' against this most notorious of British mass murders. The skeletons of some of the victims are still buried in shallow graves somewhere on the bleak, peaty expanses of Saddleworth Moor, and continue to defy the best efforts of my colleagues in forensic archaeology to locate them.[20]

There are only three sorts of witch, and none of them ride broomsticks. There are those who claim to be witches (currently 150,000 of an estimated 250,000 adherents of resurgent paganism in Britain);[21] those who are claimed to be witches by others but who do not accept it (such as those scapegoated during the sixteenth-century witchcraft trials); and those who are communally accepted as functional witches (such as the traditional isangomas who practise muti).

Accepting that there is such a thing as a witch generates unease in secular minds because it is easy to confuse 'belief in witchcraft' – the belief in the existence of a set of behaviours aimed at producing seemingly supernatural effects (objectively observable and mainly achieved through inducing psychological stress);[22] and 'belief in witchcraft' – the idea that spells can produce effects by magic. In fact, the idea of a witch can be thought of in much the same way as the idea of a Catholic priest, a man whom we recognize as having a ritual role and who believes, on pain of excommunication by the Pope, that the Eucharistic bread and wine are wholly transformed into the actual flesh and blood of Jesus Christ.[23] An outsider like me does not have to believe in these special powers to accept that the Catholic priest is a real entity. It is just the same with witches.

There is nothing necessarily mystical about ritual either: it can function in the absence of a supernatural belief system as an arbitrary protocol allowing people, such as official executioners, to carry through their expected duties. Sadism is frequently choreographed in such a way that the word 'ritual' becomes appropriate to describe it. On the other hand, occult belief, especially in an evil Devil who opposes God, is not necessarily incompatible with sadistic or murderous intent (and may well have particular appeal to psychopaths).

By ritually killing children, whether as part of South African muti (over 100 documented cases in the 1990s),[24] or in a Tantric rite in northern India (ditto),[25] or in a British neo-pagan black magic ritual (for which the evidence and its correct designation remain disputed), participants feel less alone and more alive.

Muti thrives in modern South Africa because of, not in spite of, modernization. It is a traditional, comfort-zone response to a rapidly changing environment. People who ritually kill children, in whatever way they congregate and whatever they may believe they are doing, are, in a perverse and negative way, repossessing the power over life and death which modern establishment institutions have been so effective in monopolizing.

In considering the nature and potential extent of SRA we should exercise genuine scepticism, as opposed to the viscerally insulated variety. Our doubts should extend to the degree to which other people conform to the codes of conduct that we find personally acceptable. In particular, we should guard against a covert cultural imperialism: the sacrifice of children by satanists should not be inherently unbelievable just because the perpetrators might be modern Britons.

To her victims, what Myra Hindley 'truly' believed was as irrelevant to what transpired as the Rus' beliefs were to the slave-girl whose last hours Ibn Faḍlān witnessed. This is the point where relativism, so useful for getting inside the logic of cultural actions, has to stop and moral judgement begin. It is not all that difficult. When Pierre Clastres is with Baipugi in the Paraguayan rain forest as she rakes through the ashes for the remains of the 18-month-old baby son that her lover, ignoring her protests, has eaten, he sees that her tears streak her ritual make-up. He recognizes, as we do, that grief is washing away the mask of cultural difference.

Doubting not just the existence, but even the possibility, of SRA is perhaps a by-product of having habitually civilized thoughts. To the viscerally insulated sensitivity, the thought that some people actually enjoy killing is too much to bear. But our discomfort is even more deep seated: it is almost as if we do not want to believe in death itself.

Those who claim to have been the victims of SRA are nowadays scapegoated like medieval rape victims, and labelled as mentally ill. Against a background of very recent media acceptance of the existence of 'ordinary' child sex abuse, these new, more disturbing victims are the target for all the societal anger that arises when our attention is drawn to something we would rather not look at.

Visceral insulation, in prehistory and history, has led to the creation of a series of increasingly distinct and exclusive comfort zones. Finally, it is death itself that we wish desperately to insulate ourselves against, isolating it and removing it from the cycle of life. Yet an acceptance of inevitable mortality is the best spur to ethical behaviour. Death signals the end point beyond which our reputations become irrevocable because our actions, which were always indelible, have finished and any further personal reparation has become impossible.

If we have beliefs, it is easy to make the mistake of thinking that our rituals are just the way that we express them. Emile Durkheim saw things the other way round – the most significant beliefs arose, he thought, out of the established forms of rituals.[26] My interpretation of the unforeseen way in which the invention of burial created an image of the immortal soul follows this logic. Our practices in the present day, whatever our reasons for them, will almost certainly rebound on us, in unexpected ways, in future.[27] The way of doing and organizing things that I have characterized here as viscerally insulated, notwithstanding the civilizing benefits it can bring, may tempt us to relax our guard. Shielded as many of us now are from the brutal facts of life and death, it is easy to become misled about the underlying nature of our species and to be drawn into an apologetic relativism, while the cruel, the powerful and the deviant visit their unresolved existential traumas on the weak and innocent. We are still capable of scapegoating and raw uncivilized reflexes. Our reflective morality is as precious and eggshell thin as a baby's skull, barely containing what is most potent and primal.

I never saw my grandfather dead. Rationally, I know he is dead but emotionally it is less clear cut. Perhaps that is best for me. I wonder sometimes whether I should visit my grandfather's grave, if it exists, and see his gravestone. Part of me says that this will bring closure, but another part of me resists. Perhaps, having felt for so long that I killed him, I want to keep him in limbo. If I knew where his body lay I might become frightened of his disembodied and vengeful soul.

Notes

Introduction

1. Pynchon 1997: 696.
2. I Samuel 28: 15
3. Hancock and Faiia 1998; Knight & Lomas 2000.
4. Mowatt 1999; the prize remained unclaimed on the 1 January 2000 deadline.
5. The age estimates vary from 5 to 7, with Scholz *et al.* 1997 arguing for closer to 7.
6. A number of archaeologists at the Department of Archeological Sciences in Bradford act as consultants for the National Crime Faculty (the British counterpart of the FBI) at Bramshill in Hampshire; in this case, a radio report alerted me to the potential muti dimension and DS Graham Nunn of the NCF came to Bradford to discuss the case on 9 Nov. 2001. South African experts with direct experience of muti were subsequently brought in to aid the investigation.
7. 'Muti' means traditional medicine in a general sense; it can be of plant, animal or human origin.
8. Scholz *et al.* 1997: 117.
9. Ngubane 1986.
10. Darwin 1872; Baron-Cohen 1998; Cowgill 2000: 732 in response to Tarlow 2000.
11. The investigation subsequently focused on communities where African isangomas or 'witches' might operate. In South Africa, Nelson Mandela made an appeal for help (Vasagar 2002). On 9 July 2002 a woman of West African origin was arrested in Glasgow and taken to London for questioning in connection with the case.
12. Until analyses are complete the maximum numbers remain

unknown. See Wahl & König 1987; Keeley 1996, 1997. The number of those apparently killed in a single event may rise well into the high hundreds at sites like Herxheim; the preceding Mesolithic was hardly peaceful: Thorpe 2000.

13. *ka* (the 'double'); *bai* (the soul proper, a human-headed bird); *ikh* (spirit bird); and *khaibit* (the shadow): see Hall 1949; Hornung 1992: Chapter 9.

14. Derrida 1995.

15. Mortalness is an attractive 17th-century word which deserves dusting off.

16. 'Emotional intelligence' is a term coined by the psychologist Peter Salovey (see Salovey & Sluyter 1997) and given wide currency by Daniel Goleman (1995); on issues of certainty of knowledge see also Taylor 2001a.

Chapter 1

1. Egg & Spindler 1993: 65. The original reads: 'In weitere Folge fanden sich bei den Toten vom Hauslabjoch zwei Stücke von Baumpilzen. Der "Mann im Eis" schnitt beide aus einem Baumschwamm heraus, durchlochte sie, zog einen unten verknoteten Leder- bzw. Fellriemen durch das Loch, um sie so an seinem Gürtel . . . befestigen zu können. Baumschwämme wurden bis vor noch nicht allzu langer Zeit sowohl zum Entzünden eines Feuers als auch als Verbandsmaterial, dem man eine blutstillende und entzündungshemmende Wirkung nachsagt, benutzt.' (For this find see also the admirable popular account of the discovery and early phases of analysis in Spindler 1994).

2. Holden 2001.

3. e.g. Polet *et al.* 1996; Schutkowski *et al.* 1996; I opened my book *The Prehistory of Sex* with a discussion of Ötzi in another context, but my negative characterization of the Neolithic period later on seems to have been strengthened by subsequent analyses.

4. Greenwell 1870; Barber *et al.* 1999, 2000.

5. The existence of a form of slavery in the Neolithic seems likely: see references to Gronenborn in Taylor 2001b.

6. The analysis of the material was done by Clutton-Brock & Burleigh;

I am most grateful to Gillian Varndell for information concerning this find.

7. There is little agreement about the correct social interpretation of the 'beaker' phenomenon. See Vander Linden 2001 for literature and a useful recent summary.

8. Barber *et al.* 2000: 28, citing estimates by Longworth & Varndell.

9. Dent 1985 for Wetwang Slack; Cunliffe 1991 for overview.

10. J. Chapman 1994, referring to Davies.

11. General orientation can be found in Haviland 2000; for the earliest stone tools see Semaw *et al.* 1997. The subtitle to *The Prehistory of Sex: Four million years of human sexual culture* exploited an ambiguity in the use of the complex word 'culture', which is used both by primatologists (e.g. de Waal 2001) to characterize the learned and transmitted routines of chimpanzees on the one hand, and by cultural commentators to designate the most refined types of modern human achievement; I am more specific in this book, connecting culture in its generic human sense most closely to the controversial origin of language, perhaps emerging with the genus *Homo* some two million years ago; but that is not to say that the period from 4 to 2 million years ago can be unproblematically decribed as 'natural'.

12. Haddenham analyses have been carried out by Mary Baxter; for Stoney Middleton see English Heritage 1996.

13. Gimbutas 1991.

14. Lewis 2001; see also Renfrew 1979; Hedges 1984; J. Barber 1988.

15. Ritchie & Ritchie 1991: 30.

16. Bendann 1930: 197f citing Codrington *The Melanesians*; Rivers, *History of Melanesian Society* Vol II: 277; Brown, *Melanesians, Polynesians*, Wheeler *Archiv für Religionwissenschaft* 17 (1914): 64; the ethnographic description of burial practices has been confirmed by archaeological work: Spriggs 1997.

17. Thomas 1965.

18. I am grateful to Paul Bloom for a discussion of this; his view is that although saying prayers in the presence of the deceased could be soul related, sitting shiva, which he first told me about, should be understood only as intensive mourning.

19. Dart 1959.

20. Berger & Clarke 1995, 1996; Hedenstrom 1995.

21. Taylor 1996: figs 1.5, 1.7, 1.8.

22. Pfeiffer 1982.

23. Rowley-Conwy 1993 (cf Leroi-Gourhan 1975).

24. Trinkaus 1983.

25. Noble & Davidson 1996.

26. Lieberman 1992.

27. Ovchinnikov *et al.* 2000; Krings *et al.* 1997; Ward & Stringer 1997.

28. Duarte *et al.* 1999.

29. Grün *et al.* 2002 (in press).

30. I am grateful to Alistair Pike for a discussion of how the various physics-based dating techniques share some systematic sources of error and uncertainty (that is, they do not simply independently corroborate one another).

31. For Qafzeh see Vandermeersch 1966 and subsequent publications by him; Garrod's excavation standards were good for their time; the stratigraphic (relative and, by extension often absolute) dating difficulty lies in the way that the fossil bones and other archaeological evidence become mixed and fragmented by short-term geological processes in these caves; see also Bar-Yosef *et al.* 1992.

32. Toren 1998.

33. Sherratt 1997: 419.

34. It is a moot philosophical point whether humanists can be said to hold religious beliefs. According to definition, religion may not necessarily extend beyond a belief in transcendental ethics to any specific belief or disbelief in God.

35. Peta 2001; cf for Shanidar see Dettwyler 1991.

Chapter 2

1. Edmund Spenser 1596, *An Hymn in Honour of Beauty*: 1.90: 132.

2. Friesinger & Vacha 1987.

3. Atkins 1994: 143.

4. Many physicists are happy to speak of 'M theory' and the '11-dimensional multiverse' while castigating theologians such as Keith

Ward (see 1996) as mystics; others manage, more humbly perhaps, to do physics and also have religious faith (e.g. Polkinghorne 1996).

5. Memento mori means 'remember that you have to die' in Latin. Its English plural could be 'mementoes mori' (the *OED* is silent) and I have taken a cue from modern Italian because I think it sounds better.

6. Ellis 2000: 1 & 4.

7. Polkinghorne 1996: 61. He goes on to say that 'No adequate account of reality could fail to recognize that we live in a world suffused with value' despite the fact that as 'part of its own peculiar style of inquiry, science may choose officially to neglect this dimension'. (But this too could be countered: as the anthropologist Pascal Boyer notes in developing his cognitive theory of religion 'Lack of humanistic "significance" or interest is often the price to pay for causal relevance'. Boyer 1994: 112.)

8. Robert Redford 2002: 24.

9. Wittgenstein 1953: 178.

10. This is very different from the much-criticized idea of the 'Ghost in the Machine' (the phrase was coined by the philosopher Gilbert Ryle in characterizing an aspect of Cartesian duality).

11. Congregation for the Doctrine of Faith, 'De quibusdam quaestionibus', 1979, cited in Fergus Kerr 1986: 178.

12. Luce 1992: 35.

13. I say 'appears to have provoked' because the *Sunday Telegraph* article maintained an atheistic, logical positivist line; this, however, is inconsistent with important personal testimony from those close to Ayer at the time, including the doctor who attended him, Dr Jeremy George. George claims Ayer told him 'I saw a divine being.' A succinct account of the issues (which also questions the veracity of the smoked salmon part of the story) can be found in Cash 2001; for Ayer's professional philosophy see Ayer 1936 and subsequent works.

14. Atwater & Morgan 2000; Bailey 1996.

15. French 1992; the existentialist philosopher Martin Heidegger provides a terse warning in a more general context: *Being and Time*, section II.1.49: 'a psychology of "dying" gives information about the "living" of the person who is "dying", rather than about dying itself' (1962: 291).

16. Bendann 1930 and Vulliamy 1926 provide useful summaries of Frazer, *Belief in Immortality*; Jochelson *The Koryak*; Roth, *Superstition, magic and medicine*; and so on.

17. Vulliamy 1926: 5.

18. As Ludwig Wittgenstein observed, the meaning of 'soul' is contained by its use; he developed this, saying that 'The idea of the human soul, which one either apprehends or fails to apprehend, is very similar to the idea of the meaning of a word, which stands next to the word, whether as a process or an object'. Translation adapted from Last Writings on the Philosophy of Psychology. Preliminary Studies for Part II of Philosophical Investigations (1982), edited by G.H. von Wright & H. Nyman and translated by C.G. Luckhardt & M.A.E. Aue, Vol.1: 127e, No.979 (Oxford: Blackwell): the German reads 'Die Idee vom Geist des Menschen, den man sieht oder nicht sieht, ist sehr ähnlich der Wortbedeutung, die als ein Vorgang oder Objekt beim Wort steht'.

19. Kant, Kritik der reinen Vernunft, 74: 669 = edited English language version in Palmer 1983: 103.

20. Part XIV of the second section of the Law of Homicide, in *King Magnus Eriksson's Law of the Realm: a medieval Swedish code* = Donner 2000: 119.

21. The events occurred in November 1994. The Guy's Hospital, London, case notes were reviewed as 'Case 38' in an unpublished University of Bradford Department of Archaeological Sciences dissertation by Tegwen Owen.

22. Ariès 1974, 1981; Metcalf & Huntington 1991: 206 ff.

23. Distinctively: see L.V. Thomas 1980, 'L'odeur du mort', in *Le Mort* 1980; for the chemistry, see Evans 1963.

24. Smith 1928; Sells 1994.

25. Raban 2002: 5.

26. see e.g. Thompson 1996.

27. Sometimes (mis)translated as a 'death instinct'.

28. Bettelheim 1982: 109.

Chapter 3

1. Cited in Alberry *et al.* 1997:125.
2. Transcript from the television series, *Cannibal* (for which I was the academic consultant): see Korn *et al.* 2001: 34. The series dealt with some but not all of the material covered in this chapter.
3. Taylor 2001c.
4. Rivière 1980.
5. Leakey and Lewin 1977: 132.
6. Post-Arens, some scholars (among them Lewis Binford) have thought that the cannibalism pattern that Leakey and Lewin deduce may have been caused by hyenas getting at the Zhoukoudian dead (Binford & Ho 1985; Binford & Stone 1986). The arguments are hard to reassess as the original fossils were lost during the Japanese invasion of mainland China; for Oxford Companion see Fagan 1996.
7. Baker 1974: 113.
8. Goodall 1986: 112–13; the cannibalization of adults has not, as far as I know, been observed.
9. Darwin 1872; for a positive review of the new edition see Baron-Cohen 1998.
10. Polis *et al.* 1984 cited in Petrinovich 2000: 85. More species have almost certainly by now been added as new observational data come in.
11. Gilmore *et al.* 1990; Elwood 1980.
12. Silverberg and Gray 1992; De Waal 2001 with references to earlier studies; Maestripieri 1999 for unconstructive aggression.
13. Taylor 1996: 95 with reference to the work of Paul Vasey.
14. Bad Planet 1998: despite placenta-eating being a widespread mammalian and human practice with clear adaptive advantages, Fearnley-Whittingstall's television programme was successfully censured by the Broadcasting Standards Authority in the UK which upheld complaints that it had offended a dozen viewers nationwide.
15. Baker 1974: 391ff citing Du Chaillu 1861 and then Schweinfurth 1873; Baker provides extensive extracts and commentary on both these authors in relation to cannibalism.

16. Chen & Chen 1998; Stephen Hallett pers. comm; compare Gordon-Grube 1988.

17. Sahlins 1981; Thomas 1989: 103ff.

18. Sources in Beaglehole 1955, 1961, 1962, 1967.

19. Korn *et al.* 2001: 17–19.

20. Keenleyside *et al.* 1997: 41f.

21. Keenleyside *et al.* 1997: Tabs. 3 & 4 and Figs 2–6.

22. Degusta 1999, 2000, with references to Gifford; Spennemann 1987.

23. Tim White first identified human hair as a regular feature in archaeologically-preserved faeces/coprolites (1992: 340); the human origin of the Cowboy Wash coprolite now seems beyond doubt and must be considered prima facie evidence for cannibalism at the site: Marler *et al.* 2000. For other important southwestern US sites and evidence see Turner 1993; Turner & Turner 1992, 1999; and Novak & Kollmann 2000 for Fremont cooking sequences. For an Arensite view see Bahn 2001.

24. Parry 1998, 1999; see also Darling 1999.

25. Gajdusek 1977 – his Nobel Prize acceptance speech. Gajdusek's work paved the way for the discovery of infectious proteins (and the award of another Nobel Prize in 1997 to Stanley Prusiner who gave them the name 'prion'). Gajdusek's convictions for sexual abuse are cited by Arens in a rather desperate attempt to cast doubt on the established epidemiology of kuru (Arens 1997).

26. Lindenbaum 1979; see also Glasse 1977 and Rhodes 1997.

27. Gillison 1983: 34; I have only had space for an abbreviated version of the Gimi rites and Gillison's interpretation.

28. Gillison 1983: 39f.

29. Transcript of Delgado interview: Korn, Radice, Hawes 2001: 116; see also Read 1974.

30. Transcript of Paez interview: Korn, Radice, Hawes 2001: 116; I have unfortunately not been able to track down Concetti's original *Osservatore Romano* article.

31. Clastres 1972 (1998): 235. (Clastres, a social anthropologist of immense potential and insight, died young, leaving a much freer field for Arens' subsequent blanket denial of custom cannibalism.)

32. Clastres 1972 (1998): 219.

33. Pickering, White & Toth 2000.

34. White 1986: 508.

35. Fernández-Jalvo *et al.* 1999.

36. Bahn 1999: 28; cf White & Toth 1991.

37. Stringer 2000.

38. Villa *et al.* 1986; Villa 1992.

39. Hdt 4.26 in David Grene's translation (1987).

40. Taylor 2001b.

41. Taylor 2001c; Taylor & Zhuravlyov in prep.

42. Bendann 1930: 205, citing Smyth, *The Aborigines of Victoria* Vol. 1: 121.

43. Murphy & Mallory 2000; realizing that Herodotus' description of funerary cannibalism matched the archaeological data these authors present very neatly, I accidentally misrepresented their conclusions in Taylor 2001c, and there was a subsequent correspondence with Paul Bahn over this in the pages of *British Archaeology*.

44. e.g. Toren 1998.

45. Hdt 3.38; David Grene (Bk 3, footnote 4) adds that Pindar, reported in Plato (Gorgias 484B) actually says something longer and less provocative, abbreviated by Herodotus to make his point.

46. Gillison 1983: 42f, footnote 10.

Chapter 4

1. Eco 1989: 164.

2. There are many English versions of this famous piece, most of them inadequate or partially misleading. Proper interpretation depends critically on a close-reading of the original Arabic, and the presentation and commentary in this chapter and in Chapter 7 have benefited immensely from discussions with James Montgomery over the best translation of specific terms. The English text reproduced here closely follows Montgomery 2000, with minor alterations signalled in the endnoting.

3. Swedish coin finds are reported in the *Corpus Nummorum Saeculorum IX–XI qui in Suecia Reperti Sunt*. Scholars such as Brita Malmer estimate that 35% of a quarter-million Viking-Age coins in all

Scandinavia were oriental: i.e. 87,500, mainly Arabic dirhams struck in the Caliphate; cf Campbell 1980: 110.

4. Palsson & Edwards 1989.

5. The most up-to-date source information with further readings can be found in Montgomery 2000, 2001, forthcoming a & b; see also discussions in Crumlin-Pedersen & Thye 1995 and cultural background in Jones 1968.

6. Montgomery pers. comm. others have previously suggested that he was a diplomat or a religious expert (e.g. Warmind 1995: 132), but there is no firm evidence for this.

7. Warmind 1995.

8. Müller-Wille 1974; Carver 1995; Ingstad 1995.

9. for Gnezdovo see *Time-Life* 1993: 68–9.

10. Warmind 1995: 134; all subsequent direct quotations from Warmind are from pages 134–5 of his short article.

11. Váňa 1983: 84–5.

12. Flon (ed.) 1985: 180; cf 'willing victims': Armstrong in Fagan 1996: 730.

13. Sherratt 1997: 419.

14. Prescott 1857: 347; Díaz 1963.

15. Townsend 1992: 28, fig 10.

16. Clendinnen 1991: 110; for a different overall perspective see Harner 1977; Harris 1977; cf Vayda 1970.

17. See Derrida 1995 with further references.

18. Clendinnen 1991: 103.

19. As Clendinnen puts it: 'There are haunting echoes of childhood here, and the possibility of a process of infantilization' (1991: 102).

20. Clendinnen 1991: 104 quoting the *Florentine Codex* 9: 14: 16.

21. Parker Pearson 1999: 17.

22. Clendinnen 1991: 104.

23. Dennis Hughes, in his study of *Human Sacrifice in Ancient Greece* warns that 'there are many possible occasions for the ritual slaying of human victims, and it would be erroneous and misleading to group all forms of ritual killing of humans together under the term "human sacrifice"' (1991: 8).

24. Taylor 1997 provides a background to the archaeological corre-

spondence between eastern European Iron Age archaeology and the descriptions of Herodotus' *History*, Book 4 (Grene 1987).

25. As Walter Williams pointed out in his groundbreaking book on native American sexuality, *The Spirit and the Flesh* (1986), such a thing is anathema even in those many communities where male–male or female–female consortships are approved. Without exception, one partner has to dress as male and the other as female, so that all marriages, even homosexual or lesbian ones (and they did exist), were *heterogender*.

Chapter 5

1. Zbarsky & Hutchinson 1998: 181.
2. Metcalf, 'The living and the dead: a re-examination of Hertz': Ch 4 in Metcalf & Huntington 1991.
3. Van Gennep 1960: 189.
4. Van Gennep 1960: 11.
5. *Année Sociologique* X (1907) translated by R & C. Needham (punctuation modernized) as 'A contribution to the study of the collective representation of death' (see Hertz 1960).
6. Doutté cited in Van Gennep 1960: 50.
7. Van Gennep 1960: 51.
8. Batchelor cited in Van Gennep 1960: 53.
9. Sheehan 1994; O'Sullivan & Sheehan 1996; Monk & Sheehan 1998; perhaps murder victims too, for rather different reasons (I guess that these might be fruitful places to target for traces of the vanished victims of the most recent round of Irish 'troubles').
10. A term first used by Thomas Aquinas in his *Summa* and later popularized by Dante in the *Divine Comedy*.
11. Van Gennep 1960: 53f (punctuation emended).
12. Hertz 1960: 84.
13. Important contributions to this debate from the standpoint of philosophical bioethics are Tooley 1983; Genevieve Lloyd 'Women and Philosophy', 1986 suppl. to *Australasian Journal of Philosophy*, criticizes Tooley for ignoring the 'emotional contexts of pregnancy and infancy'.

14. Compare Parker Pearson 1999: 11, where he claims a knife can *symbolize* such cutting.

15. Van Gennep 1960: 146.

16. Cited by Metcalf & Huntington 1991: 81.

17. Hertz's writings are dense and full of nuance so these are rough characterizations; Peter Metcalf and Richard Huntington in their standard anthropological textbook, *Celebrations of Death*, devote a whole chapter to his ideas; my interest in Hertz was begun by the art historian, Sasha Borin, in Sofia, and was continued by Rodney Needham's post-graduate anthropology seminars at All Souls, Oxford in 1984 (Rodney and Claudia Needham were Hertz's translators into English).

18. Hertz 1960: 37.

19. Hertz 1960: 76.

20. E.g. Van Gennep 1960: 157.

21. This is highlighted in the 'Equality Now' annual report for 2000 (info@equalitynow.org); textbook anthropology rarely refers to the possibility of dissatisfaction with ritual prescriptions, which is why political activism and investigative journalism are so important.

22. Taylor 1994; Sulimirski & Taylor 1990.

23. The English version running with commentary over the next few pages starts from Herodotus Book 4.71; the translation mainly follows Grene 1987. The word given here as 'sweet-smelling sedge' – *kuperos* – could have been any of the cyperaceae, marsh-plants such as sweet galingale and adrue, which contain volatile oils and astringent substances, smelling of lavender: see Bown 1995, *The Royal Horticultural Society Encylopedia of Herbs and their Uses*: 271.

24. Taylor 1994: 393f.

25. Calculations by Jäger VBI Engineering, Göttingen, in Rolle, Murzin & Alekseev 1998, Vol. 1: 64; abb 24.

26. Taylor 1994: 392: ii.

27. I have been reliably informed that the seeds of current strains of cannabis have no known narcotic effect; as with so many other plants, the precise strain may have been important.

28. Sulimirski & Taylor 1990.

29. Hdt 4.126–7.

30. The Morozov estate was renamed in 1922 after the Soviet play-

wright Maxim Gorky. For details on personages from this period see Brown 1990.

31. The so-called 'liquidation of the kulaks'.

32. Zbarsky & Hutchinson 1998: 17.

33. Brown 1990: 73; Zbarsky & Hutchinson 1998: 104.

34. Zbarsky & Hutchinson 1998.

35. Abrikosov quoted in Zbarsky & Hutchinson 1998, chapter 6.

36. The *Mozga Institut Akedemiya Meditsinskikh Nauk SSSR*.

37. Zbarsky & Hutchinson 1998: 205.

Chapter 6

1. Babel 1957: 60; I am grateful to my wife, Sarah Wright, for this translation. A published English version exists as Babel, 'The life and adventures of Matthew Pavlichenko' (Babel 1974: 92f).

2. Heaney 1998: 64.

3. Stead & Turner 1985; Stead, Bourke & Brothwell 1986.

4. Van der Sanden 1996: 167; I have mentioned Himmler's unfortunate enthusiasm for archaeological interpretation before, in *The Prehistory of Sex* (1996: 234 & 241).

5. *De Bello Gallico* 5.14; *vitrum* was for long translated as 'woad', a plant-based bluish dye, but it is now thought likely that it was a mineral-based cosmetic.

6. The total of 9 radiocarbon-14 date estimates for Lindow II and the further 11 for Lindow III have overlapping ranges, tightly packed between AD 50 and AD 200.

7. Van der Sanden 1996: 116; this conclusion was supported by electron spin resonance spectroscopy, indicating that the cereals had been heated to 200–250°C for a short period.

8. Mabey 1988: 105 etc.

9. Cornelius Tacitus, in his book *Concerning the Geography, the Manners and Customs, and the Tribes, of Germany* – Tacitus's *Germania*, for short – written in AD 98.

10. Taylor 1992; Randsborg 1995: 207.

11. Mallory 1989: 128.

12. Váňa 1983: 83.

13. Taking his title from Shakespeare, as I have also done for this chapter: 'Thou know'st 'tis common – all that live must die,/Passing through nature to eternity' (Gertrude, Queen of Denmark in Shakespeare, *Hamlet*, Act I, Scene II); see also end-note 42 below.

14. Van der Sanden 1996: 43; Pringle 2001.

15. Van der Sanden 1996: 165.

16. Van der Sanden 1996: 18; for Maillard reactions see Kurti, This-Benckhard & Aukland 1994: 13–20.

17. Van der Sanden 1996: 23.

18. Van der Sanden 1996: 23.

19. This estimate represents the 2-Sigma or 95% confidence interval, on the basis of two date determinations made by the Copenhagen laboratory and calibrated using the Gronigen curve. Van der Sanden 1996: 77, No.13 and p.195, Cat No.117.

20. *Ergotamine, ergotoxine* and *ergometrine*: Mass ergotism poisoning still occurs in parts of Europe when infected grain is wilfully or carelessly milled into flour. Grünewald's Isenheimer altarpiece, made for an ergotism hospital chapel, shows the crucified Jesus afflicted by St Anthony's Fire.

21. Van der Sanden 1996: 118.

22. These finely-woven girdles may have been of both ethnic and social significance.

23. Green 2001: 117 & 202f.

24. Van der Sanden 1996: 141.

25. This theory is largely confined to the German scholarly literature, where the term *Wiedergänger* meaning literally 'again-wanderer', is used; 'undead' is my idiomatic translation; see Turner & Scaife 1995; Briggs 1995.

26. Ross 1986.

27. *De Bello Gallico* VI, 13–14.

28. Tacitus *Annals* 14.30.

29. Pliny, *Natural History* 16.95; Lucan, *Pharsalia* 1, 444–6; see also Green 2001: 209.

30. Green 2001: 186.

31. Mabey 1988: 85 citing S. Rosell & G. Samuelsson, 1966, *Toxicon* 4: 107; Deni Bown, in the Royal Horticultural Society's *Encylopedia*

of Herbs says, 'the constituents of V. album appear to vary according to the host plant, which may explain why the Druids regarded mistletoe on oak as superior' (Bown 1995: 370).

32. Van der Sanden 1996: 161.
33. Van der Sanden 1996: 180.
34. Van der Sanden 1996: 178f.
35. Van der Sanden 1996: 178.
36. Van der Sanden 1996: 180.
37. Taylor 1996: 219f.
38. *Lex Gundobada* (34,1) 'Si qua mulier maritum suum, cui legitime est iuncta, dimiserit, necetur in luto'; van der Sanden gives this as 'when a woman repudiates the man with whom she is united in wedlock, she shall die in a swamp' but *necetur* must be taken as more active (putting to death), while *luto* is slightly less specific than swamp or bog.
39. Van der Sanden 1996: 41.
40. Taylor 1996: 221.
41. Van der Sanden notes this, but then seems to accept all water mires and swamps as equally liminal; eventually this prevents him from making any specific explanation of the choice of raised bogs, and he ends up considering the flesh-free fen skeletons and the preserved bog bodies as two archaeological dimensions of the same original social phenomenon.
42. Shakespeare, *King Lear* Act 5, Sc. 3, lines 314–16.
43. Clendinnen 1991: 91.
44. Indeed, before the decipherment of their script, this is exactly what was believed of the Aztecs' equally bloodthirsty neighbours in Mesoamerica, the ancient Maya.

Chapter 7

1. 'So – werf ich den Brand im Walhalls prangende Burg': *Der Ring des Nibelungen. Dritter Tag: Die Götterdämmerung* (The Ring of the Nibelungen. Day Three: The Twilight of the Gods) Act 3, Scene 3, by Richard Wagner = 1913. *Der Ring des Nibelungen. Vollständiger Text mit Notentafeln der Leitmotive* (my trans.).
2. Jones 1968: 317.
3. Campbell 1980: 183.

4. Whereas the Norse *Niflheim* was thought of as cold, the Anglo-Saxon king Alfred wrote of it in AD 888 in terms of burning and fire – more like Hell as we think of it. The translation of Judaic *Sheol* or Classical *Hades* by the word Hell is a relatively late phenomenon (Bernstein 1993); the name Hel, from Old Teutonic feminine noun **haljâ* 'the coverer up' or 'hider' is cognate with *Hell*.

5. Crumlin-Pedersen & Thye 1995; Campbell 1980: 182f; Davidson 1998; Freyja was equivalent to Germanic *Nerthus* – a 'Mother Earth' figure. The tracing of female deities is made difficult by their more localized character and the fact that they are less frequently and less consistently mentioned. Odin was married to Frig, while Freja's brother is Frey. Their cult is to an extent interchangeable and thus often sexually ambiguous, existing either in some accommodation with Odinism, or hidden, or in open opposition.

6. Davidson 1998: 173, citing the Elder Edda: Helgakviȝa Hundingsbana II.

7. Jones 1968: 325.

8. Montgomery 2000: 76.

9. Jones 1968; compare Eliade 1972.

10. Palsson & Edwards 1989: 58 (*Vikings in Russia: Yngvar's Saga and Eymund's Saga*); the early thirteenth-century Icelandic text reproduces a lost Latin original of *c.* AD 1180.

11. Montgomery 2001: 76.

12. Warmind 1995: 135; Campbell 1980: 175f.

13. Sherratt 1997.

14. Jago 2002; I am grateful to Daphne Nash-Briggs for pointing out the significance of autumn as the end of the fighting season.

15. Montgomery pers. comm.

16. Bown 1995: 318; *Ocimum sanctum* is second in sacredness only to the lotus in Indian religions.

17. Warmind 1995: 134.

18. It could also be read as 'Say that *you* have done this . . .'

19. Van Gennep 1960; the tent-lords are supernaturally dangerous in a way that Tolkien, as a profound scholar of Norse mythology, understood precisely when he created the Nazgûl, or ring-wraiths, in *The Lord of the Rings*; see also Shippey 1982.

20. Metcalf & Huntington 1991: 114: Ireland makes a good comparison: in many parts of medieval northern Europe men were responsible for the digging of graves, the building of pyres and the actual disposal of the body, while women were responsible for corpse preparation. Here, prior to the burial or burning, the men would organize lively games and sports while the women lamented. In Ireland in historical times, Gearóid Ó Crullaóich views the keening woman, the *bean chaointe*, as 'an agent of the transition of the individual deceased to an other-world' while the role of the rowdy male master of ceremonies, the *borekeen*, is to 'assert the continuing vitality of the community so that it can re-establish itself in the face of death' (Ó Crullaóich 1990: 146f, cited in Davidson 1998: 172).

21. While small child brides, as young as four, are known to have been tied to the funeral pyre in suttee as they could not be expected to fulfil their duty otherwise, the slave-girl is clearly significantly older.

22. Hdt. Book 5.5: the word I have translated as 'throat cut' here, *sphazein*, can have a sacrificial connotation; but it appears in this context to denote no more than the mode of death, which Herodotus is careful to distinguish from Scythian strangulation in similar circumstances; cf. Hughes 1991: 9.

23. Taylor 2001b.

24. Chadwick 1899.

25. James Montgomery pers. comm.

26. Page 1990: 38.

27. *Time-Life* 1993: 67. In this they were like their Iron Age precursors: Taylor 1992.

28. This would have added a further frisson to the deception the Rus play on their Arab visitor.

29. Montgomery pers. comm.

30. '*Gulfaginning*': Davidson 1998: 179.

31. E.g. McKinley 1997; see also Wahl 1981.

32. Jones 1968: 319ff.

33. Page 1990: 36; for the route of preservation in Snorri's Edda see Shippey 1982: 275.

34. Banks 1990: 41.

Chapter 8

1. Roy 1997: 251.
2. Svoboda pers. comm.; see also Klima 1987, 1988; Roebroeks *et al.* 2000.
3. Eitzmann 1958; Bednarik 1966; Morris 1994.
4. See e.g. Baron-Cohen *et al.* 1996.
5. One objection to this kind of inference about the possible significance of the Makapansgat pebble is that the distinction between the animate and the inanimate might be drawn differently in different human-ancestor and early hominid groups. It can be argued that in terms of ontology (the theory of being), there are peoples who have apparently considered clay idols or wooden totems to be imbued with spirit and thus somehow 'alive'. But in fact people only consider such totems alive in very circumscribed ways: human interaction depends on recognizing each other as agents with similar mental states to those we are familiar with in ourselves, and so on. So this objection, as far as modern humans go, is weak. As Pascal Boyer technically expresses it: 'There is just no evidence in cross-cultural investigations . . . for the existence of cultural environments that would do without a mentalistic spontaneous psychology *[an intuitive grasp of the existence of other people]* or an ontological divide between artifacts and living beings or an essentialistic understanding of living kinds' (Boyer 1994: 291). There is obviously another level of problem in theorizing about Australopithecines.
6. An alternative view to Cutler's (Cutler 1978), and equally problematic, was presented by the psychologist Julian Jaynes in his widely-read book of 1976, *The Origin of Consciousness in the Breakdown of the Bicameral Mind*, when he advanced an idea that until as recently as the last two thousand years or so, the living, because they hallucinated the voices of the dead, actually thought that the dead were somehow still alive; it was for that reason, Jaynes reasoned, that the corpse continued to be fed, even though it had begun to decompose: 'The food and drink at the tomb door may have been like an emergency measure . . .' This patently ignores the anthropological insights of van

Gennep and Hertz and leads to a preposterous misinterpretation (Jaynes 1976: 164).

7. Clastres 1998.

8. A sequence of stills credited to Mohamed Armin of Camerapix is reproduced in Williams 1989: 38.

9. Smirnov 1989: 199.

10. Page 163 of the 7th edition; the current 10th edition (Fagan 2001) is slightly more circumspect. Those who believe that the first known burials provide real evidence for the actual origin of religion wrap up together at least four things that in reality are separable: (i) the emergence, by whatever means, of religious sensibilities, (ii) the emotional impact of death as intelligence increases, (iii) particular treatment patterns for corpses (e.g. burial), and (iv) belief in souls. Following the nineteenth-century American ethnographer E.B. Tyler, many social anthropologists have assumed that the beliefs and actions of a community should be thought of as religious if they connect to a belief in spiritual beings – the souls of the dead, angels, fairies, God. A contrasting idea, first put forward by the nineteenth-century French sociologist Emile Durkheim, was that religion was a term that separated 'the sacred' from the everyday or 'profane'. But both Tyler and Durkheim ignored the possibility that their own unquestioned understanding of 'religion' as a distinct, separable, zoned dimension of life might really have been based on their own experience of atomized industrial existence. In fact, most small-scale tribal societies had no word equivalent to our term 'religion.' More challengingly, as the anthropologist R.R. Marett once observed, religious behaviour does not require any further meaning, any *raison d'être* – it was something that might as well be 'not so much thought out as danced out'. *The Threshold of Religion* 1914: xxxi (cited in Kerr 1986). The problem of the sacred-profane distinction is tackled by Boyer 1994: 46.

11. Gargett 1989, 1999.

12. Defleur 1993.

13. Defleur 1993: 140ff.

14. Gargett 1999: 49.

15. Stiner 1991.

16. Russell 1987; cf Trinkaus 1985. The issues are widespread: see e.g. Haverkort & Lubell 1999.

17. As reported in *Science* by Culotta (1999: 286: 19).

18. V. Teilhol 2001.

19. Villa 1992: 97.

20. Herrmann writes: 'Da das Individuum von Combe Capelle unzweifelhaft bestattet wurde, könnte eine angenommenen Anthropophagie nur rituellen Character gehabt haben' (1972: 56).

21. Girard 1977: 13.

22. Girard 1977: 25.

23. Kerr 1986: 181.

24. Girard 1977: 1.

25. Heidegger 1962: 302 (*Being and Time* II.1.52); he continues: 'Everyday concern makes definite for itself the indefiniteness of certain death by interposing before it those urgencies and possibilities which can be taken in at a glance, and which belong to the everyday matters that are closest to us'.

26. On the physical similarities, see Alt *et al.* 1997.

27. Malinowski 1927: 88–91 excerpted in Girard 1977: 59–60.

28. For Barma Grande see Churchill & Formicola 1997; for Sungir see Bader 1978; for Romito see Frayer *et al.* 1988; comparative pictures, including DV, in Svoboda 1999: figs 83–6; for issues of deviancy and death see Shay 1985; for the significance of red ochre see Marshak 1981.

29. Duarte *et al.* 1999.

30. Hershkovitz *et al.* 1993.

31. Mussi, Roebroeks and Svoboda 2000.

32. Jurmain & Nelson 1994: 456, fig. 16–19. (NB. 'Neandertal' is a variant spelling of Neanderthal, used more commonly in the US); general background for Neanderthals in Stringer & Gamble 1993.

33. Thieme 1997; the spears were made in the Reinsdorf interglacial between 380,000 and 400,000 BP; see also Dennell 1997.

34. Bronowski 1973.

Chapter 9

1. Keillor 1986: 289f.
2. I am grateful to Roger Matthews for alerting me to the existence of Ayşa's grave and to Funda Odemis for her care in interpreting for Osman and me.
3. Larsson 1983–4, 1997; see also Saxe 1971; Clark & Neeley 1987; Schulting 1998.
4. Byrd & Monahan 1995.
5. That there was conflict is dramatically demonstrated at one of the largest cemeteries known from this period, over one hundred burials at Jebel Sahara in the Sudan, which contains virtually no individual man, woman or child who did not die a violent death: Byrd & Monahan 1995.
6. There is a vast literature on the site. Accessible starting points are Hodder 1990; Taylor 1996.
7. Mike Richards pers. comm.
8. Odent 1992.
9. Lévi-Strauss 1969.
10. I am grateful to Sarah Wright (my wife) for making this connection so clearly.
11. The hunt continued at an elite level, of course, with a changing function.
12. Hepper 1990: 54.
13. Wooley 1934.
14. Pynchon 1997: 289.
15. Parker Pearson 1999: 55f; Barley 1995.
16. Yordanova 1978 with further references.
17. Hårde 2001.
18. Vladimov 1979, noting Michael Glenny's introduction.
19. Rawson 1996: 163ff.
20. Neugebauer 1991.
21. *The Times* 1974a, b, c.
22. *Lettre à l'Archevêque de Paris*, cited by Barber 1987 and reprinted in Dundes 1998: 109.
23. Abels & Schröter 1993.
24. Murgoci 1926 in Dundes 1998: 12.

25. Murgoci 1926 in Dundes 1998: 21.

26. Hutton was William Wyse Professor of Social Anthropology at Cambridge in the 1920s and wrote the extensive entry 'lycanthropy' in the *Enclopaedia Britannica* for 1949 and previous editions. I have not researched its first appearance, but Hutton's latest reference is to his colleague Margaret Murray's 1921 *Witch Cult of Western Europe*.

27. Bondeson 2001.

28. Summers 1929; the luminescence of dead animals and humans must have been much more obvious in prehistory, when light pollution was far less; the phenomenon is caused by micro-organisms such as *Photobacterium fischeri* active on the dead skin surface: P. Barber 1987: 131 with references to Airth and Foerster 1960, and Evans 1963.

29. Perkowski in Dundes 1998: 39; Barber in Dundes 1998: 128.

30. Dumitrascu in Murgoci 1926: A report made by the ethnographer and peasant sociologist, N.I. Dumitrascu in 1914 relating to events in the village of Amărăşti, Province of Dolj, Romania.

31. Barber 1988.

32. Paul Barber makes the interesting suggestion that the mass shift in burial practice from inhumation to the almost exclusive cremation cemeteries of the late Bronze Age 'Urnfield' culture may have been in response to a disease epidemic.

33. Čajkanović 1974.

34. Fine 1987 in Dundes 1998: 57–66.

35. In technical terms, it was not *deduced* that Ayşa was something of the kind we might call a vampire, but *abduced*; in his cognitive theory of religion, Pascal Boyer describes this as the way in which surprising data is made unsurprising through an assumption, from which the data would follow as a normal consequence; so, when judging 'magical' causes for illness (for example), people 'say that the person is ill because he or she is a member of a certain cult, they claim that the divination ritual failed because someone infringed the ritual prohibitions, or that the magical spell failed probably because the ancestors were angry'. (Boyer 1994: 147f.).

36. Tsaliki 2001 in press.

37. Daim 2001.

Chapter 10

1. Melville 1851: Ch 110: 'Queequeg in His Coffin': 379f.
2. Schore 2001: 235, cited in Balbernie 2001: 248.
3. Durkheim 1912 = 1995: 392.
4. Data from Spencer and Gillen 1899.
5. Spencer and Gillen 1899: 516f.
6. Spencer and Gillen knew one woman who had accustomed herself to this to such a degree that, although not physically dumb, she had communicated exclusively in sign-language for 24 years (noted in Durkheim 1995: 395).
7. Such a healing impulse coupled with social sensitivity is paralleled in advice given to Renaissance chirurges concerning 'places wherein we wolde that no cycatryce shulde appere, as in yᵉ face': OED: 'cicatrice', quoting R. Copland 1541, *Guydon's Quest. Chirurg.*
8. I am grateful to Daphne Nash-Briggs for her careful professional appraisal and analysis of these matters.
9. I was working under the direction of Elvira Toth and Attila Horvath.
10. The story appears in Jacob and Wilhelm Grimm's *Kinder- und Hausmärchen*; its history and variants are traced by Krohn 1926 = 1971. In Indian variants of the tale, it is often a girl who is to be married who is murdered, and who reappears alive when a musical instrument, made from the wood of a tree that grew over the well or pit where her body was hidden, is played (or when it accidentally breaks); the murderer is then killed in her place.
11. Thomas 2000 provides an entertaining and serious account of the events as they unfolded; for general background see Talmage 1982; Deloria 1992; Jones & Harris 1997.
12. Van der Sanden 1995: 41.
13. Novak & Kopp 2002 in press.
14. Reproduced in Novak & Kopp 2002 in press.
15. Thomas 2000: xxxix.
16. I am grateful to Chris Chippindale for a discussion of these rites.
17. The disjunction between the beliefs observed by early ethnographers such as Spencer and Gillen and the modern presentation of aboriginal cosmology does not result from the fact that the Victorians

got it wrong, rather that the past has been reinvented, for understandable reasons.

18. Barry Raftery pers. comm. Raftery's father, Joseph Raftery, was the excavator and did not know what to make of the stratigraphic relationship he revealed; the observation has remained unpublished.

19. Confirmed by experimental work conducted by one of my PhD students, Dave Cowland (who also identified the Lough Crew artefacts as bullroarers).

20. Bran the Blessed appears in the Mabinogion, set down in writing in the 14th–15th centuries.

21. Carrasco 1999; on this subject see also Trigger 1993; Green 1998; Isserlin 1997; Booth 1992.

22. Daphne Nash-Briggs pers. comm.

23. I am grateful to Gillian Riley for a candid discussion of the interface between professional conduct and human emotion on modern hospital wards.

24. Seligman 1992.

25. I saw this on a television programme; the intention appeared genuine.

26. Tew 1990. The only major glitch in the hospital figures is during the Second World War. It is informative and, in a quiet way, damning: the significantly fewer perinatal deaths in the war years can only sensibly be correlated with a sharp reduction in male obstetricians, all of whom had been called up on military service, leaving hospital midwives.

Conclusion

1. Allende 1993: 183.

2. The identification was confirmed by my colleague, Anthea Boyleston of the Calvin Wells Laboratory in Bradford; for infant killing in general see Brown 1991; Hurst 1994; Kahr 1995.

3. Evans 1984; Cunnington 1929; Gibson 1998 for cultural background.

4. Pitts et al. 2002.

5. Express, 3 April 2000, lead article: 'Hospital "stole" the soul of our Baby' pp. 1 & 4 (Ellis 2000). The idea of 'visceral insulation' was stimulated by lectures from Colin Renfrew when I was a student on

the insulating aspects of the social formation we call civilization. I have tried to develop it in a direction that might be considered 'cognitive' (cf Renfrew & Zubrow 1994), but there have in fact been a wide range of stimuli (among them Becker 1973; Baudrillard 1993; and Goody 1997).

6. Thompson Rowling 1989.

7. Jackie Lyn Rose, embalmer, interviewed in *Naked Body* (Rose 1998: 26).

8. Metcalf & Huntington 1991: 14.

9. Although Malinowski famously claimed to have brought anthropology down from the colonial verandah for the first time so as to conduct it among the real lives of native peoples, this was a misrepresentation: Du Chaillu, Schweinfurth, Baldwin Spencer and others, despite their occasional race-based thinking, had previously undergone far greater privations and run far greater personal risks to make their observations.

10. Briggs 1996.

11. 'Last nail in the coffin for satanic ritual abuse?' (www.saff. connectfree.co.uk/eppingcs.htm). See La Fontaine 1998 for a well-articulated but essentially wholly sceptical view of a selection of major cases.

12. *The Times* 8/8/1989: 3. McKenzie's sentence was one of the longest ever handed down for child sex abuse in Britain, reflecting the particularly horrendous nature of the rapes; he served seven years and has since vanished.

13. Much of the SRA polemic takes place on the web; this type of dismissal is typical of the 'apologist' school whose views are well represented by Baddely 2000.

14. Sinason 1994. NB poor archaeology can deepen confusion: Earl 1995.

15. La Fontaine 1998; see also 1994, *The extent and nature of organized ritual abuse.* The pattern of SRA denial in relation to claims of insanity fits other patterns by which people get labelled, clearly described by the French social thinker M. Foucault; the labelling of people who give credit to witness reports (both perpetrator and victim) of SRA as 'hysterical' is an equally well-covered theme in the historiography of psychotherapy.

16. Tiedemann 1996, republished in paperback = 2000.

17. Tiedemann 2000: 95 and reference 86.

18. Kerr 1986: 162.

19. Source: Calendar News 20.03.2002.

20. There is a vast literature on the Hindley & Brady abuse and murders.

21. Estimated figures from pagan society surveys presented on BBC Radio 4 'Beyond Belief' 18.03.02.

22. Briggs 1996; Martin Seligman's similar conclusions (Seligman 1992).

23. As reasserted by the Council of Trent (1545–63).

24. Scholz, Phillips, and Knobel 1997.

25. Savile 1999; see also Padel 1995.

26. Durkheim 1912 = 1995: 406.

27. The following diagrams summarize some of the ideas I have developed and presented in this book; the bibliographic references that follow them relate in the first place to the specific notes above, but also contain a few more general works, unreferenced above, that represent standard background readings across a range of disciplines which influenced the formulation of my ideas.

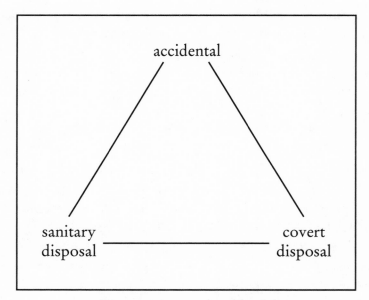

Diagram 1: non-ritual burial

314

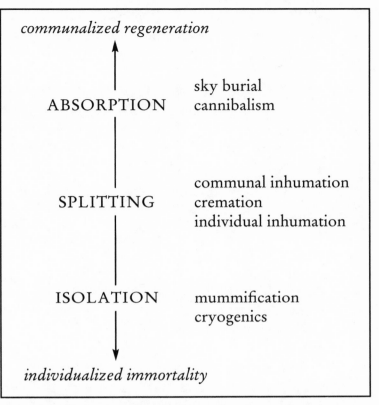

Diagram 2: absorption–isolation spectrum

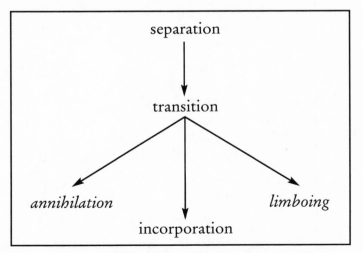

Diagram 3: the fate of the soul

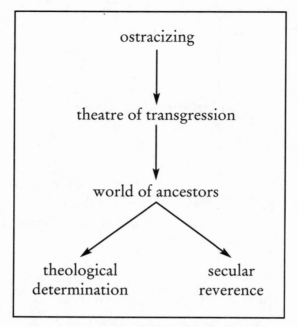

Diagram 4: ritual burial

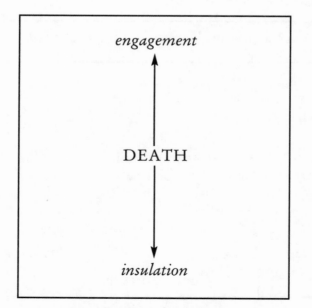

Diagram 5: visceral response

Bibliography

Abels, B.-U. & P. Schröter. 1993. Drei Sonderbestattungen von der Ehrenbürg, Schlaifhausen, Gemeinde Wiesenthau, Landkreis Forchheim, Oberfranken, *Das archäologische Jahr in Bayern* 1992: 80–86.

Airth, R.L. & G.E. Foerster. 1960. Some aspects of fungal bioluminescence, *Journal of Cellular and Comparative Physiology* 56: 173–82.

Alberry, N., G. Elliot & J. Elliot (eds.). 1997. *The new natural death handbook*. London: Rider.

Allende, I. 1993. *The infinite plan*. London: HarperCollins.

Alt, K., S. Pichler, V. Vach, B. Klíma, E. Vlcek & J. Sedlmeier. 1997. Twenty-five-thousand-year-old triple burial from Dolní Věstonice: an Ice-Age family?, *American Journal of Physical Anthropology* 102: 123–31.

Arens, W. 1979. *The man-eating myth: anthropology and anthropophagy*. New York: Oxford University Press.

— 1997. Man is off the menu, *The Times Higher*, 12/12/97 Perspective: 19–20.

Ariès, P. 1974. *Western attitudes toward death from the Middle Ages to the present*. Baltimore: Johns Hopkins University Press.

— 1981. *The hour of our death*. Harmondsworth: Penguin.

Armstrong, J.A. 1996. Ur, in B. Fagan (ed.), *The Oxford companion to archaeology*: 730. New York/Oxford: Oxford University Press.

Atkins, P. 1994. *Creation revisited: the origin of space, time and the universe*. Harmondsworth: Penguin.

Atwater, P. and D. Morgan. 2000. *The complete idiot's guide to near death experience*. London: Alpha.

317

Ayer, A.J. 1936. *Language, truth and logic.* Oxford: Clarendon Press.

Babel, I. 1957. 'Zhizneopisanie Pavlichenki, Matveya Rodeonycha', in *Konarmiya* (Russian Titles for the Specialist 68): 56–60. Letchworth: Prideaux Press/Short-Run Books.

— 1974. 'The life and adventures of Matthew Pavlichenko', in *Collected Stories* (Penguin Modern Classics. Translated/revised by W. Morrison). Harmondsworth: Penguin.

Bad Planet 1998. Placenta-eating cooking show condemned, *Bad Planet*, Tabloid (www.tabloid.net) 29–31.05.1998.

Baddely, G. 2000. *Lucifer rising: sin, devil worship and rock 'n' roll.* London: Plexus.

Bader, O.N. 1978. *Sungir: verkhnepaleoliticheskaya stoyanka.* Moscow: Nauka.

Bahn, P. 1999. Atapuerca's double contribution to the cannibalism debate, *Journal of Iberian Archaeology* 1: 27–31.

— 2001. Le cannibalisme humain à l'épreuve des faits, *La recherche* 338: 73.

Bailey, L.W. 1996. *The near-death experience: a reader.* London: Routledge.

Baker, J.R. 1974. *Race.* London: Oxford University Press.

Balbernie, R. 2001. Circuits and circumstances: the neurobiological consequences of early relationship experiences and how they shape later behaviour, *Journal of Child Psychotherapy* 27(3): 237–55.

Banks, I. 1990. *The Wasp Factory.* London: Abacus.

Bar-Yosef, O., B. Vandermeersch, B. Arensburg, A. Belfer-Cohen, P. Goldberg, H. Laville, L. Meignen, Y. Rak, J.D. Speth, E. Tchernov, A-M. Tillier & S. Weiner. 1992. The excavations in Kebara Cave, Mt Carmel, *Current Anthropology* 33(5): 497–551.

Barber, J. 1988. 'Isbister, Quanterness and the Point of Cott: the formulation and testing of some middle range theories', in J.C. Barrett and I.A. Kinnes (eds.), *The archaeology of context in the Neolithic and Bronze Age: recent trends*: 57–62. Sheffield: University of Sheffield, Department of Archaeology and Prehistory.

Barber, M., D. Field & P. Topping. 1999. *The Neolithic flint mines of England.* Swindon: English Heritage.

Barber, M., D. Field, & P. Topping. 2000. *Grime's Graves* (RCHME Survey Report) Swindon: Crown Copyright.

Barber, P. 1987. Forensic pathology and the European Vampire, *Journal of Folklore Research* 24: 1–32.

— 1988. *Vampires, burial, and death: folklore and reality*. New Haven: Yale University Press.

Barley, N. 1995. *Dancing on the grave: encounters with death*. London: John Murray.

Baron-Cohen, S. 1998. Review of Darwin, C. 'The expression of the emotions in man and animals', 3rd edition, *Nature* 392: 459–60.

Baron-Cohen, S., A. Riviere, P. Cross, M. Fukushima, C. Bryant, M. Sotillo, J. Hadwin, & D. French. 1996. Reading the mind in the face: a cross-cultural and developmental study, *Visual Cognition* 3: 39–59.

Baudrillard, J. 1993. *Symbolic exchange and death* (trans. I. Hamilton Grant). London: Sage.

Beaglehole, J. C. (ed.). 1955. *The journals of Captain James Cook on his voyages of discovery. Volume I. The voyage of the Endeavour, 1768–1771.* Cambridge: Hakluyt Society.

— 1961 (ed.). *The journals of Captain James Cook on his voyages of discovery. Volume II. The voyage of the Resolution and Adventure, 1772–1775.* Cambridge: Hakluyt Society.

— 1962 (ed.). *The Endeavour journal of Joseph Banks, 1768–1771.* Sydney: Public Library of New South Wales/Angus & Robertson.

— 1967 (ed.). *The journals of Captain James Cook on his voyages of discovery. Volume III. The voyage of the Resolution and Discovery, 1776–1779.* Cambridge: Hakluyt Society.

Becker, E. 1973. *The denial of death*. New York: Free Press.

Bednarik, R.G. 1966. The Makapansgat pebble, *The Artefact* 19: 107.

Bendann, E. 1930. *Death Customs: an Analytical Study of Burial Rites.* London: Kegan Paul, Trench, Trubner (reprinted 1969, London: Dawsons)

Beneke, M. 1999. First report of nonpsychotic self-cannibalism (autophagy), tongue splitting, and scar patterns (scarification) as an extreme form of cultural body modification in a western civilization, *American Journal of Forensic Medicine and Pathology* 20: 281–5.

Berger, L.R. & R.J. Clarke. 1995. Eagle involvement in accumulation of the Taung child fauna, *Journal of Human Evolution* 29: 275–99.

— 1996. The load of the Taung child, *Nature* 379: 778–9.

Bernstein, A.E. 1993. *The formation of Hell: death and retribution in the ancient and early Christian worlds*. London: UCL Press.

Bettelheim, B. 1982. *Freud and man's soul*. London: Penguin.

Binford, L.R. & C.K. Ho. 1985. Taphonomy at a distance: Zhoukoudian, 'the cave home of Beijing Man'?, *Current Anthropology* 26: 413–42.

Binford, L.R. & N.M. Stone. 1986. Zhoukoudian: a closer look, *Current Anthropology* 27: 453–75.

Blake, W. 1996. *Selected Poems of William Blake*. London: Penguin.

Bloch, M. & J. Parry (eds.). 1982. *Death and the regeneration of life*. Cambridge: Cambridge University Press.

Bocquet-Appel, J-P. 2000. Population kinetics in the Upper Palaeolithic in Western Europe, *Journal of Archaeological Science* 27: 551–70.

Bondeson, J. 2001. *Buried alive: the terrifying history of our most primal fear*. New York: W.W. Norton.

Booth, J. 1992. Human sacrifice in literature: the case of Wole Soyinka, *Ariel: A Review of International English Literature* 23(1): 7–24.

Bown, D. 1995. *The Royal Horticultural Society Encyclopedia of Herbs and their Uses*. London: Dorling Kindersley.

Boyer, P. 1994. *The naturalness of religious ideas: a cognitive theory of religion*. Berkeley: University of California Press.

Bräuer, G., Y. Yokoyama, C. Falguères & E. Mbua. 1997. Modern human origins backdated, *Nature* 386: 337–8.

Briggs, C.S. 1995. Did they fall or were they pushed? Some unresolved questions about the bog bodies, in R.C. Turner & R.G. Scaife (eds.), *Bog bodies: new discoveries and new perspectives*: 168–82. London: British Museum.

Briggs, R. 1996. *Witches and neighbours: the social and cultural context of European witchcraft*. London: HarperCollins.

Bronowski, J. 1973. *The ascent of man*. London: BBC.

Brothwell, D. & J.B. Bourke. 1995. The human remains from Lindow Moss 1987–8, in R.C. Turner & R.G. Scaife (eds.), *Bog bodies: new discoveries and new perspectives*: 52–58. London: British Museum.

Brown, A. (ed.). 1990. *The Soviet Union: a biographical dictionary*. London: Weidenfeld and Nicolson.

Brown, J. 1995. On mortuary analysis: with special reference to the Saxe-Binford research program, in L.A. Beck (ed.), *Regional approaches to mortuary analysis*: 3–25. New York: Plenum Press.

Brown, S. 1991. *Late Carthaginian child sacrifice and sacrificial monuments in their Mediterranean context*. Sheffield: Sheffield University Press.

Byrd, B.F. & C.M. Monahan. 1995. Death, mortuary ritual and Natufian social structure, *Journal of Anthropological Archaeology* 14: 251–87.

Čajkanović, V. 1974. The killing of a vampire. *The Folklore Forum* 7: 260–71.

Campbell, J. 1976. *The masks of God: primitive mythology*. Harmondsworth: Penguin.

Campbell, J. Graham. 1980. *The Viking world*. London: Frances Lincoln/Book Club Associates.

Carbonell, E. *et al.* 1995. Lower pleistocene hominids and artifacts from Atapuerca-TD6 (Spain), *Science* 269: 826–30.

Carr, C. 1995. Mortuary practices: their social, philosophical-religious, circumstantial, and physical determinants, *Journal of Archaeological Method and Theory* 2: 105–200.

Carrasco, D. 1999. *City of sacrifice: violence from the Aztec empire to the modern Americas*. Boston, MA: Beacon Press.

Carver, M. 1995. Boat-burial in Britain: ancient custom or political signal? In O. Crumlin-Pedersen & B. Munch Thye (eds), *The ship as symbol in prehistoric and medieval Scandinavia*: 111–24. Copenhagen: PNM.

Cash, W. 2001. Did atheist philosopher see God when he 'died'? *National Post*, 3 March 2001 (National Post Online).

Chadwick, H.M. 1899. *The cult of Othin*. London: C.J. Clay and Sons.

Chagnon, N.A. 1992. *Yanomamo: the last days of Eden*. San Diego: Harcourt Brace Jovanovich.

Chapman, J. 1994. The living, the dead and the ancestors: time, life cycles and the mortuary domain in later European prehistory, in

J. Davis (ed.), *Ritual and remembrance: responses to death in human societies*: 40–85. Sheffield: Sheffield Academic Press.

Chapman, R.W. 1981. Archaeological theory and communal burial in prehistoric Europe, in I. Hodder, G. Isaac and N. Hammond (eds.) *Pattern of the past: studies in honour of David L.Clarke*. Cambridge: Cambridge University Press.

— 1995. Ten years after – megaliths, mortuary practices and the territorial model, in L. Anderson Beck (ed.) *Regional approaches to mortuary analysis*: 29–51. New York: Plenum.

Chapman, R.W., I. Kinnes & K. Randsborg (eds.). 1981. *The archaeology of death*. Cambridge: Cambridge University Press.

Chen, T. & P. Chen. 1998. Medical cannibalism in China, *The Pharos*, Spring 1998: 23–5.

Churchill, C. & V. Formicola. 1997. A case of marked bilateral asymmetry in the upper limbs of an Upper Palaeolithic male from Barma Grande (Liguria) Italy, *International Journal of Osteoarchaeology* 7: 18–38.

Clark, D. (ed.) 1993. *The sociology of death: theory, culture, practice*. Oxford: Blackwell/The Sociological Review.

Clark, G.A. & M. Neeley. 1987. Social differentiation in European Mesolithic burial data, in P. Rowley-Conwy, M. Zvelebil & H.P. Blankholm (ed.), *Mesolithic Northwest Europe: recent trends*: 121–127. Sheffield: Department of Archaeology, University of Sheffield.

Clastres, P. 1998. *Chronicle of the Guayaki Indians* (trans.P. Auster). London: Faber & Faber. (First published as P. Clastres. 1972. *Chronique des indiens Guayaki*. Librairie Plon.)

Clendinnen, I. 1991. *Aztecs: an interpretation*. Cambridge: Cambridge University Press.

Cowgill, G. 2000. 'CA comment' on S. Tarlow, Emotion in archaeology, *Current Anthropology* 41(5): 713–47.

Crumlin-Pedersen, O. & B. Munch Thye (ed.). 1995. *The ship as symbol in prehistoric and medieval Scandinavia*. (Studies in Archaeology & History vol.1.) Copenhagen: Publications from the National Museum (PNM).

Culotta, E. 1999. Neanderthals were cannibals, bones show, *Science* 286: 18–19.

Cunliffe, B. 1991. *Iron Age communities in Britain* (3rd edition). London: Routledge.

Cunnington, M.E. 1929. *Woodhenge: a description of the site as revealed by excavations carried out there by Mr and Mrs B.H. Cunnington 1926–7–8*. Devizes: George Simpson.

Cutler, R.G. 1978. Evolutionary biology of senescence, in J.A. Behnke, C.E. Finch & G.B. Moment (eds.), *The biology of aging*. New York/London: Plenum Press.

Darling, J.A. 1999. Mass inhumation and the execution of witches in the American Southwest, *American Anthropologist* 100: 732–52.

Daim, F. 2001. Ein völkerwanderungszeitliches Grab mit Zaumzeugen aus Untersiebenbrunn, Niederösterreich, in F. Daim & T. Kühtreiber (eds.) *Sein & Sinn/ Burg & Mensch* (Katalog des Niederösterreichischen Landesmuseums (New Series) 434): 142–7. St Pölten: Niederösterreich Kultur.

Dart, R. 1959. *Adventures with the Missing Link*. New York: Harper & Brothers.

Darwin, C. 1872. *The expression of the emotions in man and animals*. London: John Murray.

Davidson, H.E. 1998. *Roles of the northern goddess*. London: Routledge.

Day, J. 1989. *Molech : a god of human sacrifice in the Old Testament*. Cambridge: Cambridge University Press.

Defleur, A. 1993. *Les Sépultures Moustériennes*. Paris: C.N.R.S.

Degusta, D. 1999. Fijian cannibalism: osteological evidence from Navatu, *American Journal of Physical Anthropology* 110: 215–41.

— 2000. Fijian cannibalism and mortuary ritual: bioarchaeological evidence from Vunda, *International Journal of Osteoarchaeology* 10: 76–92.

Deloria, V. Jr. 1992. Indians, archaeologists, and the future, *American Antiquity* 57: 595–8.

Dent, J.S. 1985. Three cart burials from Wetwang, Yorkshire, *Antiquity* 59: 85–2.

Derrida, J. 1995. *The Gift of Death*. (trans. D. Wills). Chicago & London: Chicago University Press.

Dennell, R. 1997. The world's oldest spears, *Nature* 385: 767–8.

Dettwyler, K.A. 1991. Can palaeopathology provide evidence for 'compassion'? *American Journal of Physical Anthropology* 84: 375–84.

De Waal, F. 2001. *The ape and the sushi master*. London: Allen Lane.

Díaz, B. 1963. *The conquest of Spain* (translated with an introduction by J.M. Cohen). Harmondsworth: Penguin.

Donner, R. (ed.) 2000. *King Magnus Eriksson's Law of the Realm: a medieval Swedish code* (translated and edited by Ruth Donner with an introduction by Richard Tötterman). Ius Gentrum Ry – Acta Societatis Fennicae Iuris Gentuum CII.

Duarte, C., J. Mauricio, P.B. Pettitt, P. Souto, E. Trinkaus, H. van der Plicht. 1999. The early upper Paleolithic human skeleton from the Abrigo de Lagar Velho (Portugal) and modern human emergence in Iberia, *Proceedings of the National Academy of Sciences, USA* 96: 7,604–9.

Du Chaillu, P.B. 1861. *Explorations & adventures in equatorial Africa: with accounts of the manners and customs of the people, and of the chace of the gorilla, crocodile, leopard, elephant, hippopotamus, and other animals*. London: Murray.

Dundes, A. (ed.). 1998. *The vampire: a casebook*. Madison: University of Wisconsin Press.

Durkheim, E. 1912 = 1995. *The Elementary Forms of Religious Life* (transl. Karen E. Fields). New York: Free Press.

Earl, J. 1995. The dark truth about the 'dark tunnels of McMartin', *Issues in child abuse accusations* 7(2). Northfield, Minnesota: Proceedings of the Institute for Psychological Therapies.

Eco, U. 1989. *Foucault's pendulum* (trans. W. Weaver). London: Secker & Warburg.

Egg, M. & K. Spindler. 1993. *Die Gletschermumie: vom Ende der Steinzeit aus den ötztaler Alpen*. Jahrbuch des RGZM 39 (1992), Sonderdruck. Mainz.

Eitzman, W.I. 1958. Reminiscences of Makapansgat limeworks and its bonebreccial layers, *South African Journal of Science* 54: 177–82.

Eliade, M. 1972. *Zalmoxis the vanishing god: comparative studies in the religions and folklore of Dacia and Eastern Europe*. Chicago & London: Chicago University Press.

Ellis, R. 2000. Hospital 'stole' the soul of our Baby, *Express*, 3 April 2000: 1 & 4.

Elwood, R. 1980. The development, inhibition and disinhibition of pup-cannibalism in the Mongolian gerbil, *Animal Behaviour* 28: 1,188–94.

English Heritage. 1990. *Human remains on historic properties*. London: English Heritage.

— 1996. 5,000 year-old 'death' platform discovered by English Heritage. Press release 892/1069; 15.09.1996.

Evans, J.G. 1984. Stonehenge – the environment in the late Neolithic and early Bronze Age and a Beaker age burial. *Wiltshire Archaeological and Natural History Magazine* 78: 7–30.

Evans, W.E.D. 1963. *The chemistry of death*. Springfield, IL: Charles C. Thomas.

Fagan, B. (ed.). 1996. *The Oxford companion to archaeology*. New York/Oxford: Oxford University Press.

— 2001. *People of the earth: an introduction to world prehistory* (10th edn). New Jersey: Prentice Hall.

Fehr, E. & S. Gächter. 2002. Altruistic punishment in humans, *Nature* 415: 137–40.

Fernández-Jalvo, Y., J.C. Díez, I. Cáceres & J. Rosell. 1999. Human Cannibalism in the Early Pleistocene of Europe (Gran Dolina, Sierra de Atapuerca, Burgos, Spain), *Journal of Human Evolution* 37: 591–622.

Ferraro, G., W. Trevathan & J. Levy. 1994. *Anthropology: an applied perspective*. Minneapolis/St Paul: West.

Fine, J. 1987. In defense of vampires, *East European Quarterly* 21: 15–23.

Flon, C. (ed.). 1985. *The world atlas of archaeology*. London: Mitchell Beazley.

Frazer, J.G. 1913. *The Golden Bough: a study in magic and religion*. Part VI: *The Scapegoat*: vi. (3rd edition). London Macmillan.

Frayer, D.W., R. Macchiarelli & M. Mussi.1988. A case of chrondodystrophic dwarfism in the Italian Late Upper Palaeolithic, *American Journal of Physical Anthropology* 75: 549–65.

French, C. 1992. Factors underlying belief in the paranormal: do sheep and goats think differently? *The Psychologist: Bulletin of the British Psychological Society* (1992) 5: 295–9.

Friesinger, H. & B. Vacha. 1987. *Der vielen Vater Österreiches*. Vienna: Compress Verlag.

Gajdusek, D.C. 1977. Unconventional viruses and the origin and disappearance of *kuru* (Nobel Prize acceptance speech), *Science* 197: 943–60.

Gamble, C. 1999. *The Palaeolithic Societies of Europe* Cambridge World Archaeology. Cambridge: Cambridge University Press.

Gargett, R.H. 1989. Grave shortcomings: the evidence for Neanderthal burial, *Current Anthropology* 30: 157–90.

— 1999. Middle Upper Palaeolithic burial is not a dead issue: the view from Qafzeh, Saint-Césaire, Kebara, Amud, and Dederiyeh, *Journal of Human Evolution* 37: 27–90.

Garn, S.M. & W.D. Block. 1970. The limited nutritional value of cannibalism, *American Anthropologist* 72: 106.

Gibson, A.G. 1998. *Stonehenge and Timber Circles*. Stroud: Tempus.

Gillison, G. 1983. Cannibalism among women in the eastern highlands of Papua New Guinea, in P. Brown & D. Tuzin (ed.), *The ethnography of cannibalism*: 33–50. Washington D.C: Society for Psychological Anthropology.

Gilmore, R.G., D.M. Scheidt & P.A. Linley. 1990. *Reproductive biology of lamnoid sharks*. Abstract of the American Elasmobranch Society 1990 Annual Meeting, Charleston, South Carolina.

Gimbutas, M. 1991. *The civilization of the goddess: the world of old Europe*. San Fransisco: HarperCollins.

Girard, R. 1977. *Violence and the sacred*. Balitimore: Johns Hopkins University Press. (Translated by P. Gregory from R.Girard 1972. *La violence et le sacré*. Paris: Bernard Grasset.)

— 1987. Generative scapegoating, in R.G.Hamerton-Kelly (ed.) *Violent origins: ritual killing and cultural formation*: 73–105. Stanford: Stanford University Press.

Glasse, R. 1977. Cannibalism in the kuru region of New Guinea, *Transactions of the New York Academy of Sciences* 29: 748–754.

Glob, P.V. 1969. *The bog people: Iron Age man preserved*. London: Faber & Faber.

Goleman, D. 1995. *Emotional intelligence*. New York: Bantam.

Goodall, J. 1986. *The Chimpanzees of Gombe: patterns of behaviour*. Cambridge MA: Belknap Press of Harvard University Press.

Goody, J. 1962. *Death, property and the ancestors*. Stanford: Stanford University Press.

— 1997. *Representations and contradictions. Ambivalence towards images, theatre, fiction, relics and sexuality*. Oxford: Blackwell.

Gordon-Grube, K. 1988. Anthropophagy in post-Renaissance Europe: the tradition of medicinal cannibalism, *American Anthropologist* 90: 405–9.

Graslund, B. 1994. Prehistoric soul beliefs in northern Europe, *Proceedings of the Prehistoric Society* 60: 15–26.

Green, M. Aldhouse 1998. Humans as ritual victims in the later prehistory of western Europe, *Oxford Journal of Archaeology* 17(2): 169–189.

— 2001. *Dying for the gods: human sacrifice in Iron Age and Roman Europe*. Stroud: Tempus.

Greenwell, W. 1870. On the opening of Grime's Graves in Norfolk, *Journal of the Ethnological Society of London* (New Series) 2: 419–39.

Grene, D. (trans.) 1987. *The history. Herodotus*. Chicago/London: University of Chicago Press.

Grün, R., C. Stringer, F. McDermott, S. Robertson, L. Taylor, G. Mortimer & M. McCulloch. 2002 in press. Dating the human burials from Skhul, *Journal of Human Evolution* (forthcoming).

Hall, H.R.H. 1949. Egypt: Religion, *Encylopaedia Britannica* 8: 58–61. Chicago: University of Chicago Press.

Hancock, G. & S. Faiia. 1998. *Heaven's mirror: quest for the lost civilization*. London: Michael Joseph.

Harner, M. 1977. The ecological basis for Aztec sacrifice, *American ethnologist* 4: 117–35.

Hårde, A. 2001. Warfare in the Nitra culture (early Bronze Age in southwestern Slovakia and eastern Moravia). Conference abstract: *Warfare, violence and slavery in prehistory and protohistory*. University of Sheffield, 2–3 February 2001.

Harris, D.R. (ed.). 1996. *The origins and spread of agriculture and pastoralism in Eurasia*. London: UCL Press.

Harris, M. 1977. *Cannibals and kings: the origins of culture*. New York: Random House.

Harrold, F.B. 1980. A comparative analysis of Eurasian Palaeolithic burials, *World Archaeology* 12(2): 195–211.

Hassan, F.A. 1981. *Demographic archaeology*. New York: Academic Press.

Haverkort, C. & D. Lubell. 1999. Cutmarks on Capsian human remains: implications for Maghreb Holocene social organization and palaeoeconomy, *International Journal of Osteoarchaeology* 9(3): 147–69.

Haviland, W.A. 2000. *Human evolution and prehistory* (5th edition). Fort Worth: Harcourt College.

Heaney, S. 1998. The Tollund Man, *Opened ground: poems 1966–1996*: 64–5 (originally from the 1972 collection *Wintering Out*). London: Faber & Faber.

Hedenström, A. 1995. Lifting the Taung child, *Nature* 378: 670.

Hedges, J. 1984. *Tomb of the eagles*. London: John Murray.

Heidegger, M. 1962. *Being and time* (trans. J. Macquarrie & E. Robinson). Oxford: Basil Blackwell.

Hepper, F.N. 1990. *Pharaoh's flowers: the botanical treasures of Tutankhamun*. London: Royal Botanic Gardens, Kew/HMSO.

Herrmann, B. 1972. Das Combe Capelle-Skelet, *Ausgrabungen in Berlin* 3: 7–69.

Hershkovitz, I., G. Edelson, M. Spiers, B. Arensburg, D. Nadel & B. Levi. 1993. Ohalo II man – unusual finding in the anterior rib cage and shoulder girdle of a 19,000-year-old specimen, *International Journal of Osteoarchaeology* 3: 177–88.

Hertz, R. 1907, Contribution à une étude sur la représentation collective de la mort, *Année Sociologique* 10 : 48–137.

— 1960. *Death and the right hand* (trans. R. Needham & C. Needham). New York: Free Press.

Hill, K. & A.M. Hurtado. 1991. The evolution of premature reproductive senescence and menopause in human females: an evaluation of the 'grandmother hypothesis', *Human Nature* 2(4): 313–50.

Hodder, I. 1990. *The domestication of Europe*. Oxford: Blackwell.

Holden, C. 2001. Ötzi death riddle solved, *Science* 293: 795.

Hornung, E. 1992. *Idea into image: essays on ancient Egyptian thought*. New York: Timken.

Hughes, D.D. 1991. *Human Sacrifice in Ancient Greece*. London: Routledge.

Hurlbut, S.A. 2000. The taphonomy of cannibalism: a review of anthropogenic bone modification in the American Southwest, *International Journal of Osteoarchaeology* 10(1): 4–26.

Hurst, H. 1994. Child sacrifice at Carthage, *Journal of Roman Archaeology* 7: 325–8.

Hutton, J.H. 1949. Lycanthropy, *Encyclopaedia Britannica*.

Ingstad, A.S. 1995. The interpretation of the Oseberg find, in O. Crumlin-Pedersen & B. Munch Thye (ed.), *The ship as symbol in prehistoric and medieval Scandinavia*: 139–148. Copenhagen: PNM.

Isserlin, R.M.J. 1997. Thinking the unthinkable: human sacrifice in Roman Britain, in K. Meadows, C. Lemke, and J. Heron (ed.). *Proceedings of the 6th Annual Theoretical Roman Archaeology Conference (TRAC) Sheffield 1996*. 91–100.

Jago, L. 2002. *The Northern Lights*. Harmondsworth: Penguin.

Janaway, R.C. 1996. The decay of buried human remains and their associated materials, in J.R. Hunter, C. Roberts and A.L. Martin (ed). *Studies in crime: an introduction to forensic archaeology*: 58–85. London: Batsford.

Jaynes, J. 1976. *The origin of consciousness in the breakdown of the bicameral mind*. Boston: Houghton Mifflin.

Jones, D.G. & R.J. Harris. 1997. Contending for the dead, *Nature* 386: 15–16.

Jones, G. 1968. *A history of the Vikings*. Oxford: Oxford University Press.

Jurmain, R. & H. Nelson. 1994. *Introduction to physical anthropology* (6th edition). Minneapolis/St Paul: West.

Kahr, B. 1994. The historical foundations of ritual abuse: an excavation of ancient infanticide, in Sinason, V. (ed.) *Treating survivors of satanist abuse: an invisible trauma*: 45–56. London: Routledge.

Keeley, L. 1996. *War before civilization: the myth of the pacific past*. Oxford: Oxford University Press.

— 1997. Frontier warfare in the early Neolithic, in D. Martin &

D. Frayer (eds.) *Troubled times: violence and warfare in the past*: 303–19. Australia: Gordon & Breach.

Keenleyside, A., M. Bertulli & H.C. Fricke. 1997. The final days of the Franklin expedition: new skeletal evidence, *Arctic: Journal of the Arctic Institute of North America* 50(1): 36–46.

Keillor, G. 1986. *Lake Wobegon Days*. London: Faber & Faber.

Kelly, F. 1988. *A guide to early Irish law*. (Early Irish law series III.) Dublin: School of Celtic Studies, Dublin Institute for Advanced Studies.

Kerr, F. 1986. *Theology after Wittgenstein*. Oxford: Blackwell.

Klíma, B. 1987. A triple burial from the Upper Palaeolithic of Dolní Věstonice, *Journal of Human Evolution* 16: 831–5.

— 1988. A new male burial from Dolní Věstonice, *Journal of Human Evolution* 16: 827–30.

Knight, C. & R. Lomas. 2000. *Uriel's machine: the ancient origins of science*. London: Arrow.

Korn, D., M. Radice and C. Hawes 2001, *Cannibal: a history of the People-Eaters*. London: Channel 4/Macmillan.

Krings, M., A. Stone, R.W. Schmitz, H. Krainitzki, M. Stoneking & S. Pääbo. 1997. Neandertal DNA sequences and the origin of modern humans, *Cell* 90: 19–30.

Krohn, K. 1926 = 1971. *Folklore methodology: formulated by Julius Krohn and expanded by Nordic researchers* (trans. R.L. Welsch) publications of the American Folklore Society, Bibliographical and Special Series vol 21. Austin/London: University of Texas Press.

Kurti, N., H. This-Benckhard & G. Aukland, 1994. 'A pinch of science' in R. Blanc, *Blanc Mange: the Mysteries of the Kitchen Revealed*: 13–20. London: BBC.

La Fontaine, J. 1998. *Speak of the Devil: tales of satanic ritual abuse in contemporary England*. Cambridge: Cambridge University Press.

Larsson, L. 1983–4. The Skateholm project – a late mesolithic settlement and cemetery complex, *Meddelanden fran Lunds Universitets Historiska Museum* 1–38.

— 1997 (unpublished lecture). *The dead do tell tales: burial practice in southern Scandinavia during the late Mesolithic*. University of Bradford, Department of Archaeological Sciences 12.03.1997.

Leakey, R. & R. Lewin. 1977. *Origins: what new discoveries reveal about the emergence of our species and its possible future*. London: Macdonald & Jane's.

Leroi-Gourhan, A. 1975. The flowers found with Shanidar IV, a Neanderthal burial in Iraq, *Science* 190: 562–4.

— 1989. Comments on 'Grave shortcomings: the evidence for Neanderthal burial by R.Gargett', *Current Anthropology* 30: 183.

Lévi-Strauss, C. 1969. *The raw and the cooked* (trans. J. & D. Weightman). London: Jonathan Cape.

Lewis, J. 2001. *The communal potential of the Neolithic chambered cairns of Orkney*. Bradford: Unpublished M.A. dissertation.

Lieberman, P. 1992. On the Kebara 2 hyoid and Neanderthal speech, *Current Anthropology* 33: 409–10.

Lindenbaum, S. 1979. *Kuru sorcery: disease and danger in the New Guinea highlands*. New York: CUNY.

Lubbock, J. 1902. *The origin of civilisation and the primitive condition of Man: mental and social condition of savages* (6th edition). London: Longmans, Green & Co.

Luce, J.V. 1992. *An Introduction to Greek Philosophy*. London: Thames & Hudson.

McKinley, J. 1997. Bronze Age 'barrows' and funerary rites and rituals of cremation, *Proceedings of the Prehistoric Society* 63: 129–45.

Mabey, R. (ed.). 1988. *The complete new herbal*. London: Elm Tree.

— 1996. *Flora Britannica*. London: Sinclair-Stevenson.

Maestripieri, D. 1999. Fatal attraction: interest in infants and infant abuse in rhesus macaques, *American Journal of Physical Anthropology* 110: 17–25.

Malinowski, B. 1927. *The father in primitive society*. (1966 reprint) New York: W.W. Norton.

Marler, J., R. Marler, K. Reinhard, B. Leonard, P. Lambert & S. Billman. 2000. Microscopic and molecular evidence for the human origin of the coprolite from the 'cannibalism' site at Cowboy Wash 5MT100100, *Southwestern Lore (Journal of Colorado Archaeology)* 66(4): 14–22.

Marshack, A. 1981. On Palaeolithic ochre and the early uses of colour and symbol, *Current Anthropology* 22(2): 188–91.

Marwick, M. (ed.). 1970. *Witchcraft and sorcery*. Penguin Modern Sociology Readings. Harmondsworth: Penguin.

Mauss, M. 1990. *The gift: the form and reason for exchange in archaic societies* (trans. W.D. Halls). London: Routledge.

Melville, H. 1851 = 1964. *Moby-Dick or the white whale*. New York: Airmont.

Metcalf, P. & R. Huntington. 1991. *Celebrations of Death: the anthropology of mortuary ritual* (2nd edition). Cambridge: Cambridge University Press.

Mildenburger, G. 1977. *Sozial- und Kulturgeschichte der Germanen. Von den Anfängen bis zur Völkerwanderungszeit*. Stuttgart: Verlag W. Kohlhammer.

Mithen, S. (ed.) 1998. *Creativity in human evolution and prehistory*. London: Routledge.

Monk, M.A. & J. Sheehan. 1998. *Early medieval Munster: archaeology, history and society*. Cork: Cork University Press.

Montgomery, J. 2000. Ibn Faḍlān and the Rūsiyyah, *Journal of Arabic and Islamic Studies* 3: 1–25.

— 2001. Ibn Rusta's lack of 'eloquence', the Rūs, and Samanid cosmography, *Edebiyât* 12: 73–93.

— forthcoming a. Pyrrhic scepticism and the conquest of disorder: prolegomena to the study of Ibn Faḍlān, in M. Maroth (ed.) *Theoretical problems in Arabic literature: proceedings of a conference held at the Pazmany Peter University, Hungary, Easter 1999*.

— forthcoming b. Spectral armies, snakes and a giant from Gog and Magog: Ibn Faḍlān among the Volga Bulghars. *Medieval Islamic autopsies* 1 (Paris conference, 2001). Maison des Sciences de l'Homme.

Morwood, M.J., F. Aziz, G.D. Van den Bergh, P.Y. Sondaar and J. De Vos. 1997. Stone artefacts from the 1994 excavation at Mata Menge, West Central Flores, Indonesia, *Australian Archaeology* 44: 26–34.

Morris, D. 1994. *The human animal*. London: BBC Books.

Morris, I. 1991. The archaeology of ancestors: the Saxe/Goldstein hypothesis revisited, *Cambridge Archaeological Journal* 1: 147–169.

Mowatt, T. 1999. Oil-seeker to youth-finder: Geron Corporation co-founder Miller Quarles on exercise, lifestyle and telomeres, *LE Magazine*, October 1999.

Müller-Wille, M. 1974. Boat-graves in northern Europe. *International Journal of Nautical Archaeology and Underwater Exploration* 3(2): 187–204.

Murgoci, A. 1926. The vampire in Roumania, *Folklore* 37: 320–49.

Murphy, E.M. & J.P. Mallory. 2000. Herodotus and the cannibals, *Antiquity* 74: 388–94.

Mussi, M., W. Roebroeks & J. Svoboda. 2000. Hunters of the Golden Age: an introduction, in W. Roebroeks, M. Mussi, J. Svoboda & K. Fennema (ed.), *Hunters of the Golden Age: the Mid Upper Palaeolithic of Eurasia 30,000–20,000 BP*. Leiden: University of Leiden.

Nadel, D. 1995. The visibility of prehistoric burials in the southern Levant: how rare are the Upper Palaeolithic/early Epipalaeolithic graves? in S. Campbell and A. Green (eds.), *The Archaeology of death in the ancient Near East*. Oxbow Monograph 51: 1–8.

Nadel, D. & I. Hershkovitz. 1991. New subsistence data and human remains from the earliest Levantine Epipalaeolithic, *Current Anthropology* 32(5): 631–5.

Nemeskéri, J. 1989. An attempt to reconstitute demographically the Upper Palaeolithic populations of Europe and the Mediterranean region, in I. Hershkovitz (ed.), *People and culture change. Proceedings of the second symposium on the Upper Palaeolithic, Mesolithic and Neolithic populations of Europe in the Mediterranean basin*. BAR International series 508 (ii).

Neugebauer, J-W. 1991. Die Beraubung von Grabstätten in der Frühbronzezeit, in J-W. Neugebauer (ed.), *Die Nekropole F von Gemeinlebarn, Niederösterreich* (Römisch-Germanische Forschungen 49): 112–29. Mainz: Phillip von Zabern.

Newton, M. 1996. Written in blood: a history of human sacrifice, *The Journal of Psychohistory* 24(2): 104–31.

Ngubane, H. 1986. 'The predicament of the sinister healer: some observations on "ritual murder" and the professional role of the inyanga', in M. Last and G.L. Chavunduka (eds.), *The Professionalisation of African Medicine*. Manchester: Manchester University Press.

Noble, W. & I. Davidson. 1996. *Human evolution, language and mind:*

a psychological and archaeological inquiry. Cambridge: Cambridge University Press.

Novak, S. & D. Kollmann. 2000. Perimortem processing of human remains among the Great Basin Fremont, *International Journal of Osteoarchaeology* 10: 65–75.

Novak, S. & D. Kopp. 2002 in press. To feed a tree in Zion: osteological analysis of the 1857 mountain meadows massacre, *Historical Archaeology* (forthcoming).

Ó Crullaóich, G. 1990. Contest in the Irish 'merry wake', in A. Duff-Cooper (ed.). *Contests* (Cosmos 6): 145–160.

Odent, M. 1992. *The nature of birth and breastfeeding*. Westport, CT: Greenwood.

Offner, J.A. 1980. Aztec political numerology and human sacrifice: the ideological ramifications of the number six, *Journal of Latin American Lore* 6(2): 205–15.

O'Sullivan, A. and J. Sheehan. 1996. *The Iveragh Peninsula. An archaeological survey of South Kerry*. Cork: Cork University Press.

Ovchinnikov, I.V., A. Götherström, G.P. Romanova,. M. Kharitonov, K. Liden & W. Goodwin. 2000. Molecular analysis of Neanderthal DNA from the northern Caucasus, *Nature* 404: 490–3.

Padel, F. 1995. *The sacrifice of human beings: British rule and the Konds of Orissa*. Delhi: Oxford University Press.

Pader, E.J. 1982. *Symbolism, social relations and the interpretation of mortuary remains*. Oxford: BAR supplementary series 130.

Page, R.I. 1990. *Norse Myths*. London: British Museum Publications.

Palmer, H. 1983. *Kant's Critique of Pure Reason: an introductory text*. Cardiff: University College Cardiff Press.

Palsson, H. & P. Edwards. 1989. *The Vikings in Russia: Yngvar's Saga and Eymund's Saga* (translated and introduced by Hermann Palsson and Paul Edwards) Edinburgh: Edinburgh University Press.

Parker Pearson, M. 1993. The powerful dead: archaeological relationships between the living and the dead, *Cambridge Archaeological Journal* 3(2): 203–229.

— 1999. *The archaeology of death and burial*. Stroud: Sutton.

Parry, R.L. 1998. *What Young Men Do*. Cambridge: Granta.

— 1999. Apocalypse now (Richard Lloyd Parry with the cannibals of Borneo), *Independent* 25/03/99.

Peta, B. 2001. Mugabe orders secret burials of his soldiers killed in Congo, *Independent* 25/08/01.

Petrinovich, L. 2000. *The Cannibal Within*. New York: Aldine de Gruyter.

Pettitt, P.B. 1997. High resolution Neanderthals? Interpreting Middle Palaeolithic intrasite spatial data, *World Archaeology* 29(2): 208–24.

Pfeiffer, J.E. 1982. *The creative explosion*. New York: Harper & Row.

Pickering, T.R., T.D. White & N. Toth. 1999. Stone tool cut marks on Stw 53, an early hominid from Sterkfontein, South Africa, *Journal of Human Evolution* 36: 4–17.

— 2000. Brief communication: cutmarks on a Plio-Pleistocene hominid from Sterkfontein, South Africa, *American Journal of Physical Anthropology* 111(4): 579–84.

Piggott, S. 1965. *Ancient Europe from the beginnings of agriculture to classical antiquity*. Edinburgh: Edinburgh University Press.

Pitts, M., A. Bayliss, J. McKinley, A. Boylston, P. Budd, J. Evans, C. Chenery, A. Reynolds & S. Semple. 2002. An Anglo-Saxon decapitation and burial at Stonehenge, *Wiltshire Archaeological and Natural History Magazine* 95: 131–46.

Polet, C., O. Dutour, R. Orban, I. Jadin & S. Louryan. 1996. A healed wound caused by a flint arrowhead in a Neolithic human innominate from the Trou Rosette (Furfooz, Belgium), *International Journal of Osteoarchaeology* 6(4): 414–20.

Polis, G., C. Myers & W. Hess. 1984. A survey of intraspecific predation within the class Mammalia, *Mammal Review* 14: 187–98.

Polkinghorne, J. 1996. *Beyond science*. Cambridge: Cambridge University Press.

Polson, C.J. & T.K. Marshall. 1975. *The disposal of the dead* (3rd edition). London: English Universities Press.

Prescott, W.H. 1857. *History of the conquest of Mexico: with a preliminary view of the ancient Mexican civilization and the life of the conqueror, Hernando Cortez* vols 1&2. London: George Routledge & Co.

Pringle, H. 2001. *The mummy congress: science, obsession and the everlasting dead*. London: Fourth Estate.

Pugh-Smith, J. & J. Samuels. 1996. *Archaeology in law*. London: Sweet & Maxwell.

Pynchon, T. 1997. *Mason & Dixon*. London: Jonathan Cape.

Raban, J. 2002. Truly, madly, deeply devout, *Guardian*, 02/03/02.

Randsborg, K. 1995. *Hjortspring: Warfare and Sacrifice in Early Europe*. Aarhus: Aarhus University Press.

Rawson, J. (ed.). 1996. Mysteries of ancient China. London: British Museum.

Read, P.P. 1974. *Alive: the story of the Andes survivors*. London: Secker & Warburg.

Redford, R. 2002. Quoted in *Observer*, 'They said what . . . ?', 13.01.02: 24.

Renfrew, A.C. 1976. Megaliths, territories and populations, in S.J. de Laet (ed.) *Acculturation and continuity in Atlantic Europe*: 198–220. Bruges: De Tempel.

— 1979. *Investigations in Orkney* (Society of Antiquaries Research Report 38). London: Society of Antiquaries.

Renfrew, A.C. and E. Zubrow (eds.). 1994. *The ancient mind: elements of cognitive archaeology*. Cambridge: Cambridge University Press.

Rhodes, R. 1997. Gourmet cannibalism in a New Guinea tribe, *Nature* 389: 11.

Richards, C. 1988. Altered images: a re-examination of Neolithic mortuary practices in Orkney, in J.C.Barrett and I.A.Kinnes (ed.) *The archaeology of context in the Neolithic and Bronze Age: recent trends*. Sheffield: University of Sheffield Department of Archaeology and Prehistory.

Rinpoche, S. 1992. *The Tibetan book of living and dying*. London: Rider.

Ritchie, G. & A. Ritchie. 1991. *Scotland: archaeology and early history*. Edinburgh: Edinburgh University Press.

Rivière, P.G. 1980. Review of Arens 1979, *Man* 1,980: 203–5.

Roberts, C. & K. Manchester. 1995. *The archaeology of disease* (2nd edition). Sutton: Stroud/Ithaca: Cornell University Press.

Roebroeks, W., M. Mussi, J. Svoboda & K. Fennema. (eds.). 2000.

Hunters of the Golden Age: the Mid Upper Palaeolithic of Eurasia 30,000–20,000 BP. Leiden: University of Leiden.

Rolle, R., V. Ju. Murzin & A. Ju. Alexeev. 1998. *Königskurgan Čertomlyk: Ein skythischer Grabhügel des 4. vorchristlichen Jahrhunderts*, Vol. 1. Mainz: Philipp von Zabern.

Rose, J.L. 1998. interviewed in *Naked Body*, Summer 1998: 26. London: The Body Shop/Forward Publishing.

Ross, A. 1986. Lindow Man and the Celtic tradition, in I. M. Stead, J.B. Bourke & D. Brothwell. (eds.). 1986. *Lindow Man: the body in the bog*: 162–9. London: British Museum Publications.

Rowley-Conwy, P. 1993. Was there a Neanderthal religion? in G. Burenhult (ed.), *The first humans: human origins and history to 10,000 B.C.* San Francisco: HarperCollins.

Roy, A. 1997. *The God of Small Things*. London: Flamingo.

Russell, M.D. 1987. Mortuary practices at the Krapina Neandertal site, *American Journal of Physical Anthropology* 72: 381–97.

Sahlins, M. 1981. *Historical metaphors and mythical realities: structure in the early history of the Sandwich Island kingdom*. Ann Arbor: University of Michigan Press.

Salovey, P. and D. Sluyter (eds.). 1997. *Emotional development and emotional intelligence: implications for educators*. New York: Basic Books.

Sanday, P.R. 1986. *Divine hunger: cannibalism as a cultural system*. Cambridge: Cambridge University Press.

Savile, C. 1999. Suffer little children, *Bizarre* 17: 64–67. London: John Brown.

Saxe, A.A. 1971. Social dimensions of mortuary practices in a Mesolithic population from Wadi Halfa, Sudan, in J. Brown (ed.) *Approaches to the social dimensions of mortuary practices*. Washington DC (Memoir of the Society for American Archaeology 25): 39–57.

Scarre, C.J. 1984. Kin groups in megalithic burials, *Nature* 311: 512–13.

— 1994. The meaning of death: funerary beliefs and the prehistorian, in C. Renfrew and E. Zubrow (ed.) *The ancient mind: elements of cognitive archaeology*: 75–82. Cambridge: Cambridge University Press.

Scholtz, H.J., V.M. Phillips, and G.J. Knobel, 1997. 'Muti or ritual murder', *Forensic Science International* 87: 117–23.

Schore, A.N. 2001. The effects of early relational trauma on right brain development, affect regulation, and infant mental health, *Infant Mental Health Journal* 22(1–2): 201–69.

Schulting, R.J. 1998. Creativity's coffin: innovation in the burial record of Mesolithic Europe, in S.Mithen (ed.) *Creativity in human evolution and prehistory*. London: Routledge.

Schutkowski, H., M. Schultz, & M. Holzgraefe. 1996. Fatal wounds in a Late Neolithic double inhumation – a probable case of meningitis following trauma, *International Journal of Osteoarchaeology* 6(2): 179–84.

Schweinfurth, G. 1873. *The heart of Africa. Three years' travels and adventures in the unexplored regions of central Africa. From 1868 to 1871.* 2 vols. London: Sampson Low, Marston, Low, & Searle.

Seligman, M. 1992. *Helplessness: on depression, development, and death.* New York: W.H. Freeman.

Sells, M. 1994. *Foundations of Islamic Mysticism.* Classics of Western Spirituality. Paulist Press.

Semaw, S., P. Renne, J.W.K. Harris, C.S. Feibel, R.L. Bernor, N. Fesseha & K. Mowbray. 1997. 2.5-million-year-old stone tools from Gona, Ethiopia, *Nature* 38: 333–5.

Shay, T. 1985. Differentiated treatment of deviancy at death as revealed in anthropological and archaeological material, *Journal of Anthropological Archaeology* 4: 221–41.

Sheehan, J. 1994. Caherlihan: early ecclesiastical site and ceallunach, in I. Bennett (ed.), *Excavations 1993. Summary accounts of archaeological excavations in Ireland*: 41–2. Bray.

Sherratt, A. 1997. Sacred and profane substances: the ritual use of narcotics in later Neolithic Europe, in A. Sherratt (collected papers), *Economy and society in Prehistoric Europe*: 403–430. Edinburgh: Edinburgh University Press.

Shippey, T. 1982. *The road to Middle Earth: how J.R.R. Tolkien created a new mythology.* London: HarperCollins.

Silverberg, J. & J.P. Gray. 1992. *Aggression and peacefulness in humans and other primates.* Oxford: Oxford University Press.

Sinason, V. (ed.) 1994. *Treating survivors of satanist abuse: an invisible trauma*. London: Routledge.

Smirnov, Yu. A. 1989. Intentional human burial: Middle Palaeolithic (last glaciation) beginnings, *Journal of World Prehistory* 3(2): 199–233.

Smith, M. 1928. *Rabi'a the Mystic*. Cambridge: Cambridge University Press.

Solecki, R. 1971. *Shanidar, the first flower people*. New York: Alfred A. Knopf.

Spencer, B. and F.J. Gillen. 1899. *The native tribes of Central Australia*. London: Macmillan.

Spennemann, D.H.R. 1987. Cannibalism in Fiji: the analysis of butchering marks on human bones and the historical record, *Domo-domo: Fiji Museum Quarterly* 2: 29–46.

Spindler, K. 1994. *The man in the ice*. (trans. E. Osers). London: Weidenfeld & Nicolson.

Spriggs, M. 1997. *Island Melanesians*. Oxford: Blackwell.

Stead, I.M., J.B. Bourke & D. Brothwell. 1986. (eds.). *Lindow Man: the body in the bog*. London: British Museum Publications.

Stead, I.M. & R.C. Turner. 1985. Lindow Man, *Antiquity* 59: 25–9.

Stiner, M.C. 1991. The faunal remains from Grotta Guattari: a taphonomic perspective, *Current Anthropology* 32(2): 103–17.

Stringer, C. 2000. The Gough's Cave human fossils: an introduction, *Bull. Br. Mus. Nat. Hist. (Geol.)* 56: 135–139.

Stringer, C. & C. Gamble. 1993. *In search of the Neanderthals. Solving the puzzle of human origins*. London: Thames and Hudson.

Sulimirski, T. & T. Taylor. 1990. 'The Scythians', Chapter 33a in Boardman *et al.* (eds.). *The Cambridge Ancient History* Vol III, part 2 (2nd edn): 547–90. Cambridge: Cambridge University Press.

Summers, M. 1929 *The Vampire in Europe*. London: Kegan Paul, Trench, Trubner.

Svoboda, J. 1999. *Čas Lovců: dějiny paleolitu, zvláště na Moravě*. Brno: Archaeology Branch of the Academy of Sciences of the Czech Republic.

— 2000. The depositional context of the Early Upper Palaeolithic human fossils from the Koněprusy (Zlatý kůň) and Mladeč Caves, Czech Republic, *Journal of Human Evolution* 38: 523–536.

Talmage, V.A. 1982. The violation of sepulture: is it legal to excavate human remains?, *Archaeology* 35: 44–49.

Tarlow, S. 2000. Emotion in archaeology, *Current Anthropology* 41(5): 713–747.

Taylor, T.F. 1992. The Gundestrup Cauldron, *Scientific American* 266(3): 84–89.

— 1994. Thracians, Scythians, and Dacians, 800 BC–AD 300, Ch 11 in B.W. Cunliffe (ed.). *The Oxford Illustrated Prehistory of Europe*: 373–410. Oxford. Oxford University Press.

— 1996. *The prehistory of sex: four million years of human sexual culture*. London: Fourth Estate/New York: Bantam.

— 2001a. Explanatory tyranny, *Nature* 411: 419.

— 2001b. Believing the ancients: quantitative and qualitative dimensions of slavery and the slave trade in later prehistoric Eurasia, *World Archaeology* 33(1): 27–43.

— 2001c. The Edible Dead, *British Archaeology* 59: 8–12.

Teilhol, V. 2001. *Contribution à l'étude individuelle des ossements d'enfants de La Chaise de Vouthon (Charente, France). Aspects paléodémographique, paléoethnologique. Etude morphologique et métrique. Place phylogénique des enfants de La Chaise*. Perpignan: University of Perpignan doctoral dissertation.

Tew, M. 1990. *Safer childbirth? a critical history of maternity care*. Oxford: Oxford University Press.

The Times. 1974a. Court told of naked girl dancing among coffins, *The Times* 12/6/1974: 5.

— 1974b. Stakes driven into corpses in cemetery, *The Times* 13/6/1974: 4.

— 1974c. Four years, eight months' jail for 'ritual' trial man, *The Times* 18/7/1974: 3.

— 1989. Self-styled wizard who ensnared girls jailed for fifteen years, *The Times* 8/8/1989: 3.

Thieme, H. 1997. Lower Palaeolithic hunting spears from Germany, *Nature* 385: 807–810.

Thomas, D.H. 2000. *Skull wars: Kennewick man, archaeology and the battle for Native American identity*. New York: Basic Books.

Thomas, L-V. 1980. *La mort: le cadavre de la biologie à l'anthropologie.* Paris: Payot.

Thomas, N. 1965. A double beaker burial on Bredon Hill, Worcestershire, *Birmingham Archaeological Society, Transactions & Proceedings* 82: 59–76.

Thomas, N. (Nicholas) 1989. *Out of time: history and evolution in anthropological discourse* (Cambridge Studies in Social Anthropology 67). Cambridge: Cambridge University Press.

Thompson, D. 1996. *The End of Time: Faith and Fear in the Shadow of the Millennium.* London: Sinclair-Stevenson.

Thompson Rowling, J. 1989. The rise and decline of surgery in dynastic Egypt, *Antiquity* 63: 312–19.

Thorpe, N. 2000. Origins of war: Mesolithic conflict in Europe, *British Archaeology* 52: 8–13.

Tiedemann, M. 2000. *'In Auschwitz wurde niemand vergast': 60 rechtsradikale Lügen und wie man sie widerlegt.* Munich: Goldman.

Time-Life 1993. *Vikings: raiders from the north.* Alexandria, Virginia: Time-Life.

Tobias, P.V. 1971. *Man's past and future.* (Raymond Dart Lectures 5). Johannesburg: Witwatersrand University Press.

Tooley, M. 1983. *Abortion and Infanticide.* Oxford: Clarendon Press.

Toren, C. 1998. Cannibalism and compassion: transformations in Fijian concepts of the person, in V. Keck (ed.) *Common worlds and single lives: constituting knowledge in Pacific societies.* London: Berg.

Townsend, R. 1992. *The Aztecs.* London: Thames & Hudson.

Trigger, B.G. 1993. *Early civilizations: ancient Egypt in context.* Cairo: The American University in Cairo Press.

Trinkaus, E. 1983. *The Shanidar Neandertals. Vol. 2. Shanidar Cave (Iraq).* New York: Academic Press.

— 1985. Cannibalism and burial at Krapina, *Journal of Human Evolution* 14: 203–16.

Tsaliki, A. 2001 in press. Vampires beyond legend: a bioarchaeological approach, *Journal of Palaeopathology* (forthcoming).

Turnbaugh, W.A., R. Jurmain, H. Nelson & L. Kilgore. 1996. *Under-*

standing physical anthropology and archaeology (6th edition). Minneapolis/St Paul: West.

Turner, C.G. 1993. Cannibalism in Chaco Canyon: the charnel pit excavated in 1926 at Small House Ruin by Frank H.H. Roberts, Jr., *American Journal of Physical Anthropology* 91: 421–39.

Turner, C.G. & J.A. Turner. 1992. The first claim for cannibalism in the southwest: Walter Hough's 1901 discovery at Canyon Butte Ruin 3, northeastern Arizona, *American Antiquity* 57(4): 661–682.

— 1999. *Man corn: cannibalism and violence in the prehistoric American southwest.* Salt Lake City: University of Utah Press.

Turner, R.C. & R.G. Scaife (ed.). 1995. *Bog bodies: new discoveries and new perspectives.* London: British Museum.

Ucko, P.J. 1969. Ethnography and the archaeological interpretation of funerary remains, *World Archaeology* 1: 262–280.

Váňa, Z. 1983. *The world of the ancient Slavs* (trans. T.Gottheiner). London: Orbis.

Van der Sanden, W.A.B. 1996. *Through nature to eternity: the bog bodies of northwest Europe* (trans. S.J. Mellor). Amsterdam: Batavian Lion International.

Vander Linden, M.M. 2001. Perpetuating traditions, changing ideologies: the Bell Beaker culture in the British Isles and its implications for the Indo-European problem, in M.E. Huld, K. Jones-Bley, A.D. Volpe and M.R. Dexter (ed.), *Proceedings of the Twelfth Annual UCLA Indo-European Conference* (JIES Monograph 40): 269–86. Washington: Institute for the Study of Man.

Vandermeersch, B. 1966. Découverte d'un objet en ocre avec traces d'utilisation dans le Moustérien de Qazfeh (Israël), *Bulletin de la Société Préhistorique Française* 66: 157–8.

Van Gennep, A. 1960. *The rites of passage* (trans. M.B. Vizedom & G.L. Caffee). London/Henley: Routledge & Kegan Paul.

Vasagar, J. 2002. Mandela appeals for aid in murder inquiry, *Guardian* 20/04/02: 8.

Vayda, A.P. 1970. On the nutritional value of cannibalism, *American Anthropologist* 72: 1,462–3.

Villa, P. 1992. Cannibalism in prehistoric Europe, *Evolutionary Anthropology* 1(3): 93–104.

Villa, P., C. Bouville, J. Courtin, D. Helmer, E. Mahieu, P. Shipman, G. Belluomini & M. Branca. 1986. Cannibalism in the Neolithic, *Science* 233: 431–7.

Vladimov, G. 1979. *Faithful Ruslan* (trans. & foreword by M. Glenny). Harmondsworth: Penguin.

Vulliamy, C.E. 1926. *Immortal Man*. London: Methuen.

Wahl, J. 1981. Beobachtungen zur Verbrennung menschlicher Leichname, *Archäologisches Korrespondenzblatt* 11: 271–9.

Wahl, J. & H. König. 1987. Anthropologisch-traumatologische Untersuchung der menschlichen Skelettenreste aus dem bandkeramischen Massengrab bei Talheim, Kreis Heilbronn, *Fundberichte aus Baden-Württemburg*, 12: 65–194.

Walker, A. & R. Leakey (eds.). 1993. *The Nariokotome* Homo erectus *skeleton*. Cambridge: Harvard University Press.

Ward, K. 1996. *Religion and creation*. Oxford: Clarendon Press.

Ward, R. and C. Stringer. 1997. A molecular handle on the Neanderthals, *Nature* 388: 225–6.

Warmind, M.L. 1995. The funeral of the Rus-chief, in O. Crumlin-Pedersen & B. Munch Thye (eds.), *The ship as symbol in prehistoric and medieval Scandinavia*: 136–7. Copenhagen: PNM.

Wendorf, F. 1968. *The prehistory of Nubia* Vol. 2. Fort Burgwin Research Centre and Southern Methodist University Press.

Wheatley, P. 1971. *The pivot of the four quarters: a preliminary enquiry into the origins and character of the ancient Chinese city*. Chicago: Aldine.

White, T.D. 1986. Cut marks on the Bodo cranium: a case of prehistoric defleshing, *American Journal of Physical Anthropology* 69: 503–9.

— 1992. *Prehistoric cannibalism: at Mancos 5 MTUMR-2346*. Princeton: Princeton University Press.

White, T.D. & N. Toth. 1991. The question of ritual cannibalism at Grotta Guattari, *Current Anthropology* 32(2): 118–24.

White, R. 1993. Technological and social dimensions of 'Aurignacian-Age' body ornaments across Europe, in H. Knecht, A. Pike-Tay & R. White (ed.), *Before Lascaux: the complex record of the Early Upper Palaeolithic*. Boca Raton: CRC Press.

Williams, H. 1989. *Sacred Elephant*. London: Jonathan Cape.

Williams, W. 1986. *The Spirit and the Flesh: sexual diversity in American Indian culture*. Boston: Beacon Press.

Wittgenstein, L. 1953. *Philosophical Investigations* (G.E.M. Anscombe & R. Rhees, eds.; translated by G.E.M. Anscombe). Oxford: Blackwell.

— 1982. *Last Writings on the Philosophy of Psychology*. Preliminary Studies for Part II of Philosophical Investigations, ed. by G.H. von Wright & H. Nyman and trans. by C.G. Luckhardt & M.A.E. Aue, Vol.1. Oxford: Blackwell.

Wooley, L. 1934. *Ur excavations. Volume 2: The royal cemetery*. London: British Museum.

Yordanov, Y.A. 1978. Anthropologic study of bone remains from persons buried in the Varna Eneolithic necropolis, *Studia Praehistorica* 1–2: 50–67.

Zbarsky, I. & S. Hutchinson 1998. *Lenin's Embalmers* (trans. B. Bray). London: Harvill.

INDEX

Borromose women, 153, 159
Boystown squatter camp, Cape
  Town, 8
Brady, Ian, 284, 313 *n*
Bran the Blessed, 266–7, 312 *n*
Brockman, John, 26–7
Bronowski, Jacob, 220
Bronze Age, 244; cave burial, 275;
  cenotaph burial, 236; grave
  robbing, 238; live burial, 99–100;
  round barrows, 22; sacrifice, 276
Brown, A.R., 48
Buddha (Gautama Siddartha), 45,
  185
Bulgars, 105
burial: *Australopithecus africanus*,
  29–30; cave, 32, 33, 34, 35,
  205–22; cemetery, 225– 40, 310 *n*;
  cenotaph, 235–6; child, 120, 273,
  276, 299 *n*; earliest ceremonial, 4,
  14, 17–38; foetal position, 24,
  225; gradual movement from
  communal long barrows to
  individual round barrows, 22–6,
  29; graves, equation of beds with
  214–15; grave goods, 24, 32–3,
  41, 115, 127, 128, 129, *130*, 131–4,
  131, 208, 237–9, 247; grave
  robbery, 126, 237–9; *Homo
  sapiens* (AMHS) of Cro-Magnon
  type, 31–2, 34–5; horse, 20–1,
  36–7; Iron Age, lack of evidence
  for, 22–3; isolation, 120, 213,
  218–27, 230–1, 233, 235–48, 299
  n; live, 35, 99–100; mass graves,
  11–12, 36, 235, 236, 261–3,
  289–90 *n*; mortuary symbolism,
  232; multiple 31, 197, 200–22, 308
  n; Neanderthal, 31–3, 204–22,
  207; Neolithic, 225–40; primary
  and secondary, 27, 28, 122–4,
  126–34, 138, 177–8, 209, 215, 240,
  264, 267, 269; reburial, 54,
  259–65; reverential, identifying
  first, 35–6; shared logic of

worldwide, 28–9; ship, 90–100,
  103–12; sky, 14, 229; Theatre of
  Transgression, 214–22, 245;
  water, 25–6; World of Ancestors,
  226–40, 247 *see also* funerals
Burial Act (1857), 275
Bush, George W., 267–8

Caesar, Julius, 156, 157
Californian Asatruans, 260
Cambyses, 83–4
cannibalism: abandonment of, 84–5;
  aggressive, man-hunting, 64, 70,
  80; Andes air crash, 73–4;
  australopithecine, 77; Catholic
  Church opinion on, 74;
  chimpanzee, 60–4, 65; Cook's
  accounts of, 67–70; criminal or
  psychotic, 64, 65; defleshing, 208;
  doubts over evidence for, 12–13,
  14, 58–9, 65, 68, 69, 280; earliest
  evidence for, 76–81; *Erebus* and
  Terror, 68–9; gustatory or
  culinary, 64, 66, 76, 81; *Homo
  antecessor*, 77; *Homo erectus* 77;
  Homo heidelbergensis, 77; *Homo
  sapiens*, 77–80, *78*, *79*, *80*;
  imagery of The Last Supper and,
  74; Mappi Mundi depictions of,
  56–7, 58; medicinal, 64; Miocene
  Ape, 76; Neanderthal, 207–22;
  Peking Man, 60; placenta-eating
  64, 295 *n*; reverential funerary,
  14, 73, 78, 82–4, 204, 207–22,
  280, 297 *n*; ritual, 77–82; self-
  edibility, innate knowledge of,
  64–5; signatures, 57, 70; survival,
  64, 65, 70, 73–4, 80, 209; tribes,
  58, 65–7, 70–2, 75, 280, 295 *n*;
  triggers, 63; warfare driven, 14,
  81
Carleton, J.H., 262
Carrasco, David, 267
Catalhöyük, Turkey, 223–4, *224*,
  227–30, *228*, *229*, 233, 245, 246

348